Not magic but work

Manchester University Press

theatre
theory · practice
· performance ·

series editors
MARIA M. DELGADO
PETER LICHTENFELS

advisory board
MICHAEL BILLINGTON
SANDRA HEBRON
MARK RAVENHILL
JANELLE REINELT
PETER SELLARS
JOANNE TOMPKINS

This series will offer a space for those people who practise theatre to have a dialogue with those who think and write about it.

The series has a flexible format that refocuses the analysis and documentation of performance. It provides, presents and represents material which is written by those who make or create performance history, and offers access to theatre documents, different methodologies and approaches to the art of making theatre.

The books in the series are aimed at students, scholars, practitioners and theatre-visiting readers. They encourage reassessments of periods, companies and figures in twentieth-century and twenty-first-century theatre history, and provoke and take up discussions of cultural strategies and legacies that recognise the heterogeneity of performance studies.

The series editors, with the advisory board, aim to publish innovative challenging and exploratory texts from practitioners, theorists and critics.

also available

The Paris Jigsaw: Internationalism and the city's stages
DAVID BRADBY AND MARIA M. DELGADO (EDS)

Theatre in crisis? Performance manifestos for a new century
MARIA M. DELGADO AND CARIDAD SVICH (EDS)

World stages, local audiences: Essays on performance, place, and politics
PETER DICKINSON

Performing presence: Between the live and the simulated
GABRIELLA GIANNACHI AND NICK KAYE

Jean Genet and the politics of theatre: Spaces of revolution
CARL LAVERY

'Love me or kill me': Sarah Kane and the theatre of extremes
GRAHAM SAUNDERS

Trans-global readings: Crossing theatrical boundaries
CARIDAD SVICH

Negotiating cultures: Eugenio Barba and the intercultural debate
IAN WATSON (ED.)

Not magic but work

An ethnographic account of a rehearsal process

GAY MCAULEY

Manchester University Press
Manchester and New York

distributed in the United States exclusively by Palgrave Macmillan

The right of Gay McAuley to be identified as the author of this work has been asserted by her in accordance with the Copyright, Designs and Patents Act 1988.

Published by Manchester University Press
Oxford Road, Manchester M13 9NR, UK
and Room 400, 175 Fifth Avenue, New York, NY 10010, USA
www.manchesteruniversitypress.co.uk

Distributed in the United States exclusively by
Palgrave Macmillan, 175 Fifth Avenue, New York,
NY 10010, USA

Distributed in Canada exclusively by
UBC Press, University of British Columbia, 2029 West Mall,
Vancouver, BC, Canada V6T 1Z2

British Library Cataloguing-in-Publication Data
A catalogue record for this book is available from the British Library

Library of Congress Cataloging-in-Publication Data applied for

ISBN 978 0 7190 85437   hardback

First published 2012

The publisher has no responsibility for the persistence or accuracy of URLs for any external or third-party internet websites referred to in this book, and does not guarantee that any content on such websites is, or will remain, accurate or appropriate.

Typeset by Servis Filmsetting Ltd, Stockport, Cheshire
Printed in Great Britain
by TJ International Ltd, Padstow

for
Derek Nicholson
Russell Emerson
and
Kim Spinks
who made it all possible
and in memory of
Rex Cramphorn
who was our friend and inspiration

CONTENTS

LIST OF FIGURES

ACKNOWLEDGEMENTS

My thanks are due first and foremost to Neil Armfield and the actors (Richard Roxburgh, Russell Dykstra, Monica Maughan, Justine Clarke and Guy Edmonds) for so generously permitting me to watch their work process and to share in the camaraderie of the rehearsal room, answering my many questions and entering into the spirit of my project with characteristic wit and grace. To the playwright (Michael Gow), the designers (Paul Charlier, Ralph Myers, Tess Schofield and Damien Cooper) and the production team (Kylie Mascord, Liam Fraser, Chris Mercer, Shaun Poustie and Joshua Sherrin), my thanks for your acceptance of my presence and your preparedness to stop and talk to me, however busy you were. To Eamon Flack, a special thank you for some very illuminating discussions, both during the process and long afterwards. The company staff in the office, in particular John Woodland and Christine Sammers, also made me welcome, providing me with information and many useful insights into the working processes of the company.

This study would not have been possible without the years of work undertaken with my colleagues at the University of Sydney and the many theatre artists who became involved in our projects as we explored the nature of rehearsal and refined the techniques and methods required for effective observation, documentation and analysis. I would like to acknowledge in particular my academic colleagues Tim Fitzpatrick, Terry Threadgold, Paul Dwyer, Laura Ginters and

Kate Rossmanith, whose scholarly insights and analytical skills have so greatly enriched our numerous joint projects over the years and whose generosity of spirit always made collaboration such an enjoyable experience. Even more important to the development of the rehearsal observation projects has been the practical involvement of the small group of theatre practitioners employed at the university's Theatre Workshop before it merged with the Department of Performance Studies. They were equal partners in the work from the beginning, bringing a wealth of theatrical expertise to the planning and execution of projects, and insights that have shaped our evolving research questions. In dedicating this book to Derek Nicholson, Russell Emerson and Kim Spinks, I wish to express my appreciation and thanks for many years of professional collaboration and friendship.

The fourth person named in my dedication is Rex Cramphorn, the director who made such a profound contribution to the theatre culture of Sydney and Melbourne before his tragically early death in 1991. Rex entered wholeheartedly into the academic enterprise represented by these rehearsal projects, enjoyed the opportunity they gave him for deeper reflection and analysis and, by his example, encouraged other theatre artists to participate. I take this opportunity to acknowledge the enormous debt I owe to him for the insights into the theatre making process he so generously shared and for the intellectual rigour he brought to our projects.

Many people have assisted the production of this book and have given me encouragement and support. I should like to thank Matthew Frost, head commissioning editor at the University of Manchester Press, for all his help and advice, Maria Delgado and Peter Lichtenfels, directors of the 'Theatre: Theory Practice Performance' collection, for including this book in their collection and for their perceptive comments during the publication process, and Randall Collins for graciously permitting me to reproduce his diagram of a model interaction ritual. Heidrun Löhr has been photographing theatre in Sydney for many years, and her archive of images of both rehearsal and performance will constitute a major resource for future theatre historians. I am grateful for permission to publish some of her wonderfully revealing rehearsal shots of *Toy Symphony* here and for our many conversations about the art and craft of performance photography.

On a personal note, I should like to thank Jennifer and Angela Beeching and Fred Jameson for their generous hospitality, which made such a difference to the final months of work on the book in London, and Mary Roberts in Sydney who not only gave wise advice but much practical support. Finally and most importantly, there is my family. My children, Sam and Hannah Williams, are both involved in scholarly research of their own but they have always been prepared to engage with the issues arising from mine and to bring their disciplinary perspectives to bear on my reflections. For all those conversations around the kitchen table, the emails misleadingly headed 'Quick query,' and the phone calls at inopportune moments across the world's time zones, my loving thanks to you both. And also to David, no longer here in person but always with us in spirit.

Writing about rehearsal: some preliminary observations

> And let him observe
> That this is not magic but
> Work, my friends.
> (Bertolt Brecht, *The Curtains*)

A good place to begin to think about rehearsal is via the word itself. According to the *Oxford English Dictionary*, 'rehearsal' comes from the Old French word 're-herser,' which is a term used in agriculture. It refers to the practice of preparing the soil before planting seeds, and the implement used, the 'herse,' is a frame with metal spikes that pierce the soil when dragged along the ground. The English word, both noun and verb, is 'harrow' but as is often the case in English, the original French word has also been retained with another meaning. A 'herse' is the wooden or metal frame with prickets set up in the sanctuary of a church, upon which the faithful may place lighted candles that each represent a prayer or an appeal to God. In the Anglican church, this practice was particularly connected with the funeral rite, hence the slippage from 'herse' to 'hearse,' from the frame carrying the prayers of the faithful that was placed over the coffin to the vehicle carrying the coffin to the grave. Interestingly, in modern French, the word 'herse' designates the agricultural implement, the liturgical candelabra and also a batten from which stage lights are hung in the theatre. The theatrical connection does not,

however, extend to rehearsal, for which the modern French word is *répétition*. Victor Turner demonstrated on numerous occasions that tracing
the etymology of key words revealed them to be 'crystallised secretions of
once living human experience' or, what he called 'a "laminated" semantic
system' (Turner 1982, 17) in that meanings are layered onto one another,
some superseded but nevertheless still present. The semantic system
indicated by the etymology of the word 'rehearsal' provides an extremely
rich context for consideration of the theatrical practice: nurturing the
soil, providing the organic conditions for new growth and providing
illumination are obviously relevant connotations, and the sense of some
appeal to the supernatural or sending a message into the unknown is
also part of the mix. Modern rehearsal practice, thus, seems to draw on
a complex set of meanings and connotations embedded in the word and
it becomes clear why, over the past couple of centuries, this is the word
that has come to the fore amongst English speaking theatre practitioners
rather than words like 'repetition' or 'trial,' used in earlier times (Stern
2000, 23–4) and still the norm in other European languages.[1]

This book is an attempt to describe a single rehearsal process, the six
weeks of intensive work involved in the making of *Toy Symphony*, a new
play by Michael Gow, directed by Neil Armfield and brought to the stage
for the first time in December 2007 by Company B at the Belvoir Street
Theatre in Sydney. I was a participant-observer of the whole rehearsal
process, made welcome by the director and the actors, by the company
staff in the offices and the production crew in the theatre, even though
no one had much of an idea what kind of book I would be writing. In
keeping with contemporary ethnographic practice, I make no attempt
to disguise my own presence as narrator in this account for so much of
it depends on my responses to the fragments of performance that were
created, discarded, adjusted and refined day by day over the weeks of
painstaking, repetitive work. Like the director, I was the unconditional
spectator, as Ariane Mnouchkine once put it (Mnouchkine 1973),
always attentive to the performers and ready to respond, but I was also
observing the director and trying to keep track of what was done and
what was said throughout the process. In this introductory chapter, the
story of the process is preceded by some comments concerning the task
of rehearsal observation and the lessons learned from ethnography and
micro-sociology that have inflected what I see as a central element in
the academic study of performance; the chapter also includes a short
account of the prior creative work of the three main protagonists in the
work process: Neil Armfield, the director, Michael Gow, the writer and
Richard Roxburgh, the actor who played the huge role of the central
character and was never off the stage. The fourth protagonist is the

Belvoir Street Theatre itself, with its idiosyncratic corner stage and its historic role in the formation of a theatre culture in Sydney. It, too, is briefly described here.

It is a somewhat surprising fact that, notwithstanding a century or so of scholarly concern with theatrical performance, relatively little has been written about the rehearsal practices from which these performances emerge. In part this can be explained by the historical emphasis in the discipline of theatre studies as it sought in its early years to find a place in the contested field of the humanities (see Vince 1989, Fischer Lichte 1999, Carlson 2001, Jackson 2004). The well-documented difficulties involved in talking about performance in bygone periods are greatly compounded when the question turns to rehearsal for, if public performance is ephemeral and leaves little trace, the private work processes that precede it are even more deeply buried in the past. As Tiffany Stern has shown, however, even in relation to the distant past, the inability to find material has been due perhaps more to a lack of scholarly enterprise than genuine absence of information. According to her, 'much more data than has been assumed survives about rehearsal from 1576 to 1780. Sources are diverse and scattered, however, and there is no single logical place to look for material concerning theatrical practice' (Stern 2000, 18).

Once the focus shifts from historical to contemporary performance, there is no shortage of material evidence for scholars who seek it, but the reluctance to engage seriously with rehearsal practice has continued. Paul Atkinson, author of an ethnographic study of the Welsh National Opera, is criticising scholars in cultural studies as well as theatre and performance departments, when he speaks of 'collective failure' in relation to the dearth of studies examining 'the social worlds of cultural production as collective work in socially organised settings' (Atkinson 2004, 94). In this one phrase, Atkinson foreshadows a whole intellectual programme and it resonates with my own evolving concern with rehearsal practice.[2]

In setting out to describe the creative process involved in the making of Michael Gow's *Toy Symphony* by Company B Belvoir in 2007, I am drawing on many years of experimentation and reflection on how best to approach the 'hidden world' of rehearsal, to use Susan Letzler Cole's telling phrase (Cole 1992), and the methodologies and conceptual frameworks that can best assist in dealing with the complex aesthetic and social issues involved. In the early days of this research, the focus of my interest was the production emerging from the rehearsal process. Concern with the semiotics of performance meant that what I noticed most was the way dominant signifiers came to be selected, the discussions that surrounded this selection process and the traces of things tried and discarded that were left in the performance. Already at this early stage, however, I was struck by the wide range of practices and people involved in the creative work, the collaborative nature of what went on, the way an element that later proved to be essential might have been originally introduced almost by accident, and the way a good director drew on the creativity of everyone in the room. As a result, I became more and more uneasy with the authorial role being attributed to the director in relation to performance, which seemed as misleading and reductive as claiming the same for the playwright. The issue of creative agency remains a central concern and, in attempting to describe how a group of artists with very different skills, working in a range of different media, come together for an intensive period and produce a single work of art, I hope to make possible a more nuanced understanding of the real artistry involved in what it is that the director does and what the playwright contributes to the process, as well as providing a deeper appreciation of the profoundly collaborative nature of theatrical creation.

The notion of creative and authorial agency, issues related to power relations between participants, and appreciation of the social and professional networks that underpin the groupings found in any rehearsal room were brought into clearer focus once I began to apply to rehearsal analytical concepts and methods derived from my reading of ethnography. I have written elsewhere about the insights that led me to place engagement with rehearsal process at the centre of the study of performance (McAuley 1998, 2006(a), 2008), and as I observed more and more rehearsals it became clear that the critical apparatus provided by theatre studies (historiography, semiotics, text and performance analysis) was insufficient when attempting to deal with the complex interpersonal relations, work practices and the collective creative process involved in rehearsal. My theatre studies colleagues, like the theatre artists I observed, engaged in the practice of rehearsal but did not write about it or theorise their experiences.

Rehearsal as we know it today in the west, is substantially an invention of the twentieth century, and it is inextricably bound up with the emergence and development of the role of director. In earlier periods, the task of preparation for performance was essentially one of organising the stage traffic and ensuring that any special effects worked. The actors' work of preparation was done privately, in their own time, and they were given the text only of their own parts, indicated by cue words, so the actor would not necessarily know even which character was the interlocutor in the exchange in question (Stern 2000). Well into the nineteenth century, the custom was to have only one full rehearsal of the whole play with all the actors present, and sometimes there was no rehearsal at all. When Edmund Kean was invited to play Shylock at the Croydon Theatre, he notified the stage manager that he would not require any rehearsal even though he knew nothing about the planned production and had not worked with the company before (Marshall, 1957, 12). Furthermore, in those rehearsals that were held, 'leading actors never troubled to read any of their speeches . . ., contenting themselves with merely giving the cues.' Norman Marshall reports that, when Macready tried to change this at Drury Lane, the actors threatened to go on strike (13).

These anecdotes provide a measure of what the advent of the director has meant for the theatre.[3] A stage production is now acknowledged to be a complex work of art and it is through the rehearsal process that this work of art is brought into being, which is why the observation of rehearsal is such a fascinating and compelling area of research. Rehearsal is the time when the multiple material elements that will constitute a unique work of art are progressively brought together and when the process of reaction between them is set in train. Rehearsal as we now know it is a process of discovery and, in the words of American actor Peter Moloney, 'the things that are to be discovered are not known by *anyone* before the work of rehearsal begins – not by the playwright, not by the director, not by the actors' (Cole 2001, 162). The role of the director in the process is absolutely crucial even when, perhaps especially when, the work is emerging from a genuinely collaborative effort by artists working in different media. While a director-auteur like Richard Foreman or Tadeusz Kantor[4] has the complex task of orchestrating a wide range of elements to meet the demands of his own vision, the work of the director in a creative process such as that described by Moloney is even more complex in that it involves stimulating and unleashing the creativity of others as well as moulding the results into an intellectually dense, artistically compelling work.

Ethnography has provided methodological guidance and concepts that 'are good to think with' (to use Lévi-Strauss's often quoted phrase), and the ethnographic turn has brought with it a significant shift from concern with the individual work of art to the social and cultural context within which that work is being created. As the above quotation from Paul Atkinson suggests, it becomes necessary to consider the institutional framework, the 'socially organised settings' that both constrain and make possible the production of the artwork as well as the work itself. *Toy Symphony* was part of a season and, for a sizable proportion of the audience who were Belvoir subscribers, it was received in the

context of all the other productions that made up that season's programme; the season's productions are embedded in and emerge from
the company set up, are seen to be the work of Company B and not just
the particular artists, some of whom might well be producing work for
other companies in the same season (actors and designers in Sydney are
essentially freelance, hired only for the given production); Company B
Belvoir is part of a wider theatre community and this in turn is part of
the urban culture of Sydney. Within the theatre community, Company
B has a certain reputation, represents certain values and work practices,
and employment there confers a certain kind of cachet on the individual
practitioner. For spectators too, and in particular for the loyal subscribers who come back year after year for the whole season, Company B
Belvoir is associated with a certain kind of theatre and certain social
values. Any production is thus embedded in a series of institutional
and cultural contexts, all of which have a part to play in relation to the
work process involved in that particular production, all of which need
to be considered alongside and around the narrative recounting details
of aesthetic choices made, interpretations discussed, stories told and
imaginary worlds constructed. James Clifford has described the task of
the ethnographic observer and analyst as

> a continuous tacking beween the 'inside' and the 'outside' of events; on the
> one hand grasping the sense of specific occurrences and gestures empa-
> thetically, on the other stepping back to situate these meanings in wider
> contexts. (Clifford 1988, 34)

In the words of Clifford Geertz, reflecting in his Jerusalem-Harvard
lectures on the experiences of a lifetime's work as an anthropologist,
the task is one that 'involves bringing figure and ground, the passing
occasion and the long story, into coincident view' (Geertz 1995, 31).
Many hours spent in rehearsal rooms showed that my colleagues and I
had been engaging in participant-observation, even though we had not
been using that term, but our reading of ethnography revealed the extent
to which the analytical practices we had been inventing were already
a form of ethnographic study. This reading also provided a broader
context within which to consider some ongoing methodological and
ethical issues, such as the vexed question of the relation between insider
and outsider.

Rehearsals are traditionally private, a time when artists work
intensively together, when actors go further and deeper into their own
and their characters' emotions and need to feel safe to experiment with
what they are finding. The demarcation between insider and outsider is

very strong in the theatre, and never more so than when it is a matter of rehearsals, for many directors fear the disruptive impact an outsider can have on the chemistry that is occurring in the room. This is why, for example, when Susan Letzler Cole was observing rehearsals for the Wooster Group's production *Frank Dell's The Temptation of Saint Antony*, she was asked to leave on one occasion when relations became fraught between members of the group, even though the tension had nothing to do with her (Cole 1992, 114–15). Many directors refuse to admit observers and others will do so only on condition that that person takes on a role in the rehearsal, such as assistant to one of the functionaries in the process (director, dramaturg, stage manager) and thereby becomes a pseudo-insider. In the circumstances, it is not surprising that most of the accounts of rehearsal that have been published have been written by insiders concerning their own work: directors, actors, playwrights (for example, Stafford Clark 1989, Hall 1983, Sher 1985 and 2005, Cox 1992, Wesker 1997) and even dramaturgs (Bly 1996 and 2001).

While these accounts are invaluable and, indeed, they are rapidly becoming canonical texts as scholarly interest in rehearsal develops, it is my view that accounts by outsiders also have a valuable contribution to make. In pursuing this intuition against the received wisdom of theatre practitioners, who are more often than not extremely reluctant to admit an observer to their rehearsal room, I found in the debates that had occurred in ethnography a decade earlier the most nuanced discussion of an issue which is, of course, utterly central to that discipline. James Clifford, writing in 1986 about the shifting power relations between anthropologists and their informants in the postcolonial world, makes two very important points about insider accounts: 'Insiders studying their own cultures offer new angles of vision and depths of understanding. Their accounts are empowered *and restricted* in unique ways' [my emphasis] (Clifford 1986, 9). Accounts such as those mentioned above describe the process from the perspective of the writer's role in it and, although they definitely have 'depths of understanding' unavailable to an outsider, this understanding does not necessarily extend very far beyond the writer's own role. The insider, engaged in an act of artistic creation, will see differently from an outside observer, and find different things important or noteworthy. Insiders are also well placed to talk informally with the other participants throughout the process and, thus, tend to elicit more valuable insights than are normally forthcoming in structured interviews after the event. On the other hand, an outsider may see things that familiarity has rendered unremarkable to the insider and may usefully broaden

the perspective by paying more attention to the experience and contribution of other participants.

Vitally important, however, is Clifford's point about the published accounts being restricted in different ways. When a person is
located within a community or group, that person is subject to the
power relations of the group, and may be reluctant to hurt people's
feelings or offend the powerful who have influence over future job
opportunities. The outsider's account is of course also subject to
constraints, albeit slightly different ones, and it may be true that, as
Georges Banu claims, anyone who has observed a rehearsal process
becomes a quasi-insider:

> It must be acknowledged that any account by an outsider will, to a greater
> or lesser extent, be a betrayal of the reality because the observer becomes
> emotionally involved with the experience he is recounting and will refuse,
> not so much to reveal it, as to describe it as fully as he could; it is as though
> he feels it would be indecent to open to scrutiny a practice located in the no
> man's land between public and private. (Banu 2005, 41)

It is not clear if Banu is speaking of his own experience here or gener-
alising from other cases, but the point is a serious one. On numerous
occasions during the rehearsals for *Toy Symphony*, Neil Armfield or one
of the actors would tell me that what had just been said should not be
included in the book and I have of course respected their wishes. There
is a good deal of story telling in the rehearsal room, often involving other
productions and other artists, sometimes quite indiscreet but, as Marion
Potts pointed out in her masters thesis, written after she had spent
several years working alongside some of the most experienced directors
in Sydney, this kind of story telling is in fact an essential part of the way
craft knowledge and theory are articulated and passed on (Potts 1995).
Jim Sharman put the point even more pithily in the first Rex Cramphorn
Memorial Lecture when he said 'theatre practitioners are like a lost
tribe with only an oral tradition handed down erratically from person
to person, usually as gossip' (Sharman 1996). Writing about rehearsal,
thus, requires navigation of a fine line between betraying confidences by
telling too much and failing to engage with the reality of the practice by
telling too little.

While there are definite advantages that flow from becoming a
quasi-insider by taking on a role within the process, my own experience has been that the task of observing and note taking is so demanding that it is not possible to undertake any further responsibilities
and nevertheless pay the requisite attention to all the aspects of the

developing work process. A day spent observing in the rehearsal room has to be followed by several hours of writing up what anthropologists call the 'scratch notes' taken during the day (Sanjek 1990, 92–121). Graduate students of anthropology preparing to go into the field are warned that failure to write up scratch notes within a period of forty-eight hours or so will render them useless. I can attest to the validity of this advice: coming back to notes taken a few days earlier if I had missed writing them up, I would find that they triggered little in the way of additional memories, so it became a simple matter of transcribing factual details, whereas writing up on the same day always triggered more memories, more details and the beginnings of theoretical speculations. The task is, thus, demanding and absorbing and would definitely be put at risk if one had also to take responsibility for part of the creative process.

The experience of ethnography is that the participant/observer in the field has to be both vitally enmeshed in the daily experiences of the people being studied and, at the same time, sufficiently distanced to make observations, write notes about what is occurring and find time to write these up in more detail. As Margaret Mead put it, the task is to 'maintain a balance between empathic involvement and disciplined detachment' (Mead in Naroll & Cohen 1973, 247). My realisation that it took many months of analysis and reflection before one rehearsal experience could be written up echoes the normal practice of ethnographers, who return home after a period in the field in order to engage in the next phase of the work: reflecting on the experience and transforming the mass of field notes into another form of discourse. The different timeframes involved in theatrical creation and academic reflection come strongly into play here: while the artists involved in the production of *Toy Symphony* have moved on to other productions, other equally intense creative experiences in the three years since the show ended, I am still living with it, still mulling over it, trying to find appropriate ways to write about it.

Undoubtedly, the single most valuable concept ethnographic practice has contributed to the study of rehearsal and performance analysis is Clifford Geertz's idea of 'thick description' (1973, 3–30) and its concomitant insistence on both the detailed minutiae that make up the 'passing occasion' and the larger structures of the 'long story' of which it is a part. Applying the idea to rehearsal means broadening the focus from concentrating on the materiality of the performance signifiers being created to greater awareness of the social and professional networks relating the participants in the rehearsal room to each other, and attempting to establish the nature of the social field within which the work is occurring. In order to discover the logic of the practice, one must be alert to all the details of rehearsal room talk, the terminology and the concepts used. Nothing can be taken for granted because the meaning attributed to a certain term may not be the same for practitioners coming from different backgrounds, and even for those with the same background, the meaning and use of key terms seems to change over time. The result is that virtually nothing can be bracketed out as irrelevant, whether it is jokes, gossip, story telling, a sudden silence or even (as happened on one occasion) an animated discussion of where to procure the best feta and avocado muffins. In rehearsal analysis as in ethnographic description, the larger picture comes into view through the accumulation of minutiae, and this is why the task requires full time presence by the observer and why it cannot be done adequately by someone dropping in at intervals to view work in progress.

In attempting to make sense of the relationships, exchanges and practices observed during the weeks of the rehearsal and the run of the show, I have found some very illuminating insights into the theory of interaction ritual, as developed by Erving Goffman and, particularly, by Randall Collins in his book *Interaction Ritual Chains* (2004). While the word 'ritual' is normally taken to refer to ceremonial practices, Collins explains that this common usage refers to what he calls 'formal rituals' and distinguishes from 'natural rituals.' The latter are far more widespread in social life and the necessary ingredients are the bodily co-presence of two or more people, boundaries to outsiders so that par-ticipants know who is included, who is excluded, a focus of attention on a common object or activity that is mutually enhanced by the focus of the other participants and a shared common mood. These four factors produce what Collins calls 'emotional energy' or, following Durkheim, 'collective effervescence.' The period of rehearsals can be seen as a classic interaction ritual chain, exemplifying the process that Collins describes 'in which participants develop a mutual focus of attention and become entrained in each other's bodily micro-rhythms and emotions' (2004, 47), a process that in turn generates feelings of solidarity, group mem-bership and social worth amongst the participants and functions to endow with particular value the objects and places that are at the heart of the activity. There are many features of the *Toy Symphony* rehearsals that might be considered somewhat peripheral to the task of producing the show, but seen in the light of interaction ritual theory, are utterly germane to the social process of which the production is a part, as will be discussed further in my final chapter.

Observation of rehearsal practice raises the question of when and where the creative process begins and perhaps also where it ends. In the case of *Toy Symphony*, as will be seen, there was the writer's process that had been going on for years with greater or lesser intensity, and this continued after the rehearsals and the run of the show with the preparation of the script for publication. The creative process for the other participants was also already well under way before the first day of rehearsals proper. A great deal of thought, discussion and planning had preceded that moment, including a reading of the whole text by the cast in the company's boardroom and reading of specific scenes during the audition process. The main role of the play was cast before the season was announced, photographs of Richard Roxburgh in the role of the child Roland were taken for the season brochure (see figure 1) so an image of the play was already imprinted in the minds of subscribers and the other artists. Michael Gow had written several drafts of his script and discussed these with Neil Armfield, making changes in response to problems raised. Ralph Myers had designed the set but he was still thinking about it, and when he met Neil, fortuitously while both were on holiday in Sicily a few weeks before rehearsals began, he decided on some radical changes. This indicates that the creative process is not confined to a particular place and time but can be bubbling along in a subliminal way even when the artist is doing something else, including being on holiday.

Ethnographers speak of the bounded nature of events and, as Tim Asch has put it: 'Observers and subjects may differ greatly in their perceptions of when an event or interaction begins and ends and whom it includes' (Asch in Rollwagen 1988, 3). This is certainly the case with rehearsals. It came as something of a surprise to Kylie Mascord, the stage manager, when I said that I wanted to attend the production meetings, held every Wednesday morning during the five weeks of rehearsal, and the 'bump in' when technical and production crew installed the set on the Belvoir stage. She had thought that my interest would be exclusively with what the actors were doing. As late as the preview performances, costume designer Tess Schofield was still finding delightful elements to add to the costume of some of the characters, which demonstrates the temporally extended nature of her creative process. And of course, there is a limit to where the observer can be in a diffuse process involving numerous artists, groups, and different types of artistic expression. Should I ask to go with the director and the playwright to lunch on the days when the latter was in Sydney, would this be an intrusion, would my presence prevent vital exchanges of views about the text? Should I have lunch in the kitchen with the group of actors who brought their own sandwiches or take the opportunity to get my own thoughts in

Figure 1. Richard Roxburgh in publicity photograph for *Toy Symphony*
Photo: Alex Craig

order somewhere else? And if I did go to the kitchen, what would I be
doing? It would clearly be inappropriate to take notes even though, of
course, the social bonding occurring at that time was a crucial part of
the process but would it not be even more unacceptable to make notes

about lunchtime discussions at some later time? Georgina Born, writing an ethnographic study of the Institute for Contemporary Music in Paris, found herself in a similar bind:

> As one intellectual informant and friend said, 'I never know when we are talking if we are simply talking, or whether you're going back home to write it up as notes;' to which I could only reply, 'both.' This touches on the inherently reflexive nature of the ethnographic encounter – a reality that makes it no less problematic for intellectual informants or ethnographer. (Born 1995, 8–9)

There is much to be learned from contemporary ethnographic practice when dealing with the practicalities and the ethics of rehearsal observation as well as in the subsequent phase of written analysis.

Neil Armfield and Company B

Neil Armfield is probably best known outside of Australia as a director of opera (his biographical note on the Opera Australia website lists eight foreign opera companies for whom he has directed: the Royal Opera Covent Garden, the Welsh National Opera, English National Opera, Zurich Opera, Houston Grand Opera, the Bregenz Festival, Canadian Opera and the Lyric Opera Chicago) but within Australia he is even better known for his theatrical productions. The 1999 tour to London, Dublin and Zurich of his acclaimed production of *Cloudstreet*, based on the novel by Tim Winton, and the success of his Broadway production of *Exit the King* in 2009, adapted by Armfield and Geoffrey Rush from Ionesco's play, have provided overseas audiences with some indication of why, in his home country, he is widely considered to be the finest theatre director of his generation. While he has directed for all the major theatre companies in Australia, it is as artistic director of Company B Belvoir for the last 16 years that he has created the works that best represent his mature style, and he has so successfully imprinted his particular artistic vision and management ethos on the company that it is difficult to remember it had a considerable life before he took over the directorship in 1994.

Neil Armfield was born in 1955, the youngest in a family of three boys living in the Sydney suburb of Concord, and he studied arts at Sydney University. He began directing plays for the Sydney University

Dramatic Society, where his talent was spotted by Paul Iles, general manager of the Nimrod Theatre, and Richard Wherrett, one of the three artistic co-directors of that theatre. In 1979, after Richard Wherrett left Nimrod in order to become the director of the newly formed Sydney Theatre Company, Armfield was invited to join John Bell and Ken Horler as artistic co-director of Nimrod, in Wherrett's place. He stayed for two years with Nimrod, then took up the position of associate director at the Lighthouse Theatre Company in Adelaide under the mentorship of Jim Sharman. It was at Lighthouse that he directed a legendary production of *Twelfth Night* in 1983 as well as plays by Patrick White, until then considered virtually unstageable but revealed by the Lighthouse directors to be among the most powerful Australian plays yet written. He returned to Sydney in 1985, at the time of the crisis that saw Nimrod moving out of the Belvoir Street theatre, the building being put up for sale to developers, and a heroic effort spearheaded by Sue Hill and Chris Westwood to raise the money from within the theatre community to purchase the building and keep it safe for theatre.[5]

Hundreds of arts, entertainment and media professionals contributed funds to form a syndicate, Company A, to purchase the building. Under a unique scheme, Company A owns the building but leases it to Company B, which has responsibility for managing the theatre and producing the annual season of shows in both the Upstairs theatre (capacity 320) and the tiny Downstairs (capacity around 80). The scheme protects the theatre itself from the risks that are inherent in the business of theatre making and ensures that, even if Company B should fold, the theatre itself will still be there. In fact, over the twenty-five years of its existence, Company B has been enormously successful both in establishing a substantial audience of enthusiastic subscribers and in attracting corporate donors to supplement the always inadequate government subsidies.

The company's annual report proudly lists the core values and principles that underpin their work:

> Belief in the primacy of the artistic process; clarity and playfulness in storytelling; a sense of the community within the theatrical environment; responsiveness to current social and political issues; equality, ethical standards and shared ownership of artistic and company achievements; development of our performers, artists and staff. (Company B *Annual Report*, 2006, 3)

These principles are not just high sounding ideals but have been implemented in such things as the parity of pay policy, which the company maintained until 2010, causing the former Prime Minister, Paul Keating, to refer to it affectionately as 'the last commune in Australia'.[6] The published principles reflect the nature of the company's relationship to both the theatre community and the wider community within which the theatre is located. They also convey Armfield's conviction that theatre, however playful or wild it might be, has something vitally important to contribute to society, perhaps more so than ever in the face of social, political and environmental problems that seem to get more and more intractable year by year. As he asked in his annual message to subscribers in the 2007 season brochure: 'How do we confront the overwhelming problems of our world without buckling under the weight of despair and anxiety?' And then answered his own question: 'by listening and teaching, by raising the standards of education, by advancing informed debate, by encouraging the telling of our stories in books, on our screens and on our stages. And that is what we're trying, in our own way, to do. That's our job: to tell the stories, to sing the songs of our land, our world, our past' (Armfield 2007, 6–7).

The annual subscription season consists of six or seven productions, two or three of which are directed by Neil Armfield. There is a pattern to the programming that juxtaposes new and classic Australian plays, classics from the international repertoire, especially Shakespeare, and contemporary works from abroad. The performance history supplied by the company (figure 2) indicates their method of categorising the works and it shows that by far the largest category is new Australian plays. As part of this, there has been a significant attempt to produce work with strong Indigenous content as well as providing mentorship and opportunities for Indigenous artists. Indeed, when Neil Armfield was awarded the Order of Australia in 2007 for 'services to the arts,' the citation read in part: 'for promotion of innovative Australian productions including Australian Indigenous drama'. For people in Sydney, Company B Belvoir represents high quality text-based theatre that still maintains something of the larrikin edge that is part of the Nimrod legacy. As Neil put it when describing the 'sing-along' performance which ended the phenomenal run of Keating!, 'Times like these are as good as it gets – and really what the ongoing experiment of Company B is all about: creating a live experience that is unforgettable, unique and specifically a fusion of the creative energy in that space on that night' (Armfield 2009, 4).

Figure 2. Company B Belvoir performance history 1985–2007

Year	Shakespeare	Classic	Classic Australian	New Australian	New International
1985			*Signal Driver* Patrick White	*Ha Ha Ha* Performing Humans	
1986				*ABC* Holman; *A Smile a Song and a Lump of Wood* Kelso/Ackroyd; *Pearls Before Swine* Watkins/Harriot; *State of Shock* Strachan	*Savannah Bay* Duras *Kids Stuff* Cousse
1987				*Cho Cho San* Daniel Keene; *Magpie's Nest* Grattan; *Europe* Michael Gow	*Lie of the Mind* Shepard; *Shakers* O'Connell; *Gertrude Stein and a Companion* Margolyes; *On Parliament Hill* Greig
1988		*Les Enfants du Paradis* Prevert Lerner *Ghosts* Ibsen *Drums of Thunder* Brecht		*Capricornia* Herbert/ Keir; *Hate* Sewell	
1989		*Diary of a Madman* Gogol/Holman *A Doll's House* Ibsen		*Greek Tragedy* Leigh	*Conquest of the South Pole* Karge; *The Wolf's Banquet* Cousse

Year					
1990	*The Tempest*		*No Sugar* Davis	*Call of the Wild* Kemp; *Words of One Syllable* Barrett; *Café Fledermaus* Archer	
1991		*The Master Builder* Ibsen		*Royal Commission into the Australian Economy* Clarke; *Buzz* Coleman/Coppin; *Headbutt* Abbot; *Diving for Pearls* Thomson	*Love and Magic in Mamma's Kitchen* Wertmuller
1992		*Diary of a Madman* Gogol *Frogs* Aristophanes		*Cosi* Nowra; *Popular Mechanicals 2*	*The Cockroach Opera* Riantiarno
1993				*Aftershocks* Brown; *The Exile Trilogy* Gilgul/Kosky; *Radiance* Nowra	*Scenes from an Execution* Barker
1994	*Hamlet*			*All of Me* Legs on the Wall; *Dead Heart* Parsons; *Blue Murder* Christian	*Picasso at the Lapin Agile* Martin
1995	*The Tempest*	*Splendids* Genet	*The Blind Giant is Dancing* Sewell	*Emma* Pitts	
1996		*The Alchemist* Jonson *View from the Bridge* Miller	*Night on Bald Mountain* White	*Up the Road* Hardinge	*Wasp* Martin

Figure 2. (continued)

Year	Shakespeare	Classic	Classic Australian	New Australian	New International
1997		*The Seagull* Chekhov *Lulu* GWPabst *The Birthday Party* Pinter		*Black Mary* Jansen; *The Governor's Family* Christian	
1998		*Caucasian Chalk Circle* Brecht *Trouble in Tahiti* Bernstein		*Cloudstreet* Enright/Monjo; *Under the Influence* Legs on the Wall; *Welcome to Broome* Melllick; *Love Burns* Nowra/Koehne	*Judas Kiss* Hare
1999	*As You Like It*		*The Small Poppies* Holman	*Burnt Piano* Fleming; *Box the Pony* Purcell/Rankin; *My Vicious Angel* Evans	*Little Cherry Orchard* Alexej Slapovskij
2000	*Twelfth Night*	*Suddenly Last Summer* Williams *Figaro* Beaumarchais	*The Ham Funeral* White	*Stolen* Harrison	*The Unexpected Man* Reza
2001		*Ubu* Jarry	*A Cheery Soul* White	*Emma's Nose* Livingstone; *Aliwa* Winmar; *Roulette* Cortese; *Cloudstreet* Enright/Monjo	*The Laramie Project* Tectonic

Year					
2002		Buried Child Shepard; Waiting for Godot Beckett	The Dreamers Davis; The Aunt's Story White	Svetlana in Slingbacks Levkowicz	The Cosmonaut's Last Message to the Woman He Loved in the Former Soviet Union Greig; My Zinc Bed Hare
2003	Macbeth	Threepenny Opera Brecht	William Yang Retrospective	Conversations with the Dead Frankland; Run Rabbit Run Valentine	The Underpants Martin; The Lieutenant of Inishmore McDonagh
2004	Midsummer Night's Dream	What the Butler Saw Orton		In Our Name Jamieson; Life Times Three (Page 8 Nowra/Page; Little Black Bastard Tovey; Gulpilil Gulpilil/Cribb); The Spook Reeves	Our Lady of Sligo Barry
2005		The Chairs Ionesco; Black Medea Euripides adapt. Enoch		The Sapphires Briggs; Ray's Tempest Rodgers	Stuff Happens Hare
2006		Peribanez de Vega	Capricornia Herbert/Nowra	It Just Stopped Sewell; Keating! Bennetto	
2007		Exit the King Ionesco; Who's Afraid of Virginia Woolf? Albee		Snugglepot and Cuddlepie Clarke/ MacLeod/John; The Gates of Egypt Sewell; Parramatta Girls Valentine; Toy Symphony Gow	Paul Brenton

Michael Gow and *Toy Symphony*

Michael Gow is the same age as Neil Armfield, born in 1955, and educated, like him, at a state high school and then, in the mid-1970s, in the
Faculty of Arts at the University of Sydney. At university, they were
rivals, as Neil recalls, acting and directing plays for the Sydney University
Dramatic Society (SUDS). It was extremely unusual for amateur or
student theatre to be reviewed by national newspaper critics, but this
is what happened for some of these SUDS productions, notably Barry
Keefe's *Gimme Shelter*, directed by Neil Armfield, in which Michael
Gow gave what Armfield still remembers as 'an amazing performance'.
This was a particularly vibrant period in Australian culture when the
New Wave was, in the words of Geoffrey Milne, 'Australianising the
Australian theatre' (Milne 2004, 6) and a new Labor government had
been elected after more than two decades of stultifying conservative rule.

Unlike Armfield, Michael Gow was an only child. He was brought
up in Como, in the Sutherland Shire, part of Sydney's vast and sprawling
southern suburbs, and he returns in his plays frequently to the experience of growing up in suburbia, the dysfunctional families, the mind-
less cruelty inflicted on homosexual teenagers, the pretensions and the
snobbery, but his dark vision is balanced by the recurring theme of the
redemptive power of art. His first play, *The Kid* (1983) won considerable
success, but it was *Away* (1986) that really seemed to strike a chord with
Australian audiences, actors and directors. Reprinted nearly every year
since it was first published, and sometimes more than once, performed
in every state capital and regional centre, read by generations of high
school students as part of the literature syllabus, it is the most frequently
revived Australian play. For Neil Armfield, who has directed three productions of it, including the 1987 production for the Playbox Theatre
in Melbourne, it is '*the* great Australian play of the last quarter of the
twentieth century'.

Michael Gow is not a prolific playwright: *Away* was followed by
On Top of the World (1986), *Europe* (1987), *1841* (a play commissioned
for the Australian Bicentennial in 1988), *All Stops Out* (1989), *Furious*
(1994), *Sweet Phoebe* (1994), *Live Acts on Stage* (1996) and then nothing
apart from an adaptation, *The Fortunes of Richard Mahoney* (2004) until
Toy Symphony in 2007. During this time, however, he was constantly
involved in theatre as a director, but no longer as an actor. He has also
written for television, and his mini series, *Edens Lost* (based on the novel
by Sumner Locke Elliott and directed by Neil Armfield) won him the

Australian Film Institute award in 1989 for Best Mini Series Screenplay. He makes no secret of the fact that writing does not come easily to him. He told Richard Crooke, in an interview published online in *Time Out*, 'I never write for pleasure. I hate it. In a masochist way. I enjoy the sense of achievement, but I have to push myself all the time' (Gow 2010(a)). This tallies with comments made during the rehearsals for *Toy Symphony*, when he said that he was happy to make amendments to what had been written but it was evident that he approached any requirement for new writing with considerable reluctance.

He was appointed artistic director of the Queensland Theatre Company in 1999 and has run the company with conspicuous success. His decision to decline the offer to continue in the position after the expiry of his contract in August 2010 was perhaps affected in some way by the extraordinary success of the Company B production of *Toy Symphony* in 2007. The production won no fewer than seven Sydney Theatre Awards and four Helpmann Awards in 2007–08, and the critical reviews were overwhelmingly positive.[7] In the press release posted on the Australian Stage website on 4 April 2010 when his resignation from the directorship had been announced, Gow spoke of a 'growing need to get back to myself as a writer' (Gow 2010 b). If this is the case, then the intermeshing of fact and fiction that is such a feature of his work will be continuing, and the redemption hinted at for Roland Henning, the central character in *Toy Symphony,* may become a reality for Michael Gow, experiencing like Roland a prolonged inability to write.

A significant part of Michael Gow's skill as a playwright is to write in such a way as to leave space for the actor and the director. Richard Roxburgh commented on numerous occasions about the power of Michael's writing for the actor in this play. He found the broken syntax and fragmented sentences extremely difficult to learn but he delighted in the scope offered by them and by such things as what he called 'the Gowian full stops'. A good example of the latter occurs in the second scene, when Roland Henning says to the copyright lawyer: 'There you are. There. You are.' (p. 9), and I frequently marvelled at the way Richard was able to load those few bland words with layers of self justification and apprehension as, guided by the punctuation, he shifted the focus from Roland convincing the lawyer to Roland realising his own predicament. Richard Roxburgh told an interviewer before the play opened, 'there are a few scenes in this play that are really Michael Gow at his absolute incisive, gobsmacking best. There are some scenes that are just so fantastically raw, there's such pleasure in the playing of it. It's a great thing for an actor to get those rewards along the way' (*Sydney Morning Herald*, 9 November 2007, 14).

Richard Roxburgh

Richard Roxburgh was born in 1962 and brought up in the New South Wales country town of Albury, the youngest of six children. He studied economics at the Australian National University but had already been deeply involved with theatre while still at school when he played Willie Loman in a school production of *Death of a Salesman*. He trained at the National Institute for Dramatic Art (NIDA), Australia's most prestigious theatre school, graduating in 1986, and has since worked in film, television and on the stage in Australia as well as contributing some notable supporting performances to international blockbuster movies such as *Mission Impossible II*, *Van Helsing* and *Moulin Rouge*. He said in an interview 'when I came out of drama school, it was all about theatre. It was what I invested all my love in and the thing that I really cared about. I did quite a lot of work with various companies. But finally, it was Belvoir Street that settled as my creative home' (Talking Heads, Australian Broadcasting Corporation (ABC), 2007).

He has worked with Neil Armfield on a number of occasions. It was Neil who directed his graduation play at NIDA (Louis Nowra's *Golden Age*), as well as his extraordinary *Hamlet* in 1994, and his Trigorin in *The Seagull* in 1997 for Company B. For the Sydney Theatre Company, his work includes Pinter's *The Homecoming*, Patrick Marber's *Closer*, and *Romeo and Juliet*. In addition to his acting, Richard Roxburgh has created some significant work as a director, both for theatre and film. He directed a highly regarded production of *Twelfth Night* for Company B in 2000 as well as *Ray's Tempest,* a play by Steve Rodgers that was based on an idea by Roxburgh and formed part of Company B's 2005 season. He collaborated with Justin Monjo on the stage adaptation of Tim Winton's novel *That Eye The Sky* and then directed it for his own company, Burning House, as part of the Sydney Festival in 1994. When he directs a work, whether for film or theatre, it tends to be something he has worked on for several years, collaborating with a writer to produce the script he will then direct. This was also the case for the film adaptation of *Romulus My Father*, clearly another labour of love, with a script written by Nick Drake in a seven-year collaboration with Roxburgh. The film, directed by Roxburgh, won several Australian Film Institute awards in 2007, including best feature film.

Belvoir Street Theatre

The Belvoir Street building was originally a factory, and was in a derelict condition when the Nimrod company transformed it into a theatre in 1974, retaining the key features of the idiosyncratic performance space they had created in the tiny mews building they had earlier occupied and that their success had forced them to quit. The theatre building itself and the particular features of the performance space it houses have played a vital role in the success of Company B and of the Nimrod Theatre before it.

There is an asymmetrical, five-sided, open thrust stage, set into the corner of the room, surrounded by three irregularly placed, steeply raked banks of seating that fan out at an angle of 58°, thus ensuring

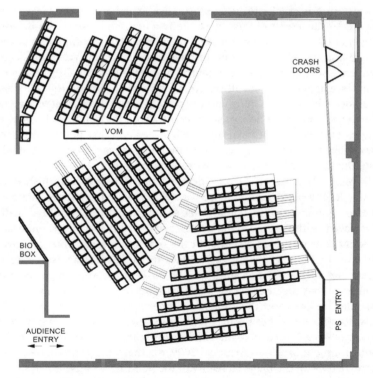

Figure 3. Floor Plan of Belvoir Street Theatre with set for *Toy Symphony*
Graphic: Russell Emerson

a kind of immediacy of access for spectators which in turn creates a particular kind of energy. As Neil Armfield has said many times, the corner stage is central to his aesthetic, and he goes even further: 'The interplay of space, light and sound is unique. It's why our company exists' (Armfield 2009, 6). This performance space affects spectators as much as practitioners and I have argued elsewhere that, for a number of historical reasons, it is at the heart of a whole way of conceptualising and experiencing theatre that is peculiar to Sydney (McAuley 2011). The shape of the stage, the dimensions of the overall space and the relationship between stage and auditorium mean that spectators are very close to the actors, they witness the performance in a direct, unmediated way, and actors get quick and undiluted feedback from the audience. Looking down at the stage is a very different experience from looking into a box set from a seat in the stalls, and the fact that the floor of the stage is always visible means that actors' moves are perceived in relation to the floor as much as to elements of the set. Another material feature of the theatre that is crucial to the performance experience is the placement of the entrance/exit points: there are two access points to the Belvoir stage, one from the wings on the audience right or prompt side of the stage[8] and the other via a vomitory that leads under the raked blocks of audience seating between the central and left hand (or OP) blocks of seats (see figure 3). While other access points can be introduced if the set includes false walls, as here with the crash doors, a significant feature of the dynamism of the Belvoir space comes from the vomitory because it means that the lines of force running between entrance points necessarily engage the audience space rather than leaving the spectators outside looking in, as with a traditional picture frame stage.

When the Belvoir Street Theatre was extensively refurbished in 2005–06, the performance space was left virtually unchanged. State of the art equipment, more comfortable seating and better backstage facilities have greatly improved the experience for both spectators and practitioners but what was essential in the old building has been retained: the size of the auditorium that allows immediacy of access between actor and spectator, the sightlines, the off-centre corner stage and the vomitory that together create a special kind of energy. To quote Neil Armfield once more: 'the audience connects with the actors at Belvoir Street unlike any other theatre. It means somehow that every show has a cast of over 300 participants, all breathing the same air, living in the same moment of story' (Armfield 2009, 6). The description I have given here focuses on the material reality of the building because it plays such an important role in determining relationships between performers and audience and because these in turn affect the emotional intensity of the performance experience for both parties. It should, however, also be pointed out that, for reasons that depend in part on these material features, in part on a complex of historical factors and in part on the work of Neil Armfield as artistic director over a period of sixteen years, the Belvoir Theatre and Company B have come to occupy a very particular place within the theatre culture of Sydney. The Sydney Theatre Company, with its prestigious theatres around the harbour foreshore and its status as the official company for the state of New South Wales, may attract a larger share of public funding and more glamorous sponsorships, but for theatre practitioners and spectators alike there is the sense that, as one of the actors put it, 'Belvoir is art house theatre and its productions have heart and are culturally richer than those of the STC.' Furthermore, the Belvoir Theatre occupies the building that Nimrod created and it is thus seen to be in a direct line of descent from the artists who first began to create an authentically Australian theatre during the so-called New Wave in the 1960s (see Milne 2004). All of these factors have some bearing on the creative process that I observed and will be discussed further in the final chapter of this study.

The project

The plan for me to observe one of Neil Armfield's productions and write a book about the experience had been discussed over a number of years but was continually deferred due to problems that arose: Neil's serious illness in 2005, a late decision to rehearse Stephen Sewell's *It Just Stopped* in Melbourne rather than Sydney, the need for the timing to coincide with my own availability. When finally, in 2007, several years after the plan was first adumbrated, everything fell into place, it was with a new Australian play and a group of actors I did not know. Michael Gow had studied French in the department in which I taught but I did not know him as an undergraduate nor did I see the SUDS productions on which he and Neil Armfield collaborated. I had, however, spent a fascinating week in 1991 watching him at work on his production of Racine's *Phaedra* and I had, of course, seen a great many of Neil Armfield's productions over the years.

Neil arranged for me to get copies of all the draft versions of the *Toy Symphony* script (the so-called Rehearsal Draft 1 with which the rehearsal process began, was in fact the fourth draft). I attended rehearsals every day for five weeks in the renovated warehouse that now houses the

Company B offices, wardrobe store and rehearsal rooms beginning on Tuesday 2 October and I also attended the weekly production meetings, held for an hour on Wednesday mornings. On 5 November I spent several hours in the theatre while the production crew were bumping in and the actors had a day off, and I then watched all the technical rehearsals, the two dress rehearsals on 9 and 10 November, and the preview performances on 10, 11 and 13 November. I was there for the party and shared some of the exhilaration of opening night on 14 November and I attended performances on numerous occasions throughout the run, sometimes sitting backstage to watch the work process from that perspective, once in the bio box with Kylie Mascord, the stage manager, as she 'called' the show, and several times in the auditorium, trying to see the production from many of the different viewing positions provided by the three banks of seats in the Belvoir Street Theatre. I attended all the sessions during the preview week when Neil delivered his 'notes' to the cast and I was given the handwritten sheets of notes posted in the actors' dressing room after performances he attended during the run when there was no formal meeting with the actors. Most of the interviews that I had arranged with the actors occurred during the run, and on some occasions I went out to supper with them after the show or was given a lift or drove one of the actors home after a performance. From the party on the final night of the run (22 December 2007) until March 2010 when I began my most intensive period of writing about the process, I did not see or speak to any of the participants. An experience that occupied most of my waking thoughts for nearly three intensive months was suddenly over, and the leap from pseudo-intimacy to complete absence provides an instructive insight into aspects of the actors' working life that are rarely discussed.

The description of the extent of my involvement and of the access I was given is an indication of the basis on which this account of the work process has been constructed. The production was special for many reasons, notably in that it was the first full length work for the stage Michael Gow had written for ten years, an enormously long period of silence from a playwright who had been able to capture the country's *Zeitgeist* so powerfully in 1986. It also marked the return to the theatre of one of Australia's most accomplished actors, Richard Roxburgh, after seven years working in film and television, much of it out of the country. It is a particularly galling fact of theatre life that actors, whose artistry is the driving force of the creative and the performance process, should be paid so poorly in the theatre compared to the remuneration they can receive for work in film and television where the creative process is handled at its most profound levels by others, long after the actors have done their bit and moved on to other things. The answer Richard gave when asked why he had stayed away from the theatre for so long raises major issues about the actor's experience, which are discussed in Part Two where I reflect on the intermeshing of real life and fiction that is so much part of an actor's work in the theatre.

A question I had pondered before rehearsals began concerned the fact that there would be three people in the room with considerable directorial experience: Michael Gow, while ostensibly the writer, is an experienced and accomplished director whose work in the theatre in recent years has been overwhelmingly as director, and Richard Roxburgh, playing the huge central role, is also a director, usually for works he has also co-written, adapted from literary works over a long period of development. Before the process began, I did wonder how the fact of having three highly skilled directors in the room would work in practice and whether it might create a degree of tension. When I spoke of this late in the run of the play to another of the actors, Monica Maughan, she was immediately dismissive of any such possibility. She said 'Oh no, they are all professionals and they know what their role is in this process. They all respect the protocol that every suggestion has to go to the director.' This is certainly true, and the three roles were scrupulously respected: every suggested cut or addition to the text was discussed with Michael by Neil in their regular phone calls and emails, Neil's authority as director was never challenged, and there was no question of either of the others taking it upon themselves to say anything that might have been construed as a 'note' for another participant. It was not uncommon for Neil to defer to Richard on the playing of a given moment, as happened for example on Day 21 when they were rehearsing the final scene. Richard said 'let me experiment, I will find it' and Neil said simply 'I know' and turned his attention to the other actor in that scene. Notwithstanding this acknowledgement of each other's strengths and what Monica referred to as the 'protocols', I think there is evidence that, as the work developed over the weeks of the rehearsals and also over the weeks of the run, there were some significant differences between these three key players as to directions into which to take the material. This fascinating question will also be explored further in Part Two.

The quotation from Brecht that serves as epigraph to this chapter, and indeed to the book as a whole, encapsulates with admirable concision the central premise of my study. In choosing to write an extended description of a single rehearsal process rather than extrapolating from the many productions I have observed, my purpose is to give an account of the day-to-day work, the hard graft involved in repeating a given

fragment over and over again, trying to find the optimum arrangement of all the variables, the incremental advances in knowledge and
understanding, the hesitations, anxieties and compromises as well as
the thrill of discovery, the tensions that arise as well as the emotional
warmth of the relations between the participants. As indicated earlier in
this introduction, I am also vitally interested in the complex nature of
collective creativity. It seemed to me that an account of rehearsal process
involving references to a range of productions could mislead the reader
by showing only the high points of discovery without the repetitive work
process that precedes the moment of discovery, but I acknowledge the
possibility that focusing on the day-to-day work of a single production
may overwhelm the reader with a plethora of what seem to be minute
details.

The great anthropologist E. Evans-Pritchard once said that for the
ethnographer 'the decisive battle is not fought in the field but in the study
afterwards' (in Sanjek 1990), and his comment draws attention to the
sheer difficulty of what is being attempted. As Evans-Pritchard knew all
too well, any period in the field produces an enormous amount of material that has to be ordered and analysed before a useful account can be
produced, and in the case of rehearsal, the danger is always present that
the written account will render boring what was in fact an exhilarating
experience. The two-part structure of this book is a response to the need
to achieve an appropriate balance between detailed description of the
daily work practices and commentary on the larger social and cultural
processes within which they are located and to which they contribute.
Part One is, thus, a relatively straightforward narrative account of the
process, largely chronological but with some activities singled out for
particular attention, while Part Two consists of a number of more reflec-
tive essays. My aim has been to provide a compelling story of the day-
to-day work of the rehearsal process, maintaining where possible the
sense of not knowing ahead of time things that were not in fact known
at the time by the participants, and deferring until Part Two attempts
to draw out from the material any more general observations. Part Two
consists of four essays. The first deals with the way the rehearsal space
was haunted by figures brought into it through the story telling that
accompanied the work process, the second with the different directions
in which author, director and actor wanted to take the material, the third
examines in greater depth Neil Armfield's directorial process, and the
last one attempts to locate the whole production experience within the
larger social and cultural context of which it is a part. The two sections
of the book are interdependent and there are a number of references in
the narrative section to matters that will be dealt with in more depth in

later chapters. In order to permit the narrative a degree of autonomy, however, these references to the later commentary are used sparingly.

A final warning concerns the potential confusion for the reader confronted with a narrative involving twenty characters, the artists, technicians and craftspeople who created Company B's *Toy Symphony*, all of whom are referred to by name on numerous occasions here, and an embedded narrative constituted by Michael Gow's play which itself involves another twenty-four characters, most of them named. It is evident that this constitutes a bewildering number of names and I have tried to provide a brief indication of role or function every time I have used a name that has not been mentioned for a few pages. The Company List (reproduced on p. 33–4) formed part of the folder of essential materials handed to every participant on the first day of rehearsals and readers may need to refer back to it, as to the *dramatis personae* listed at the beginning of a play text, if my signposting proves inadequate.

Notes

1   The German *Probe*, the Italian *prova* and the Spanish *ensayo* all derive from words meaning to try; the French *répétition* and the Russian *repetitsia* foreground the idea of repetition.

2   Notwithstanding these comments, the study of rehearsal is slowly beginning to emerge as a sub-discipline in theatre and performance studies, witness the work of Josette Féral and the Working Group on Creative Processes she convenes for the International Federation of Theatre Research, the interest in theatre practices expressed by French exponents of genetic criticism (see Léger and Grésillon 2005; Kinderman and Jones 2009) and the special issues of theatre journals dedicated to rehearsal documentation and analysis in recent years (see for example Féral (ed.) 2008, and McAuley (ed.) 2006(b). Diana Taylor's theorisation of the shift from written to embodied culture via the interrelated notions of archive and repertoire represents another point of connection between bodies of research generated by performance practices (Taylor 2003). Her perception that the consequences of this shift might entail the traditional disciplines extending their boundaries to 'include practices previously outside their purview' (17) is clearly relevant to the emergence of rehearsal as the locus of scholarly interest.

3   There is an extensive literature concerning the pioneering work of directors such as Antoine, Stanislavsky, Gordon Craig, Copeau and Reinhard, who transformed the European theatre in the early years of the twentieth century and paved the way for what would be known as 'director's theatre' a couple of generations later. Norman Marshall (1957) was one of the first to draw attention to the way the whole production process was being transformed by the input of this new artist. On the later generation of directors see also

Whitton 1987; Bradby and Williams 1988; Delgado and Heritage (eds) 1996; Mitter and Shevtsova (eds) 2005; Delgado and Rebellato (eds) 2010.

4   On Richard Foreman, see for example Foreman (with Jordan) 1992; Gerald Rabkin 1999. On Tadeusz Kantor, see Michal Kobialka 1993; Denis Bablet 1980.

5   See Julian Meyrick 2008.

6   In a speech given from the stage of the theatre after a performance of *Keating!*, the satirical musical by Casey Bennetto celebrating Keating's prime ministership (1991–96), directed by Neil Armfield for Company B in 2006.

7   Sydney Theatre Awards have been conferred annually since 2005 by a group of Sydney-based theatre reviewers 'to recognise the strength and diversity of theatre in Sydney' (www.sydneytheatreawards.com). Awards for *Toy Symphony* in 2007 were: Best Mainstage Production; Best Direction (Neil Armfield); Best New Australian Work (Michael Gow); Best Actor in a Lead Role (Richard Roxburgh); Best Actor in a Supporting Role (Russell Dykstra); Best Actress in a Supporting Role (Monica Maughan); Best Lighting Design (Damien Cooper). The Helpmann Awards were established in 2001 by the Australian Entertainment Industry Association to recognise excellence in all the live performing arts. Awards for *Toy Symphony* in 2008 were: Best New Australian Work; Best Direction of a Play (Neil Armfield); Best Male Actor in a Play (Richard Roxburgh); Best Male Actor in a Supporting Role (Russell Dykstra).

8   Belvoir actors and production crew use the familiar English terminology, PS (prompt side) and OP (opposite prompt), to refer to the audience right and left respectively even though their stage is five sided and the lines of force between access points are triangulated by the vomitory.

PART ONE **The *Toy Symphony*
rehearsals**

Toy Symphony
Produced by Company B Belvoir
Opening night 14 November 2007

Company list

Richard Roxburgh	Roland Henning
Justine Clarke	Nina, Julie Pearson, Miss Beverly, Lynette McKenzie, The Alien Nanny
Russell Dykstra	Lawyer, School Principal, Dr Maybloom, Titus Oates, Steve Gooding, Headmaster, Tom, Boy, Detective, Chekhov
Guy Edmonds	Alexander the Great, Medieval Executioner, Nick, Daniel, Boy
Monica Maughan	Mrs Walkham, Nurse, Crazy Woman
Neil Armfield	Director
Michael Gow	Writer
Ralph Myers	Set designer
Tess Schofield	Costume designer
Damien Cooper	Lighting designer

Paul Charlier	Composer and sound designer
Michael Toisuta	Assistant sound designer
Matthew Lutton	Assistant director
Eamon Flack	Literary manager
Kylie Mascord	Stage manager
Joshua Sherrin	Assistant stage manager
Tirian Rodwell	Costume co-ordinator
Liam Fraser	Production manager
Shaun Poustie	Production co-ordinator and company mechanist
Chris Mercer	Technical manager

The starting point: Michael's text

Fair game for extensive tinkering. (Robert Illing)

The text of *Toy Symphony* published by Currency Press in 2008 is very different from the script that was given to the actors on the first day of rehearsals. This version, designated Rehearsal Draft 1 and dated 16 September 2007, was preceded by at least four earlier drafts; the first, second and third are undated, and the fourth is dated 30 July 2007. Rehearsal Draft 1 reverted in some important ways to the undated first draft, but it was substantially changed during the rehearsal process. All the restructuring that came out of the discussions between author, director and actors in the rehearsal room, together with many of the small details suggested by Neil and the actors that added so much to the colour and energy of the play in performance, have been retained by the author in the published version. Michael was able to be present on eight occasions over the six-week period of rehearsals and preview performances and he significantly rewrote certain scenes, sometimes reverting to earlier versions, sometimes creating new material. The other alterations and additions suggested by Neil and the actors during rehearsals when Michael was not present were submitted to him for approval by Neil in their regular phone calls and email exchanges.

The following scene by scene breakdown is a plot outline derived from Rehearsal Draft 1. While it differs considerably from the text used in performance and from the text that was subsequently published, it is necessary to begin from this point in order to appreciate the work done by Neil, Michael and the actors, designers and production crew. The scenes are not numbered in any of the scripts nor is there any indication of place or time, but I have numbered them for ease of reference and provided a brief mention of the fictional place.

Rehearsal Draft 1

ACT I

1. Nina's consulting rooms
Roland Henning, a writer suffering from writer's block, is consulting (somewhat against his better judgement) a psychotherapist, Nina. He launches into an impassioned description of the creative process. She responds by querying his drug dependence. He agrees to co-operate with her therapy.

2. Lawyer's office
Roland and a copyright lawyer discuss the case against Roland, brought by a woman who claims he stole the idea for a play from her. Roland admits that he did in fact steal the idea but agrees with the lawyer that there is a difference between an idea and the words in which it is expressed. He instructs the lawyer to go on the offensive and threaten the woman with a libel case if she does not withdraw the injunction she has taken out.

3. Nina's consulting rooms
Nina asks how he proved that he had not stolen the story and he tells her he analysed his text minutely to compare it with what the woman had written. He realises that his inability to write comes from this process which was 'like wandering through my own brain with a smoking torch, scorching everything I looked at'. He denies feeling any guilt at silencing the woman. Nina asks him to tell her about a time in his life when he could create freely.

4. Primary school classroom, Como
Mrs Walkham is talking to her class, 5A, about the history of the suburb where they live and showing overhead transparencies. She mentions the ever present risk of bush fires and ends her lesson saying 'after fire, the bush does grow back. People rebuild'.

5. Nina's consulting rooms
Roland tells Nina that when he was a child he was able show the reality
he was talking about, that characters would have been physically present
in the room. She says she believes him and they will talk more about it
in their next session.

6. Primary School classroom, Como
5A is having a poetry lesson and the children are to recite for the
Headmaster. Roland is daydreaming and tells the Headmaster he was
thinking about Alexander the Great. As the Headmaster is about to cane
Roland for inattention, Alexander the Great appears in the classroom,
humiliating the Headmaster and saving Roland from punishment.

7. Doctor's consulting rooms
The child Roland is trying to explain to a psychologist how these visions
appear. Dr Maybloom points out that they all involve people who died
violent deaths and promises to cure Roland of his 'morbid fantasies',
claiming that 'some gifts come from very very dark places'. Roland
brings a Medieval Executioner with axe and flaming torch into the
room but Dr Maybloom frightens Roland into attempting to suppress
his gift.

8. School playground
Mrs Walkham finds Roland in some distress and suggests that rather
than suppressing the apparitions, he take the notebook and pencil she
gives him and 'whenever you feel one of them wants to appear, scribble
it down'.

9. Nina's consulting rooms
Nina claims to believe that this is what happened. He tells her it continued like that until high school.

10. Outside the Headmaster's office
Roland (who has never been in trouble before and Nick Sharp (who is
always in trouble) strike up a friendship. Nick is a cockney migrant, sex
obsessed, fantasising about Miss Beverly, the English teacher. Roland
shows Titus Oates[1] staggering out into an Antarctic blizzard, to the
delight and admiration of Nick.

11. Hospital
Nick Sharp has now been diagnosed with leukaemia, Roland is visiting
him. Nick flirts with the nurses, tells Roland of the frightening experience of an erection that wouldn't go down and asks him about school.
Roland says that he is still being beaten up by the school bully. Nick asks
him to 'show me someone' and Mrs Norberry comes on, a suburban

housewife who is so full of suppressed anger she wants to beat her own little daughter. Nick is unimpressed and requests Miss Beverly. She arrives, quoting love poetry, and disappears. Nick confides his fears that he will never get better but when an attractive young nurse arrives to tell them visiting hours are over, he begins flirting cheerfully again and makes Roland promise 'to do something really bad'.

12. School yard
Steven Gooding, star rugby player and school bully, is about to bash Roland, but tells him that his father wants him to study law and, for that, he needs to pass English. Roland offers to do his English assignments for him and then conjures up Lynette McKenzie, the girl for whom Steve lusts. While Steve is transfixed by the vision, Roland initiates oral sex with him.

13. Hospital
Roland tells Nick gleefully that this arrangement is continuing at Steve's home and that he has not been bashed since. This is the 'bad' thing he has done. He has also written a play called *Toy Symphony*, about a boy with a mysterious disease who is rescued from his wicked father by a flying English nanny while all the toys in his house play *The Toy Symphony* by Haydn. The play is going to be performed at school and Roland says he has written it for Nick.

14. School yard
Steve Gooding tells Roland that the PE teacher has queried his loss of form on the rugby field and that he has realised it is due to his sessions with Roland. He grabs Roland's bag, finds the copies of the play script and tears them up to punish Roland for what he has done to him. Roland attempts to bring Caesar and Cassius but nothing happens, and Steve blackmails him into agreeing to tell Miss Beverly the play is off.

15. Nina's consulting rooms
Roland tells Nina that he had not been to visit Nick for two weeks and when he phoned he was told that Nick had died the night before. He tells her that the appearances stopped and he also stopped writing until he was in his late 20s. She then asks him about the bushfires the previous weekend during which Como public school was burnt. Roland tells her he was on the beach, watching the fires from a distance, but that he had felt nothing. A Crazy Woman appears, listening to the news of the fires.

Roland tells Nina he has realised he is not trying to begin writing again but to learn to live without it. He thanks her for her assistance in helping him quit his drug habit but, against her advice, decides to terminate the therapy.

ACT II

16. A rehearsal room
Roland comes into the empty room, followed by a young acting student, Daniel who tells him how much he has enjoyed the lecture that Roland has just delivered. Roland clearly wants to be left alone but Daniel continues to importune him. Roland then calls Daniel's bluff by offering to have sex with him there and then, and attacks him for his dishonesty in failing to recognise his own motivations (both sexual and professional). He leaves with a brutal dismissal of Daniel's hopes for a career as an actor.

17. Roland's flat
Roland is on the phone to his only friend, Jake, who lives in New York. He tells him about his mother's funeral, which has taken place that day, only six weeks after his father's funeral. He says that, instead of the eulogy, he found himself saying what was really in his mind, his rejection of any comfortable belief about an after life, and his dark vision of the tar pit that 'we all blunder into' at the end. He tells Jake he can't be bothered to write any more, that he feels he is meant to follow his parents.

18. Tom's flat
Roland has come to visit Tom, his former dealer, to attempt to buy more drugs. Tom resists, irked that Roland has ignored him for so long, but then confides that his estranged wife has agreed that he can have a trial visit from his 7 year old son. Roland pressures him into supplying the drugs by threatening to stay until the wife and child arrive, which would mean the visit would be cancelled. He says that he can feel new work taking shape but he reiterates that he does not want the tide to turn again and claims the drugs are his way to 'start my own slide down into the tar pit'.

19. Roland's flat
Roland is unpacking the drugs he has bought. Mrs Walkham appears, talking about artists who lived in or near Como. She mentions D.H. Lawrence, who had made enemies by putting people he knew into his books, and reads aloud from *Kangaroo*, the paragraph where Lawrence describes passing through Como. She urges him to open the case that is beside him; it is his old school case, full of his parents' papers, but also old school photographs, and an envelope containing a copy of the script of his play *Toy Symphony*.

20. *The Play*
The last movement of the *Toy Symphony* is played over the dumbshow of Roland's play: an English nanny is tied to a chair by a man, and words

such as Prison, Torture, Despair, Anger appear. A boy with a knife stabs the man and releases the nanny. The nanny and the boy take off in an Apollo rocket, planets and stars whirl past them and words such as Freedom, New World, Friendship and Life appear in flaming letters.

21. A bar
Roland and Daniel are having a drink, Roland begins to apologise for his conduct but Daniel cuts him off, explaining that Roland's cruelty had made him realise that if he is going to be a good actor he needs to be clear about his own motivation for wanting to act as well as being clear about his characters' motivation. So he is grateful to Roland for the insight that will sustain him in the arduous life of an actor, wondering if he will ever get to play the big roles or be condemned to making TV commercials. Roland finds words inadequate to express what he wants to say and makes Daniel a gift of the *Toy Symphony* script. While Daniel is thanking him, Anton Chekhov appears, speaking in Russian, and tells Daniel he feels that the role of Treplev must have been written for him.

In earlier versions there was no division into acts and the play consisted simply of a sequence of fluidly changing scenes that shifted the action across a number of places, times and dimensions of reality. The decision to divide the work into two acts, doubtless taken for pragmatic reasons associated with spectators' need for an interval and the main actor's need for a rest, nevertheless functions to provide an indication of dramaturgical structure. The first act thus consists of all the childhood memories, interwoven with the psychotherapy sessions with Nina, and it culminates in the burning of Como and Roland's realisation that the therapy has been less about getting back his ability to write than learning to live without it. Act II is in the present and, while time passes between the scenes, there are no flashbacks. The appearance of Mrs Walkham and the performance of the banned play are fantasies, occurring in Roland's mind.

The summary indicates how far removed this play is from any classic dramaturgical structure, notwithstanding the division into acts: Nina, the psychotherapist, who is crucial in Act I simply disappears and is not heard of again, and while the fragmented time line of Act I is organised around the narrative ostensibly recounted for Nina, the scenes in Act II are disconnected, fragmentary indications of the character's decline, with a final coda suggesting some kind of redemption. Paul Charlier, the composer and sound designer, told the actors that the musical work known as *The Toy Symphony* is a 'cassation', an eighteenth-century genre made up of fragments (Day 1), and this suggested one possible way to understand the structure of the play that shares the name of the musical work.[2] Another clue was given by Michael, when Neil told him on the phone that they were going to do a chronology for the action. Michael understood why they needed to do this but warned that they would find a ten-year hiatus because it 'is really a kind of mush that is in one person's head'. That phrase seemed to me to refer directly to the quotation from Steven Wright that figures on the title page of all the drafts as epigraph to the play: 'I'm having amnesia and *déjà vu* at the same time'.

The quote from Robert Illing that serves as epigraph to this section refers to the score of the *Berchtoldsgaden Musick* (one of the German names for *The Toy Symphony*), but as Paul pointed out with some amusement on Day 9, when describing the results of research he had done on the music, it was by that time evident that the phrase was equally appropriate in relation to Michael Gow's script. Certainly there was extensive tinkering by Neil and the actors, and some major engineering by Michael before the play as it was performed came into being, as will be shown in the account of the process that follows. It was not until Day 10 that the combined efforts of playwright, director and actors produced a clear narrative progression and scene structure for Act I but other significant changes were still being made throughout the rehearsal process right up to the first preview performance. Act II, apart from the play-within-the-play, was in a much more finished state at the beginning of the process and, while certain scenes were refined and strengthened, the basic structure of the act was unchanged.

Notes

1   The name of the Antarctic explorer was in fact Lawrence Oates (Titus Oates was a seventeenth-century Catholic perjurer). A member of the public made this point at the subscriber briefing but no change was made, perhaps because Neil was out of the country at the time. However, as Michael has maintained the error in the published text, I am using the name they used.
2   All references to the musical work in this study include the definite article, which is italicised as part of the title. The play title has no article.

The first day (2 October 2007)

Bringing new Australian work to life
is the heart of what we do. (Neil Armfield, 2007)

Company B's rehearsal room is on the top floor of the renovated warehouse that now houses the company's office staff, wardrobe, meeting rooms and storage space. After years of renting church halls for rehearsals and having minimal space for management, they have finally been able to refurbish the theatre and to procure office and working space organised to their own specifications in the newly restored building just down the hill from the theatre. The room is huge and well lit, there are big windows all along one wall and the stage space of the Belvoir upstairs theatre, utilising a corner of the room as does the Belvoir stage, is indicated with mark-up tape on the floor. It occupies only about a third of the available space. In addition to the large open space, there is a meeting room, another small room with a piano, the wardrobe production space, and a kitchen equipped with a zip water heater, a microwave oven, and a table and chairs. The floor of the rehearsal room has been sanded and varnished but it is clearly still the rough timber floor it was when the place was a warehouse, and the steep flight of gantry-like stairs that confronts anyone entering the building from the street is another reminder of the building's industrial past. At the top of the first flight there is a landing and access on the left to the open-plan offices that occupy the whole of the first floor; straight ahead a second flight of stairs leads up to the rehearsal room. People arriving for rehearsals usually got a smile and a wave from office staff on the reception desk that faces the landing.

Meeting and greeting

On the first day of rehearsals, 2 October 2007, I arrived early to find the stage manager, Kylie Mascord, and her assistant, Josh Sherrin, already hard at work. They had arranged chairs in a large circle with a table at one side where they had set out a folder for each person who would be involved (including me), containing information about the production, the crew, dates for the work schedule and phone numbers. Kylie told me that Neil does not like the actors to sit around a table for this phase of the work but that she herself needs a table for all her papers. I was glad to see later that there was another table, at right angles to Kylie's and further around the space where the designers sat when they came to watch. This was where I habitually sat as I found it much easier to write my copious notes at a table and the position gave me a good view of Neil as well as the stage space. Kylie had worked with Neil as his stage manager on all his productions for the preceding four years and it was evident that she, along with the other staff, trusted his judgement and admired his artistry as well as holding him in great affection. She told me later that Company B is the only company in Sydney she would work for. She said 'if I leave here, I will be leaving the job of stage management'.

The first day of rehearsal is always special, as anyone involved in the theatre knows. It is typically when directors bring together for the first time the creative team they have been assembling for weeks, if not months; when the actors read the script aloud together for the first time; when designers present their ideas about the set, costumes, lighting and sound, and directors articulate their vision for the production that will feed into and guide the work that will preoccupy them all over the ensuing weeks of intensive collaboration. Odette Aslan describes this first meeting as seminal and claims it is the moment when it is already possible to sense whether or not the emotional charge is going to circulate (Aslan 2005, 17). There was certainly a buzz of energy in the room as people began to arrive that

Tuesday morning, greeting each other and catching up on news and gossip while waiting for Michael Gow to arrive from the airport. It did, however, seem to me that this was something more than a normal first rehearsal buzz and that what added the undefinable something extra and created the sense of occasion was the fact that the work they had come together to create was the first production of a new Australian play by one of the country's major playwrights who had not written anything new for the past ten years (apart from a one-act play but, as Michael Gow himself commented wryly, 'noone seems to count one-act plays').

As part of Neil's inclusive management style, all the administrative staff participated in this first meeting and a lavish morning tea was provided to enhance the festive nature of the occasion. There was little opportunity to talk to the office staff once rehearsals began but, as I found out later, they were all acutely aware of what was going on 'upstairs', keen to get reports on the work in progress, buoyed up by news that it was going well, always hoping for a success and apprehensive about the possibility of a flop. Some of the people gathering for the first rehearsal had worked together in the past (see chart, figure 4), some were strangers, but whether or not they had worked together before, all were well aware of each other's reputation.

By the time Michael Gow arrived, there were thirty or so people in the room, including the five actors (Monica Maughan, Richard Roxburgh, Justine Clarke, Russell Dykstra and Guy Edmonds), the designers, known as the 'creatives' (set designer: Ralph Myers, music and sound: Paul Charlier and lighting: Damien Cooper) and the production crew (the production manager was Liam Fraser and his team included Chris Mercer, the technical manager, and Shaun Poustie, the company mechanist who was also to be production co-ordinator for the show). The only person missing was Tess Schofield, the costume designer. Neil explained that she was involved with a group of other people in caring for a terminally ill friend and was unable to come to the rehearsal that morning. Tess's friend died a few days later and she was then involved in making the funeral arrangements, which meant that it was not until the Monday of Week 2 that she was able to come and present her costume designs to the actors. She and Tirian Rodwell (the costume co-ordinator) then had to work extremely hard to catch up with the production schedule. Neil was accompanied by Matthew Lutton, a young director from Perth who was to be assistant director for *Toy Symphony*, and Eamon Flack, the company's literary manager. While Eamon's main responsibilities as literary manager relate to the selection of plays to be performed and reading unsolicited manuscripts, he does function to a limited extent as dramaturg, even though the term did not seem to be used.

The custom of referring to the designers as 'creatives' and excluding the performers from this appellation is a relatively new phenomenon in the theatre. It was probably adopted into theatre practice under the influence of the mega musicals of the 1980s, where the whole production was imported and the design had to be identical to the original in every respect. In these musicals, the performers were the only local factor and in a sense secondary to the designers. Paul Charlier told me that it had crept into theatre practice over the years and he acknowledged that the implications could be construed as somewhat offensive to actors whose creativity seems to be relegated to a rather shadowy, ambiguous area, if not excluded altogether. In writing this account of rehearsal practice, I use the term 'design team' as it is certainly useful to have a term that refers to the designers as a group, given that their contribution occurs in such different spaces and over a different timeframe from that of the actors. This avoids the insidious suggestion of a hierarchy of creativity in the now commonly used term, which seems to me extremely problematic. Neil told me later that he uses the term 'production team' for the same reason, although he acknowledged that this introduced a potential confusion between the designers and the production management crew working in the theatre.

Michael's arrival was greeted with cheers and applause, and then the business of the rehearsal began with a speech of introduction from Neil. He stressed the importance of doing new Australian works, claiming it went to the heart of why Company B exists: 'This is what we are here for.' The production of new Australian plays has for many years been the chosen terrain of the Griffin Company at The Stables and Belvoir has always had a much wider brief in constructing its seasons.[1] We talked about this when I interviewed Neil some weeks later and he told me that, in his view, the function of Company B's productions of classics and of contemporary works from other countries is 'to open up the frame by which we view new Australian work'. I asked if the 'we' in that comment referred to audiences or to the company and he said he was really thinking about the company. He said 'if Australian companies don't bring new Australian work to life, then it won't be done at all. It is so essential.' In his view, this is 'really the heart of the work' he has been doing with Company B during his fifteen years as artistic director.

The tone of Neil's speech was friendly and informal and it functioned both to introduce the artists and the company staff to each other and to underline the sense of family that is an important part of his management style and of his artistic philosophy. He mentioned everyone by

Figure 4. *Toy Symphony* cast and crew: network of prior working relations
Graphic: Russell Emerson

Company B productions directed by Neil Armfield

Production	Armfield	Gow	Roxburgh	Clark	Dykstra	Edmonds
Exit the King	X					
Snugglepot 2007	X					
Keating 2006	X					
Peribanez 2006	X					
Stuff Happens 2005	X				X	
The Spook 2004	X					
Lieutentant of Inishmore 2003	X					
The Underpants 2003	X				X	
Waiting for Godot 2002	X					
As You Like It 1999	X					
Cloudstreet 1998	X					
The Judas Kiss 1997	X					
The Seagull 1997	X		X			
Hamlet 1994	X		X			
Diary of A Madman 1989/82	X					
Company B	X	X	X		X	
Belvoir	X	X	X		X	X

	1	2	3	4	5	6	7	8	9	10	11	12	13	14	15
Maughan	X	X													
Myers	X	X								X					
Schofield	X	X	X	X	X	X	X		X					X	
Cooper	X	X						X		X	X	X	X		X
Charlier	X	X		X	X	X	X	X	X						
Toisuta	X	X											X		X
Mascord	X	X							X	X	X	X	X	X	
Sherrin	X	X													
Fraser	X	X										X	X	X	X
Poustie	X	X											X	X	X
Mercer	X	X											X	X	X

Figure 4. (continued)

		Armfield	Gow	Roxburgh	Clark	Dykstra	Edmonds
Other works	Angels in America (Melb)	X					
	All Saints (TV)					X	X
	Come in Spinner (TV)				X		
	Holding the Man 2007						X
	Romulus My Father dir: RR			X		X	
Michael Gow's plays	Sweet Phoebe		X				
	Edens Lost (TV)	X	X				
	Live Acts on Stage '03, '04		X		X		X
	Away '86 (many production)	X	X				
	The Kid (Belv '83) Griffin '88	X	X				
Company B other directors	Ray's Tempest 2005			X		X	
	Cosmonaut's Last Msge '02						
	Laramie Project 2001					X	
	Twelfth Night 2000			X			
	Ham Funeral 2000					X	
	Burnt Piano 1999						
	Popular Mechanicals 1992						

	1	2	3	4	5	6	7	8	9	10	11	12	13	14	15	16
Maughan	X	X						X						X		X
Myers					X	X										
Schofield						X		X			X					
Cooper			X		X											
Charlier					X		X		X							
Toisuta																
Mascord						X										
Sherrin																
Fraser													X			
Poustie													X			
Mercer													X			

name, explaining their function in the company (financial administrator, publicist, education officer, etc) and for this show and how long they
had worked at Belvoir. He said that Monica, a Melbourne-based actress,
had recently received an award in recognition of the fact that she had
been a professional actor for fifty years and everyone applauded, that
this was the first time Justine had worked at Belvoir, more applause,
and that Richard had been making films and had not done any theatre
work for the last seven years. He also introduced me and told them that
I would be writing a book about their work. While this had been cleared
with Michael Gow before final arrangements were made, it was evident
that this was the first any of the others had heard about the fact. The
actors' unquestioning and gracious acceptance of my presence was evidence of the faith they have in Neil's judgement, although it might also
be seen as an indication of the power he wields notwithstanding the discourse of family and his generous attempt at inclusiveness. The notion
of family is of course a complex one and, alongside the obvious connotations of relatedness, inclusion, acceptance and security, there are also
obligations, constraints and hierarchies of respect and these come into
play within the Belvoir 'family' as much as in any other.

The following brief biographies of the four actors, whose task in
Toy Symphony was to support the *tour de force* of the central role, may
not be precisely the details given by Neil in his speech of welcome but
they represent the sort of common knowledge concerning each other's
careers that was circulating in the rehearsal room.

Monica Maughan, Melbourne-based, a professional actor since 1957,
well known for continuing and guest roles in television series, has performed with all the major state theatre companies as well as in at least
50 productions for the Melbourne Theatre Company, including the
1994 production of *Angels in America*, directed by Neil Armfield. She
told me she was heartbroken that she could not accept Neil's invitation
to play Gwen in *Away* for his 1987 production due to prior contractual
agreements, but she did play the role in a later production.[2] She has won
numerous awards for best actress and best supporting actress.

Justine Clarke, a singer as well as an actress, worked extensively in
television before undertaking training at the Victorian College of the
Arts in 1993–94. Her first professional role in theatre was in Michael
Gow's *Live Acts on Stage* (Griffin Company, Sydney, 1995) directed by
the author. Most of her theatre work has been for the Sydney Theatre
Company, including the 2004 production of *Hedda Gabler* that also
enjoyed a season at the Brooklyn Academy of Music. She told me that
she had worked with all the other actors, apart from Guy, at some time

in the past. She is currently a very popular presenter on the ABC's children's programme *Playschool* and has produced two successful CDs of songs for children.

Russell Dykstra trained at Darling Downs Institute of Advanced Education and was working as an actor in Queensland when spotted by Geoffrey Rush, who encouraged him to go to the Lecoq School in Paris. After a year at Lecoq (1990–91), he undertook a further year of training with Philippe Gaulier in London. He has worked extensively for theatre, television and film, including several productions for Company B and was appointed to serve for a term on the Company B board. He performed in Richard Roxburgh's production of *Ray's Tempest* for Company B, as well as in Roxburgh's film *Romulus, My Father* and won a Helpmann Award for Best Supporting Actor for his memorable Donald Rumsfeld in Company B's production of *Stuff Happens,* directed by Neil Armfield in 2005.

Guy Edmonds, the youngest member of the cast, trained at the Queensland University of Technology (2002–04). Immediately after graduation, he landed a regular role in the television serial *All Saints* and then, in 2006, he created the demanding central role of Tim Conigrave in the Griffin Company's extremely successful production of *Holding the Man* (play by Tommy Murphy, based on Conigrave's memoir, directed by David Berthold). By late 2007, the production had already had four seasons in different theatres and it has since been taken to London for a season at the Trafalgar Studios, still with Guy Edmonds in the central role.

    Holding the Man was the play that immediately preceded *Toy Symphony* in the Belvoir Street season, which meant that Guy would be playing Tim Conigrave at night and rehearsing *Toy Symphony* by day. When someone commented one day on the heavy workload he was carrying, Monica said rather sternly, 'We've all done it.'

The set

Neil and Ralph Myers, the set designer, then talked about the set and showed the model Ralph had prepared. There was a false ceiling over the stage, sloping down slightly at the upstage corner, with a shaft at the centre through which diffuse light shone down on the empty floor below. The stage was completely empty with no visible sources of light, and the walls, floor and ceiling were painted black except for the floor under the light shaft where most of the action takes place. In an earlier design this was to be a stark white rectangle (referred to by Neil as 'the scorching') but in the model it had become a stippled pale stain that Michael said was reminiscent of a pile of cocaine (both images are pertinent to the play). Neil explained that this would have to be painted by a specialist spray painter suspended above the space as there can be no visible brush strokes. The juxtaposition of meta-phorical and material, the deeply meaningful and the immediately practical is typical of the discourse and the practice that I observed over the next three months.

There were double crash doors in the upstage wall, painted black like the wall, which I assumed (wrongly, as it turned out) would be the entry point for the apparitions. Neil and Ralph had originally thought that as so much of the action is located in the schoolrooms of Roland's childhood, the set could be a generic school hall, which would then also serve as the college rehearsal room in the second act, but they later decided against any kind of literal spatial representation. Neil said that the set did not need to represent any particular fictional place because so much of the action was taking place inside the character's head, and he loved Ralph's design because he saw it as 'a space that creates a kind of energy and releases the dynamic of the piece'. When I wrote that comment down, I had no idea how prescient it would turn out to be but I see it now as evidence of how well both these men know the Belvoir Theatre and of the extent to which Neil's staging of the play was already taking shape in his mind. Peter Brook has said 'When I begin to work on a play, I start with a deep, formless hunch which is like a smell, a colour, a shadow' (Brook 1987, 3) and the conversations that had occurred between Neil and Ralph were part of the process of giving form to the 'formless hunch'. They had decided then that most of what they had been thinking of doing through the set, could be better done by the light-ing, which would be designed by Damien Cooper.

The choice of black was not fixed but seemed to Neil to fit the idea of receding memory and the mysterious space in the shadows (by which he meant the artist's imagination), while also being relevant to 'the tar pit idea that sits under the whole play'. The central shaft created a space from which the rocket in the play-within-the-play could descend and/or blast off. Neil referred to this play-within-the-play as 'a Masque' at this stage, but they later called it simply *The Play*. He wanted the apparitions to erupt into this bleak, minimalist space in extremely colourful cos-tumes and with appropriate music and sound effects. Everybody seemed excited by the design, while acknowledging its radical nature and the difficulties it would pose for the production crew in terms of locating lights and speakers, not to mention the lack of space above the Belvoir stage for a rocket of any size. A problem that was mentioned a number of times (without any solution being proposed) was how to get the hospital bed on and off for the scenes with the dying schoolboy.

Neil said that he did not know at this stage how the movement from one fictional place to another would be managed, but he knew that he wanted the furniture to be absolutely minimal and he wanted to explore how much could be done without changing any furniture. Ralph said that his instinct was never to hide the passage between locations. Neil reiterated that he saw the visions as hugely theatrical, playful, absurd, colourful figures. He had the sense that they would make an entrance, while in contrast, the memory figures would involve minimal costume changes that could be done in full view of the audience (the small cast meant that all the actors apart from Richard would be playing multiple roles). Ralph also said that they could possibly experiment with the use of very small chairs (this idea must have been around for several months because the image chosen to publicise the play in the season brochure was of Richard Roxburgh sitting in a confined corner on a kindergarten sized chair – see figure 1). Coming back to these early notes with the hindsight provided by the actual production is fascinating both for the elements of the formless hunch that did become central to the production (minimal furniture, no set changes, no hiding or masking the passage between locations) and those that did not (some of the memory figures were as flamboyant as the conjured visions and only one involved a change in full view of the audience; the chairs were typical of a 1970s high school, and there was never any experimentation with child-sized chairs).

The music

Paul Charlier has worked with Neil and Company B on many occasions and was well known to most of the people present. He spoke briefly about the musical piece known in English as *The Toy Symphony* and played a recording which caused great hilarity. The idea was born in that moment of the actors playing all the toy instruments and doing the bird songs. Someone asked if the music had to be that very piece and Neil said 'Yes. The frothiest children's music to accompany the darkest play.' Paul said that it used to be thought that Haydn wrote

it, then that it was by Leopold Mozart but that, according to the latest
scholarly research, it was probably written around 1770 by an unknown
monk in an Austrian monastery and either passed off by others as their
own work or attributed to more famous composers by enterprising
if unscrupulous publishers. It was a publisher who invented the title
Kindersinfonie (Children's Symphony) at some time in the nineteenth
century. It had earlier been known as the *Berchtoldsgaden Musick*. The
mystery about the authorship of the music that gives Michael's play its
name and the suggestion that it may relate to an ancient story of artistic
skullduggery provided another intriguing connection to Michael Gow's
Toy Symphony, which draws heavily on the accusation of plagiarism that
was made in relation to his play *Sweet Phoebe* in 1994.[3] The plagiarism
scandal and its repercussions in the lives of some of the people involved
will be discussed in more detail later in this chapter as it was one of the
first things the actors wanted to talk about after their first reading of the
play.

The first reading

The work process proper began with a reading of the whole play, from
beginning to end without commentary, although a brief tea break was
taken at the end of Act I. There had been an earlier reading of the complete play in Michael's presence some weeks before but that was before
Monica Maughan joined the cast. It had been Justine's audition and she
told me that Judi Farr had read the parts of Mrs Walkham, Mrs Norberry
and the Crazy Woman. Scene 14 in Rehearsal Draft 1 was a completely
new scene, written by Michael after that reading to meet objections
that had been expressed to the way in which Roland's play comes to be
banned. In the new version, it is the school bully Steve Gooding who
destroys the play as retribution for having let himself be seduced by
Roland. At this reading, nobody was happy with this but they also had
reservations about the earlier version in which the headmaster inflicts
this punishment. Someone said that the play should be burnt rather than
torn up, as Roland could have retrieved the pieces. This struck a chord
with everyone, Neil saying that he liked 'the fascist undertow to book
burning'. In the end, Michael reinstated the scene with the headmaster
in a revised form, and it is the headmaster who takes the initiative in
banning the performance and incinerating the script as a punishment
for what Roland has done to Gooding.

Figure 5. Company B rehearsal room
Photo: Heidrun Löhr

Neil asked everyone who was staying for the reading to bring their chairs into the stage space taped onto the rehearsal room floor and place them in a large circle. All the reading over the next few days was done 'on stage', as it were. Neil ensured that the actors were sitting in a group, and he sat with Matthew Lutton (the assistant director) and the designers (Paul Charlier, Ralph Myers and Damien Cooper) on the opposite side of the circle. Most of the office staff apart from the publicist returned to their work downstairs. Before the reading began, Neil asked Michael for more information about the epigraph, and Michael said simply that it was a quote from Steven Wright, an American comedian 'who does a very funny kind of stream of consciousness' that had seemed to sum up what he was doing in the play. The reading itself was quite low key and unremarkable but already there were tiny indications of relationships that could develop (see figure 5[4]).

When the reading was finished, Neil said there was only half an hour to raise questions with Michael before he had to leave for the airport and his flight back to Queensland (his own production of *Who's Afraid of Virginia Woolf?* was opening a few days later). This first reading was followed over the next few days by what was called a stop/start reading of each scene (described in more detail below), a careful analysis that threw up many more issues that required textual changes, but re-reading my fieldnotes with the knowledge of the work that would eventually emerge from the process, I am struck by how perspicacious the actors were in their first reading. All the issues they raised on the first day turned out to be of crucial and ongoing importance in the creative process and all required substantial changes to the text: the status of the apparitions that Roland was able to conjure in his childhood and youth and Roland's attitude to them as an adult; the structural problem caused by the fact that Roland's 'gift' has apparently been restored to him at the end of Act I with the appearance of the Crazy Woman, thus diminishing the impact of the appearance of Chekhov at the end of Act II; the length of the telephone call scene during which Richard is alone on stage and speaking into a mobile phone; and the nature of *The Play*, ostensibly being performed by a class of high school students but very obviously the work of a much younger child. What struck me most in the discussion, however, was not so much Michael's acknowledgment that significant changes would need to be made but the fact that he seemed happy for these changes to emerge from a rehearsal process in which he would play only an intermittent part.

What is the play about?

After a late lunch, when Michael had left to go back to Queensland, the actors, design team and Neil gathered again in the rehearsal room and Neil set two tasks: firstly, he asked everyone to say what they thought the play was about, and secondly, he wanted to establish a chronology of the dramatic action. The discussion of what the play was about was fascinating because the answers ranged over a number of themes and revealed some of the tensions that would become apparent in the later work. For Neil, it was about striving for lost innocence that he felt would somehow be manifested in the links between Nick Sharp, the school friend who dies of leukaemia, and the later relationship with acting student Daniel, both characters to be played by Guy. For Justine, it was about a writer trying to understand how and why he works and how it makes him what he is. Guy agreed with this and said that Daniel's search for truth in his work as an actor is part of the same quest. For Matthew, it was about death: Roland has been disturbed by death since his earliest childhood (all the figures he conjures have died violent and in his view unnecessary deaths) and now his parents have both died and his life has become a descent into hell. Richard did not answer the question directly but commented on his character's trajectory over the course of the play. He said that the things that have hurt Roland most have silenced him: 'from being a lovely, optimistic kid he has become kind of rotten, all his talent has fermented and rotted and now he is on the edge of the tar pit. He does terrible things to other people because his own creativity has withered on the vine.'

This is evidence of a play that is either thematically very rich or in such an inchoate state that a great deal of work was going to be required and, at that stage of the process, I was not clear which was the case. With hindsight, it is probably correct to say that both statements were correct.

One thing that emerged very clearly from the discussions about the script that first day was an actors' perspective on the work process that would be involved in the performance. While Michael had written a play with a fragmented story line held together by a strong central character, surrounded by figures from his past, some remembered and some purely fanciful, the actors were concerned with the logistics involved in playing multiple roles, or indeed in having too little to do. Michael abandons Nina, the psychotherapist, at the end of Act I and does not give the actress playing the role anything else to do until the play-within-the-play, a frenetic two and a half minute dumb show near the end of Act II. Both Richard and Russell made suggestions for ways that Justine could be brought into Act II, none of which were taken up. Michael had, in fact, originally specified a cast of six, three women and two men in addition to the actor playing Roland, one woman to be in her 60s, one in her late 30s and one in her 20s, so there would have been even more waiting around for the female actors. It was Neil who reduced the number in order, as he told me, to give each one a good night's work.

Sweet Phoebe

In discussing the question of Roland's having stolen the idea for a play, someone mentioned Michael's play *Sweet Phoebe* and the plagiarism scandal he was clearly drawing on in his creation of the fictional situation. One of the actors asked Neil to provide them with more details about what happened and its relevance to this play. It came as something of a shock to everyone to find that Neil himself was quite closely involved as the person who made the charge was someone he had been friends with since primary school. This woman (who here will be called

JR) was staying in his house while he was away, looking after Kevon (Neil's dog) as well as a dog called Phoebe who belonged to another friend. Neil said that one day JR came home and found that Kevon was there but Phoebe had gone. JR and her partner searched desperately for the missing dog, putting signs on lamp posts and telegraph poles, and then began to receive phone calls from all sorts of people who claimed to have found Phoebe. When it was all over, she and her partner thought it would make the basis for a comic film and she discussed it with Michael, who then worked on her idea, turning it into a play without acknowledging her. She took out an injunction against him when she discovered what he had done, but later withdrew it and the play was performed and eventually published. Neil made it clear that JR had been a friend from primary school days, that she remained very friendly with his parents even after his friendship with her had become more distant, and now that his mother had died it was JR who accompanied his father to first nights in the theatre.

JR had been one of my students in the French Department and I had supervised her honours thesis, so I thought I should volunteer what I knew of the affair. In my recollection, it was far more than an idea that she had pitched to Michael. She and her partner had written a substantial treatment and, I thought, the dialogue for one scene and, far from giving the work to Michael, it was my understanding that she had approached him for advice about how to develop it, perhaps hoping he would suggest collaboration. Richard then commented, only half in jest, that if he had known all this back story, he doubted if he would have accepted the role. He said 'there will be a *fatwa* against us'.

The fact that Michael was drawing on real and scandalous events that had happened a relatively short time before in their own community had a rather sobering effect. Ralph put into words what many were thinking when he said he was amazed at Michael's decision to use his own story, and was in awe of his brutal honesty about himself. I began to see the play as an extraordinary public apology to JR notwithstanding the self-serving nature of some of Roland's explanations.

The events of the first day have been described in some detail as they provide a good indication of the range of activities that are involved at this stage in the rehearsal process, the intensity of the work, the number of factors that are being juggled at any one time (from practicalities like the size of the roof cavity in the theatre to methods of maintaining company cohesion), the way the various participants bring their artistry and craft knowledge to the process and the central role of the director in unleashing and channelling the creative energies of this group of people.

Notes

1   As indicated in the performance history, printed as figure 2 in the previ-
    ous chapter, the Company B seasons are made up of works selected from
    a number of categories. The policy of the Griffin Company has been, until
    very recently, to produce only new Australian plays.

2   Monica Maughan died suddenly early in 2010. She was scheduled to
    perform the major role in Tommy Murphy's play *Gwen in Purgatory*, to
    be directed by Neil for Company B in August 2010 and had already had a
    very productive meeting with the author. As Neil recounted in the moving
    eulogy he wrote for her funeral, she and Tommy Murphy 'were texting me
    ideas like a couple of love struck school kids,' another reminder of the col-
    laborative nature of the creative process in theatre and of how much of it
    occurs upstream of the actual rehearsals.

3   The first production of *Sweet Phoebe* was at the Sydney Theatre Company in
    1994, directed by Michael Gow himself with actors Cate Blanchett and Colin
    Moodie.

4   The photograph shows the actors sitting in a wide semi circle, facing Neil
    who is wearing his signature rehearsal garb of boldly patterned shirt and
    Ugg boots. Michael is present, sitting at the table next to me, where I am
    as usual writing. Josh Sherrin, the assistant stage manager is sitting at the
    table next to Neil in the seat normally occupied by Kylie Mascord, the stage
    manager, her task being to take notes of cuts and script changes. The two
    chairs in the foreground are those used in the performance.

Establishing the chronology (Day 2)

It is really a kind of mush that is in one person's head. (Michael Gow)

Creating an imaginary timeline for the action was an important stage in the actors' understanding of both the action and the play's structure. There had been no time on the preceding day to undertake this task, so it was the first thing they tackled on Day 2. After a good deal of discussion and checking of dates on the internet, the final therapy session with Nina was situated in 2001–02, the summer in which catastrophic bushfires destroyed much of Como. The scenes in the primary school are dated by Dr Maybloom, who says 'This is Australia, 1966.' Situating the Nick Sharp and Steve Gooding scenes was more tricky because Roland seems to remain quite childlike while the other boys are clearly sex obsessed teenagers. *The Play*, too, seemed much more the work of an exuberant 10 year old than that of a 16 year old and that was borne out by the way Roland describes the play to Nick Sharp. In the end, they decided that Nick, who is illiterate, may have had to repeat a year or two and that maybe Roland, being particularly smart, is ahead of his age cohort and they situated the high school scenes in 1970, when Roland is 13 and Nick and Steve are 15. The scene with the copyright lawyer is situated in 1994, as that was the year in which the *Sweet Phoebe* case occurred.

They decided that the scene with Daniel at the actor training college must have occurred some time after the bushfires and the termination of Roland's psychotherapy, so put it in 2003. Roland says in this scene that he is about to visit his father in hospital, but the next scene, the telephone call to his friend Jake, occurs immediately after his mother's funeral, which occurred six weeks after that of his father. So they put this scene a year later, in 2004. They originally placed the final reconciliation scene with Daniel in the same year but later agreed that more time must have elapsed during which Daniel would have graduated from college and begun to discover the realities of an actor's life, so put the last scene in 2005.

This is, thus, the chronology they established. Characters whose names are in italics are memories, those in bold are the apparitions Roland was able to conjure when a child and again in his teenage years.

Act I

1. Roland/Nina: first session 2001
2. *Roland/Lawyer* (1994)
3. Roland/Nina (the scorching) 2001
4. *Mrs Walkham*: slide show 1966
5. Roland/Nina: the 'gift' 2001
6. *Roland/Mrs Walkham/Julie Pearson/Headmaster/***Alexander the Great** 1966
7. *Roland/Dr Maybloom/***Medieval Executioner** 1966
8. *Roland/Mrs Walkham*: (gift of notebook) 1966
9. Roland/Nina: segue to high school 2001/2
10. *Roland/Nick Sharp/***Titus Oates**: beginning of the friendship 1970
11. *Roland/Nurse/Nick Sharp/***Mrs Norberry/Miss Beverly**: hospital 1970
12. *Roland/Steve Gooding/***Lynette** 1970
13. *Roland/Nick*: hospital 1970
14. *Roland/Headmaster*: play banned 1970
15. Roland/Nina/*Crazy Woman*: final therapy session 2001/2

Act II

16. Roland/Daniel 2003
17. Roland: phone call to Jake after funeral 2004
18. Roland/Tom: drug dealer 2004
19. Roland/Mrs Walkham: finds playscript 2004
20. The Play (fantasy, not located in time)
21. Roland/Daniel/**Chekhov** 2005

Considerable discussion was given to the status of the Crazy Woman, whether she is a memory or an apparition and the implications of each possibility. Mrs Walkham in her appearance in scene 19 is located in relation to Roland's 2004 reality but she is neither memory nor apparition. In fact she seems to belong to yet another order of reality, together with the performance of *The Play*, neither memory nor conjured apparition, occurring outside of time.

The actors' internet search threw up an awkward fact, namely that there were two catastrophic bushfires that affected Como, one in 1994 and the other in 2001/2, and that it was in the former that Como West Public School was burned down. They decided, however, to ignore that as it had to be the 2001/2 bushfires that led Roland to terminate the therapy, and Nina specifically mentions the school burning. It was fascinating to note that everyone in the rehearsal room could speak of when the worst bushfires had occurred, that these terrible events are seared into people's memories in Australia, and many had personal stories of loss, of friends or acquaintances who had lost their homes or possessions in bushfires. The major way in which the past was signposted for them was, however, the productions they were involved in: 'that's when we were doing *Godot*' or 'that was the year we did *Hamlet*'. 1994 was indeed the year of Company B's now legendary production of *Hamlet*, with Richard Roxburgh in the lead role, Neil directing, Paul Charlier doing the sound, and Tess Schofield designing the costumes; in evoking the memory of the bushfires, they also evoked the memory of that collaboration and reinforced the sense of the longstanding creative relationships that join them together.

For me, the realisation that there were two catastrophic bushfires, that one occurred in 1994, the same year as the real plagiarism scandal, and the other in the summer of 2001/2, after which Roland Henning realised he no longer wanted his creativity back, led to a very different analysis of the play's structure. As I saw it, there were two crises in the past, both connected with suppressing Roland's creativity: Dr Maybloom forcing him to suppress his 'gift' when he was 10, and Steve Gooding and the Headmaster destroying his play when he was 14. There were also two crises in Roland's adult life: the plagiarism scandal in 1994 when he 'scorched' his own mind in his attempt to exonerate himself from the charge, and the psychotherapy in 2001/2 in which he not only realised the extent of the damage done but also retrieved the memory of the shame and humiliation that accompanied the banning of his high school play. In this latter case, the attack was not only on his creativity but also, cruelly, on his sexuality. Furthermore, there were the two bushfires in Como, each one linked to these other crises: the one in 1994 burned his primary school and coincided with the shattering attack on his creativity over the accusation of plagiarism, and the one in 2001/2 devastated yet more of Como and was associated with his decision to abandon therapy and give in to despair.

This was, as I saw it, the force of the play's epigraph, for it was the combination of amnesia and *déjà vu* that permitted these events to merge and blur, which is why I thought the phrase was more than the 'tonal reflection of the play' that Neil mentioned on Day 2, but a key to its deep structure. Or rather to a potential deep structure, because the play was still in a relatively fluid state and the double helix structure that I have been describing is not really part of the play as it emerged from the rehearsal process. Indeed, it might never have worked in practice and what Neil and the actors found, with Michael's approval, is more straightforward and more character based. As Neil summarised it at the end of the second day's work, the story is that Roland had a gift as a child, which was channelled into writing by Mrs Walkham. When he scorched his brain over the plagiarism accusation, he stifled the writing, but he eventually gets it back as a gift via Daniel and the appearance of Chekhov. Michael Gow's play deals with the complexity of the writer's life, the combination of reliance on real life events and experiences and pure inspiration involved in the creation of character and plot, and with 'the dark place' (to use Dr Maybloom's phrase) from which his creativity comes, but the story line as worked out in rehearsal keeps the merging and blurring grounded within a fairly coherent narrative. Simultaneity of amnesia and *déjà vu* can work as a conceit in a writer's head, but the concrete demands of the stage mean that at some level the actors have to work it out more clearly. As Richard said when they were discussing the scene outside the headmaster's office when he first meets Nick Sharp, 'I need to know how old he is here.' As his work involves literally *embodying* the character, it is vital to know what kind of body is involved. He is either 12 or 16, but even with the magical time shifts that they are playing with, he cannot be both at once.

The stop/start reading (Days 2–4)

> Michael has been writing the play in order to discover what it is.
>
> (Neil Armfield, Day 2)

The working day was divided into four sections, beginning at 10am, with a break for morning tea around 11.30am, and a lunch break of one hour (usually between 1 and 2pm); the afternoon session ended at 6pm and was divided into two by a tea break around 4pm. It was part of Kylie Mascord's job to ensure that this schedule was adhered to and, as she had worked as Neil's stage manager for several years, she was well aware of his proclivity for losing track of the time. Choosing the moment to interrupt a creative process is a delicate matter, but she did it with great good humour and firmness as well as intuitive understanding of the process. She told me that after the rehearsals finished for the day, she usually had several hours more work to do, debriefing with Neil, contacting actors if there were changes in the calls for the next day and notifying designers or production crew about things that were needed.

A great deal of the work in the early weeks of the rehearsal concerned quite substantial changes to the text, either at the behest of the author or, more frequently, as a result of problems Neil and the actors were finding. Later in the process, the textual changes were smaller, and usually emanated from Neil (the addition of a word or two to clarify the progression of the action, or the suggestion of a more colourful word that lifted the moment or provided more scope for the actor) but at this early stage, the concern was with the overall structure, the logic of the action, and the underlying motivation for characters' responses. Michael managed to extricate himself from his commitments in Brisbane on the Friday of the first week in order to spend the whole day with the company (Day 4) and then two consecutive days at the end of the second week (Days 8 and 9), by which time the script had been radically transformed.

The so-called stop/start reading of the play took from after the lunch break on Day 2 until afternoon tea on Day 4. Everyone remained sitting in a circle in the taped indication of the stage space, where they had been for the first reading on Day 1. All the actors were present throughout with Neil, Matthew Lutton (assistant director), Eamon Flack (whose role at this stage was dramaturg), Kylie Mascord and Josh Sherrin (her assistant), and the designers Ralph Myers (set) and Paul Charlier (sound). The lighting designer, Damien Cooper, did not attend and Tess Schofield was still involved in caring for her dying friend. The actors worked through the whole play, reading scene by scene, interrupted frequently by Neil to raise issues, ponder the meaning of a word, the implications for motivation and the character's overall experience, referred to as the character's 'journey', or sometimes 'arc.'

Neil's insistence that this reading be done from within the stage space, as it were, was clearly part of his normal practice. I never asked him about his reasons, but reflecting on it now, it seems to me that sitting around a table, as is frequently done for this phase of the work, functions to anchor the reading to the materiality of the script. Sitting in a wide circle, even though people still had pencils in their hands, were still noting cuts and additions on their scripts, somehow made it freer, not only facilitated more interactions between interlocutors in the reading, little glances, embryonic suggestions of the performance to come, but also somehow set the words loose in the space. And the space was a kind of ghostly suggestion of the Belvoir stage, so familiar to many of them from earlier productions that one can certainly speak of deep body knowledge.

The reading process involved was very different from literary analysis, frequently involving director and actor latching onto a word or phrase, worrying at it, teasing it out to find a way through the character's 'journey', and gain insight into the moment a character becomes aware of something. What Neil later talked about as 'the forward progression in the play' is made up of these moments, the turning points that move relationships between characters to a new level and, in turn, tell the play's story. A good example of the process is in Scene 3 when Roland tells Nina, the psychotherapist, about the way he had to analyse his play so minutely to prove he had not committed plagiarism. She pressures him to say what he had then felt, and his answer, as given in Rehearsal Draft 1 read:

> I was incredibly self conscious. Of my own voice, style, instincts, impulses. Right. So self aware that now I can't do anything without questioning it. And when you question your basic instincts that closely, they seize up. Paralysis. And that might just stop me working.

In the stop/start reading, Richard picked out the word 'Right' in that speech, asking why is it there? What does it mean? Then he said 'Aha! That's the moment he realises that it was his self analysis that has silenced him.' So Nina has led him to this insight. It was not something he knew before he started the therapy, it is not something he is telling Nina, it is something he is discovering in that moment. Richard's perception and skill and craft led him to pick up this little word that a reader might have skated over, and he then used it to carry a huge weight of important emotional, character and plot meaning.

Richard's insight in fact led Michael to rework the scene considerably to show more clearly the way Nina leads Roland up to the emotionally climactic moment, now indicated in the text simply by the notation 'Aah' but performed by Richard as an inarticulate cry of pain. She then forces him to put this into words: 'It's like, I'm wandering through my own brain with a smoking torch, scorching everything I'm looking at.' In the first version, this strong image was almost thrown away because it came too early in the exchange, as Michael realised when he saw what Richard was doing with the scene. In the revised version, the exchange is placed after the cry of pain (done very powerfully by Richard in performance) and it acquired its true value as one of the key images in the play. The exchange then continues:

> Nina: Yes. Good, thank you, good. You can relax. You're feeling . . .
> Roland: Dandy, just, you know . . . extreme panic, but apart from that.

It is typical of the collaborative process involved here that it was Neil who suggested the inclusion of the rather quaint word 'Dandy,' which regularly got a laugh in performance, serving to defuse the tension slightly after the high emotion. It also revealed Roland to have a sense of irony, part of the charm of the character as he came into existence through the combined work of writer, director and actor.

Another example of such a moment of realisation was Roland's 'And I felt nothing' when describing the bushfires consuming Como that he watched from the beach on the other side of the bay. To Richard's consternation, the rewritten version of the scene that Michael emailed from Brisbane on Day 3 no longer included the phrase that was, for him, 'the vital part of Roland's experience of the fire', the moment when he realises he does not wish to continue the therapy, does not want to begin writing again, does not mind if the 'landscape in his mind' has been burnt along with the real place. After discussion with Michael on Day 8, it was reinstated and it ended up becoming so important in performance that Neil had to warn Richard one day that he was pausing too long between 'felt' and 'nothing' and piling too much onto the moment (Day 23).

A third telling example is the word 'Bruises,' inserted at Neil's suggestion in Scene 11, the hospital scene, at the moment when Nick shows Roland his arm with all the bruises caused by the doctors taking blood samples for testing. Richard resisted the addition, questioning why Roland would say the word if he can see the reality. Neil responded in a slightly flippant way that they are spectacular bruises (and indeed, they were, dabbed onto Guy's arm every night by Josh during the quick costume change from healthy, soccer playing schoolboy to frail figure in hospital gown trailing an intravenous drip). Once they read the scene again, however, it became evident from the way Richard said the word that this is the moment when Roland realises how seriously ill his friend is. So, again, an extremely powerful performance moment, an important part of the forward momentum of the play, and a turning point in a character's awareness comes from a single word.

In the first example, the word that triggered the actor's discovery is no longer part of the scene (which has, however, been substantially reshaped), in the second example the key phrase was cut by the playwright but later reinstated, and in the third, the word upon which so much meaning was loaded was not even in the playwright's original script. It would be completely wrong to conclude from this that the actors were compensating for something lacking in the script. On the contrary, it is evidence of how good actors use a strong script to make performance and how good playwriting leaves space for the actors to make their discoveries, find their characters' journeys.

In this stop/start reading process, it was most frequently Neil who interrupted the reading, usually with a query directed to the actor who had been speaking or to both parties in the exchange. For instance, are Roland's first responses to Nina blocking her or encouraging her? Why does he refuse to say the words 'writer's block?' What does Roland think it is if not a block? Why does he say 'my childhood' when Nina asks him for a time before he became self conscious, especially when he has just been so contemptuous of speaking to his 10 year old self? Sometimes Neil just seemed to be musing aloud, prompting general discussion, sometimes he was definitely probing a given actor's perception of their character's state. He asked 'are Roland and Daniel going to fall in love?' (Michael, who was present that day, said 'no') which prompted Russell to ask if Nina falls in love with Roland (to which Justine said 'on some level, yes' and Michael said nothing). Sometimes the questions flagged practical issues that would have to be dealt with in performance, such as the hospital bed for Scenes 11 and 13 (solved on Day 9, after Kylie and Josh had already procured a hospital bed and mattress, by Michael remembering that hospitals often have a kind of sun room and that the boys could be talking in such a room, the intravenous drip all that was needed to signify the hospital location). More complex was the discussion of the nature of the sexual seduction of the school bully, Steve Gooding (Scene 12) and how much of it would need to be seen. At that stage, the text had Roland actually initiating oral sex while Gooding was distracted by the vision of Lynette McKenzie but, to the relief of the actors, both Michael and Neil thought it did not need to be that explicit. For Neil 'it doesn't need to be seen on stage. It can be described, we have to know it happened.' But Michael then said 'It has to be pretty transgressive. We need to be aware of the dimension of the scandal, of the stakes involved. We need to feel the deep, thick texture of sexuality.' Although the scene in performance became comic rather than scandalous, this discussion fed into what later became a slightly contentious issue between Richard and Neil concerning how much detail should be included when Roland tells Nick what he has been doing (see 'Neil's Play, Michael's Play and Richard's Play' for further discussion of the issue).

Michael was not happy with the hospital scenes when he heard them read aloud on Day 1 and this led eventually to the replacement of Nick Sharp, the randy English schoolboy, by Nikolajs Eglitis, son of Latvian displaced persons (a bombshell for the actors that was announced on Day 4), and this in turn led to Miss Beverly becoming more of a romantic dream than an object of lust. The apparition of Mrs Norberry was cut, Roland having demonstrated his ability to conjure real people with the apparition of Miss Beverly, and Nick's frenzied flirting with the nurse was no longer appropriate, given the change in character. The action of the two hospital scenes was, thus, greatly simplified: in the first, Roland produces the apparition of Miss Beverly and promises to do 'something bad' to Steve Gooding; in the second, he reports that this 'something' has involved the seduction of Gooding and tells Nick about *The Play*.

Mindful of the fact that Michael had said he wanted to make some cuts to the scene with the copyright lawyer, Richard raised several issues with the scene during the stop/start reading. He said he did not understand why Roland admits to the lawyer that he had indeed stolen the idea of the play about the lost dog nor why he keeps apologising to the lawyer ('That must be frustrating for you. And I'm sorry' and later 'I'm sorry if it disappoints you'). Michael later removed some of the apologies and some other rather repetitious elements, but kept the admission (although in one later rewrite this too was cut, to the consternation of everyone involved, but Michael reinstated it after a long telephone exchange with Neil as, by that time, it had become very important in the character's overall moral trajectory). Michael's modifications simplified the scene considerably and made it more powerful while leaving unanswered the motivation for Roland's admission of guilt.

Another important issue that had been flagged the day before concerned the status of the apparitions that Roland is able to conjure up so that they are 'actually here . . . in the flesh.' During the stop/start reading of Scene 5, Richard queried his character's attitude to his 'gift.' He said, 'Does he believe he was actually able to summon fantasms into the room? What are we meant to make of that? Does he have a mental problem?' Neil's response was that the apparitions are an intensely theatrical metaphor, 'the room becomes peopled because that is what theatre is' and, while he acknowledged Richard's concern that the audience would need some explanation, felt that the gift should not be examined too much. He remembered that in one of the earlier drafts Michael had tested the possibility of providing some explanation so they read that version, discovering along the way more material to flesh out their idea that the psychotherapist, Nina, might be attracted to Roland, but finding that the explanation was indeed a mistake. In Neil's words 'the image snaps under the pressure', and he was confirmed in his belief that the status of the apparitions must be left mysterious. They are 'a metaphor for writing but they have to exist in a twilight zone' (Day 2).

A potential problem posed by the play is the way it shifts between the genres of psychological realism, memory, autobiography and the wonderfully bizarre scenes involving these apparitions. Dramatists frequently weave real events together with credible fiction, but this play draws on real events that are well within the memory of members of the audience and juxtaposes them to scenes, not of credible fiction, but of surrealistic fantasy, and Neil and the actors knew that for the play to work, the relationship of these levels had to be carefully managed. In the draft they had just read, Roland tries and fails to conjure up Julius Caesar in the Steve Gooding scene and is mocked by Gooding. They felt that this somehow made Roland's gift more ordinary, less magical. In Scene 9, Nina claims to believe Roland's assertion that he did not simply

Figure 6. Monica Maughan as the Crazy Woman (first dress rehearsal)
Photo: Heidrun Löhr

describe but actually produced the real presence of the figures and then, in Scene 15, the Crazy Woman, appears in her consulting rooms. Richard argued strongly that Nina must not say she believes Roland or appear to notice the Crazy Woman or else her character will lose all credibility. In subsequent rehearsals, considerable ingenuity was exercised in respect of the Crazy Woman, treating her as a memory rather than an apparition and using her hysterical account of the bushfire as counterpoint to Roland's claim to 'feel nothing'. In the end, but not until after the first dress rehearsal, the Crazy Woman was cut even though Monica had by then invested a good deal of effort into the character and Tess had created a wonderfully zany costume.

The major problem they pinpointed was a structural one: if the adult Roland is able to produce an apparition and it occurs at the end of Act I, then what is the point of Act II? The appearance of Chekhov is such a powerful and loaded moment and would be undermined if the ability to produce apparitions had already been returned to Roland. So the progression of the action, as they worked it out over the next weeks, was that Roland terminates the therapy in the same week that the bushfire destroys Como when he realises he does not care about the destruction of the source of his creativity and indeed, is not seeking the clarity offered by Nina but darkness, obscurity. Act II shows him slide progressively deeper into the tar pit, until he is saved again by Mrs Walkham, who appears to him and reminds him of *The Play*, which is then performed. They all agreed that the reappearance of his gift at the very end should be left mysterious.

Another important issue concerned *The Play*, the science fiction fantasy around a magical nanny based on Mary Poppins to be performed to an accompaniment of *The Toy Symphony*. They discussed the connection between the music and the ideas in Roland's play, Neil suggesting escape for Nick from an unpleasant place to somewhere beautiful. The major problem, as the actors saw it, was that Roland speaks of *The Play* as 'a skit written by a 12 year old' but it is being put on by a high school class of sexually obsessed teenagers. In fact, as Monica pointed out, the contents of *The Play*, as described by Roland in the various versions of the script, seem immature even for a 12 year old and more like something he could have written when in Mrs Walkham's fifth class at Como West Public School. The precise content of *The Play* seemed to be of little interest to Michael and it was left to the cast and crew to find a way of transforming it into something that a 'savvy kid like Roland' might have written (as Richard put it), or something that might have shocked the parents and been transgressive enough to cause the Headmaster to ban it. What they produced in the end was largely improvised by the actors in a couple of delirious sessions on the basis of one of Michael's minimal plot outlines: it no longer had the Nanny and the Boy escaping in the rocket to a better world but, on the contrary, the Nanny is an evil alien whose plan to take over the world is foiled by a Detective, who saves the Boy and blows up the Nanny's rocket as she is attempting to escape.

The Play required a large amount of creative energy, skill and imagination from the whole company, as will be seen later in this account, and the shift in tone from naive pastorale to science fiction/horror/thriller and back again plays a far from negligible role in establishing the conditions for Roland's final redemption. Roland presents Daniel with the copy of the script that has somehow escaped incineration, and this gift is linked in an unfathomable way to the mysterious return of his ability to create real presence, to wit the person of Anton Chekhov. It makes a difference if the return of Roland's gift is heralded by a reminder of the exuberance of his childhood creativity or by something darker emanating from his tortured teenage years.

One change Richard argued for strongly that was not accepted by either Neil or Michael, concerned the phone call in Scene 17, a 1,000 word monologue to be delivered by Richard into a mobile phone. He stressed the technical difficulties in doing this, and argued for the narrative of Roland's mother's funeral to be part of a scene with Nina, pointing out that it would provide something for Justine to do in Act II. But Neil really liked the scene, liked the idea of Roland being so alone at that moment of total disarray in his life, liked the way Jake (Roland's friend in New York) hovers over the play but never appears. And clearly, both Michael and Neil had the utmost confidence (rightly as it turned out) in Richard's ability to make the scene work. When I interviewed Richard during the run of the play, however, he was still of the opinion that the scene was too long and that judgement was shared by some spectators with whom I spoke.

In summary then, as a result of the queries raised in these early readings, Scenes 10 to 15 were substantially rewritten and simplified, the tone of the high school scenes was transformed through the replacement of sex obsessed Nick Sharp by the more romantic yearnings of Nick Eglitis and his early death was made more poignant; Steve Gooding was turned into a more simpleminded bully; and it became clearer that Roland's creative gift was silenced at that time by the triple onslaught of the death of his friend, the banning and destruction of his play and the Headmaster's ferocious attack on his sexuality. The function of the nurse changed once she was no longer the object of Nick Sharp's lust, one of the apparitions was cut (Mrs Norberry) and serious questions were raised about the Crazy Woman. Other rewrites gave more of a build up to the moment Nina gets Roland to acknowledge the damage done by subjecting his writing to detailed critical analysis (Scene 3), and clarified his motivation for abandoning therapy (Scene 15) although, as will be seen, the final version of this scene introduced another complication in terms of Nina's response.

Apart from the play-within-the-play, changes to Act II were relatively minor. When working on Scene 16, both Neil and Richard commented on several occasions about the powerful writing: after working on the scene on Day 11 Neil commented that 'Michael is expert at cruising sexual tension,' and Richard's assessment was that 'the scene is dynamite.' Michael told me on Day 8 that he was quite happy with the textual changes that were being made to the high school scenes and that, as they were in a very fluid state, he was happy to go with the flow in the rehearsal room, pick up ideas and take on board the actors' observations. The next day he told me that, once the narrative comes into the present, as it does in Act II, he would be less open to changes and more insistent on them making it work as he had written it.

The plot outline provided above does not reveal the full extent of the modifications introduced by Neil and the actors. Michael's comment at the first reading that certain scenes were too long and would have to be cut virtually invited Neil and the actors to become very interventionist

in relation to the text, suggesting cuts and alterations rather than search-
ing for performance solutions to problems they perceived. Neil, in particular, was extremely proactive in suggesting phrases and little details
that gave additional colour to a moment, or facilitated the discovery of
a minor character's 'voice' (a term frequently used by the actors), and
this unleashed the inventiveness of some of the actors. For others, the
changes requested were more a matter of clarification of the action or
their character's intentions.

When I talked to Kylie Mascord during the run of the play, she
said that the work process had been relatively simple as the set was so
minimal and there were no complicated props or staging issues. This
meant that, from her perspective, the fact that the play was in such an
unfinished state when rehearsals began did not cause major difficulties.
As she put it, 'the rehearsal process was as much about finalising the play
as putting it on'. From the stage manager's point of view, this may well
be the case, but I think for the actors it was a very different matter. All
the actors involved in this production were highly skilled and experienced in the work of making written texts come to life on stage, teasing
out tiny details to find character, exploring the emotional underpinnings to any exchange, using these nuances to flesh out and deepen the
experience of the moment. If the text is incomplete or extremely fluid,
these skills must in a sense be held in abeyance until the words have been
determined. Of course, the actors' own inventiveness comes into play
in such circumstances, but this is a different kind of skill, one at which
Russell Dykstra in particular excelled, perhaps because he was responsible for some of the most robustly comic characters. Or was it because of
his inventiveness that they became so comic, when they might in other
hands have been more sinister?

Certainly, some of the dramatic changes in direction made as the
work took shape caused problems for the costume and sound designers
as they had to modify elements of their design that derived from versions discarded in the collaborative creative process. On Day 19, after
reworking the music he had written for *The Play* to make it fit the darker
version that was now required, Paul Charlier was somewhat dismayed
to be reproached by Neil for not having procured a slide whistle. He
reminded everyone that his brief the week before had been to produce a
dark, sci-fi, horror thriller version and, as the slide whistle belonged to
the sunnier, childlike version which at that time was being superseded,
it had slipped down his list of priorities. Notwithstanding this kind of
slight tension, what emerged most strongly from the process involved
in producing *The Play* was the imagination, craft skill and sense of fun
shown by everyone, particularly the design and production team as they

sought to meet the shifting needs of the production. In relation to *The Play* as well as to the production as a whole, the task was less one of 'serving the play' than of helping it to come into existence.

On Day 2, when they looked at the earlier draft version of Scene 15, Neil said 'Michael has been writing the play in order to discover what it is' and that this explained why there was so much good material locked away in the earlier drafts. The amount of rewriting, reshaping and tinkering that went on was perhaps not unusual in relation to the first production of a new Australian play – Kylie told everyone that Stephen Sewell had brought a different final scene every day throughout the whole rehearsal period for his play *It Just Stopped*, produced by Company B in 2006. It may also be the case that this kind of textual intervention is a feature of Neil's mature directorial process. What strikes me as most significant, however, is the extent to which changes suggested by Neil and the actors have been retained by the author in the published version; not only were they doing what all actors and directors do, namely bringing to life on stage a written text, they were deeply involved in the writing of that text and this was a genuinely collaborative creative process.

Scene work (Days 4–14)

It's a complex ballet of meaning. (Neil Armfield, 2010)[1]

The next stage of the work was the physical exploration of each scene, establishing movements, proxemic relations between the actors in the space and the use of the furniture and props. In other rehearsals I have attended, this process is called 'blocking' but I do not remember anyone actually using that term here. Neil's practice involves painstaking exploration of the text in relation to the space, exploiting to the full the dominant axes and the tensions inherent in the five-sided Belvoir stage, mapping moves and words together with gestures, pauses and looks. The phrase used by Neil that I have quoted as epigraph to this chapter sums up in a beautifully concise way what was involved and it reminded me that Rex Cramphorn used the lovely phrase 'emotional geometry' to describe the organisation of actors' movements within the scenic space. In Neil's habitual work practice, it takes from two to three hours per scene to do this preliminary blocking and the process occupied the *Toy Symphony* cast throughout the next two weeks, interrupted by the need to backtrack when Michael sent new versions of scenes. Once they had worked through the entire play, they went back to the beginning and repeated the process.

In practice, the work proceeded by the actors doing numerous runs of short fragments of the scene on which they were working, trying different things each time, each acutely aware of the other's performance,

Figure 7. Neil Armfield, Kylie Mascord, Joshua Sherrin
Scene work in Company B rehearsal room
Photo: Heidrun Löhr

responding moment by moment to what the other was doing (this play is substantially a series of scenes between Roland and one other interlocutor, so it was frequently a matter of Richard working with one other actor). Neil, watched attentively by assistant director Matthew Lutton, intervened to comment, dig deeper or propose adjustments, Kylie noted for the prompt copy the moves that were finally agreed and kept an eye on the time to ensure that there were the appropriate tea and coffee breaks. Before rehearsals began she and her assistant, Josh, had prepared a large number of objects they thought, from their reading of the script, might be required and they seemed able to provide at a moment's notice any prop that was suggested, and if not, they would improvise (for example two rolls of mark-up tape tied together to make handcuffs, suddenly wanted for *The Play*).

The first impulse run

The process began after they had finished the stop/start reading of the final scene. It was quite late on the Friday afternoon of the first week and it was clearly quite a shock for the actors when Neil stood up and said 'Right, now let's run it.' Michael made a jocular remark about it being a bit early for a run but Neil said it was what he always did at this stage. As soon as he said 'Clear the space and we'll run it on our feet', there was a flurry of activity and it became apparent just how far the two days of sitting around discussing the text had depleted the energy level in the room. This lifted immediately as people began moving the chairs from the taped stage space, deciding where on the stage the light well would be shining onto the floor, and where the crash doors would be located. Kylie and Josh set up three tables at angles around the stage space, delineating roughly the blocks of audience seating. The central one of these was where Kylie sat throughout the rehearsal process, notating the moves for the prompt book, and Neil sat with his elbow on the corner of that table but with no table in front of him (see figure 5). He used an old office chair that enabled him to swing and even to scoot around, if he so wished. He may have used that chair for comfort or back support but the impression it gave, besides slight eccentricity, was potential mobility and multiple perspectives even though, in fact, it was nearly always located in the same spot. Mapping this onto the Belvoir Theatre space reveals his vantage point to be close to the entrance from the vomitory, an important consideration in relation to blocking the action on such an open stage (see figure 3).

The table on the OP side was where Paul Charlier normally sat when he attended rehearsals and where he set up his computer and sound system. The other designers sat at the table on the PS side and that was where I normally sat. I thought that by using a table that was already there, one that was occupied, albeit intermittently, by people with a major creative role in the process, my own presence might be less obtrusive. In the event, the actors were always aware of my presence, often as part of the rehearsal room banter demanding that such and such a comment be included in the book, sometimes to warn me that what had just been said was not for publication. One day Richard said that he was frequently bemused as to what I could be writing, that he would hear my pencil scratching and wonder whatever had struck me as so noteworthy. It did not seem, however, that the presence of an observer was an impediment to the work but as that comment indicates, the knowledge they were being observed was always present at some level of their consciousness.

Once the blocking process began, the taped stage space ceased to be a place where anyone could sit and people did not even casually walk across it. In some intangible way, it seemed to become the domain of the fiction, intently watched by the circle of people around the edge, but frequented only by the characters in the fiction. The scene work that

Figure 8. Gay McAuley, Michael Gow (rehearsal room, Company B)
Photo: Heidrun Löhr

occupied most of the next three weeks built on this first experience of spatialising the action. The actors and director worked systematically through each scene to establish points of entrance and exit, moves within the space in relation to the text, and the introduction of props where necessary. For this stage of the work, only the actors required for the scene were present and, although Neil made a number of remarks that suggested he would have ideally liked the designers to be there to watch and to participate more fully, they came only intermittently. This means that the actors were privy only to the discussions involved in their own scenes unless they arrived for a call to find that work on the preceding scene was still in progress. As a consequence, a lot of the discoveries that occurred were not shared amongst the whole group and, of course, once the play was being performed in the theatre, there was no chance for anyone to see scenes in which they did not figure. It is only the director, the 'attentive, unconditional spectator' (Mnouchkine 1973), the assistant director and stage manager who really 'know' the whole show fully.

Rehearsing a piece of text-based theatre is a creative process that consists of inventing, adjusting, and layering together minute details of gesture, intonation, look and position in space in relation to words spoken. It is extremely laborious to describe in words the difference these minute adjustments and interventions make but electrifying when you see it happening, when you see the light and shade that emerge, the nuances that inflect the words and the emotional event that is unfold-

Figure 9. Neil Armfield, Richard Roxburgh
Stop/start reading in rehearsal room, Company B
Photo: Heidrun Löhr

ing. In contemporary theatre, the words are often a kind of façade or
mask to the emotional event rather than, as in classical theatre, a poetic
statement of it. The actors' task with this kind of text is to dig beneath
the surface, explore the forces that are in play, the desires, fears and
emotions that underpin an exchange that may consist of not much more
than words like 'yeah,' 'well,' 'right,' and then make these forces manifest
through the vocal, spatial and gestural means at their disposal.

The set provided three entrance/exit points, the vom, the crash
doors and the entrance from the wings on the PS side (see figure 3).
Of these, only the crash doors were actual doors, the other two were
less literal and marked a more diffuse and potentially more mysterious
relationship between 'on' and 'off.' At the beginning of this stage in the
process, the production crew had not installed the dummy back wall
and crash doors in the rehearsal room, so all the actors had to go on
was the location of doors, taped on the floor. Before the rehearsal began
on Day 5, Josh taped the dimensions of the scorch mark on the floor
and two rather battered, hard, upright school chairs had been brought,
as requested by Neil, and on Day 7 the back wall and crash doors were
installed. All along the back (OP) wall in the rehearsal room, there
is a large beam running along at floor level, another reminder of the

building's industrial past. Neil said that it was going to cost $30,000 to have the beam removed but that it would have to be done because its presence made it difficult for actors to assess precisely how moves along that wall will work in the theatre. This seemed to me to go to the heart of the actor's process, in that while so much can be imagined (a chair on a table can be a mountain, a stick can be a rifle), the work involves a complex combination of total embodiment as well as imagination. A wall is not a wall if it has a two-foot beam jutting out at the bottom.

Work on scene 1

The following description of the work on Scene 1 provides a representative example of the mix of issues that were being dealt with at this stage of the process. This is Roland's first consultation with Nina, the psychotherapist, and it contains some sparring between the two as she presents her intentions for his therapy, his extraordinary two-page rant about the creative process, his fake breakdown in tears, the story of the charge of plagiarism, Nina's demand that he be honest, her perception of his drug dependence and his agreement to co-operate. In the first impulse run, at the end of Week 1, Richard had turned his chair away from Justine, but his immediate instinct with the upright school chair was to swing back on it, tilting it onto its back legs, thus changing his relationship to Justine and appearing more relaxed. The chair is not only semiotically loaded with connotations of time and place, but it is in a physical relationship to the other chair and, furthermore, it makes possible/impossible certain types of sitting, suggests embodied behaviours for the actor to explore.

They tried beginning with an empty stage and Roland carrying his chair in, and Nina then coming in carrying her chair and the box of tissues (she offers Roland a tissue when he begins his spectacular sobbing); Neil was of two minds whether to begin with a totally empty stage, which would mean the audience looking for a long time at the scorch/glow area, or to have the chairs in place already, or perhaps one chair. Richard asked if he would be entering in a blackout. Neil knew as part of his formless hunch that there would be no blackout to begin with or between scenes and also that he wanted to explore the possibility of doing the whole play with just the two chairs (even making the hospital bed from chairs if necessary). They tried a few different ways of handling the opening moment and eventually decided to have one chair on stage and for Richard to come on quietly from the PS entrance. Neil liked the rather ominous feeling of the single chair in the dimly lit empty space, the hint of Roland as condemned man facing the electric chair. He left it to Richard to explore what to do in those first moments that he saw as a kind of prelude to the action but said that the point would be to indicate something about his emotional state, his resistance to being there or whatever Richard found. He also said that the strength of these early moments would depend in part on the backing (music or sound) and he asked Paul what he was going to provide, thus drawing attention to the enormous advantage of having members of the design team present in the rehearsal room. Paul said he was thinking about broken toys at that stage, fragments of the *Kindersinfonie* to indicate Roland's head space rather than the full naïve form. They then spent some time determining the position of the chairs in relation to each other, for not only is each arrangement loaded with connotations, but on an open thrust stage, the problems of achieving a dynamic view of both characters from all three audience blocks have to be considered.

The scene begins in the middle of the therapy session, as Justine had pointed out in the stop/start reading, so they tried her coming on, carrying her chair, already speaking from the wings (there is quite a way to travel from the wings to the centre of the playing space at Belvoir), and they tried a number of different ways in which she could place the box of tissues, dropping it unobtrusively by the side of her chair, or overtly placing it on the floor between the two with a big gesture, or even holding it on her lap. Neil said after a few runs of the first section of the scene that placing the box of tissues on the ground needed 'to constitute a kind of statement, be big and definite rather than furtive or casual.' They began with Roland slightly turned away from Nina, hunched over and very tense. Justine said that that read as irritable to her (Nina later comments on his irritability as a symptom of drug dependence), and they decided he should be a little more open to her, more receptive. Neil suggested different moments when Roland could stand and move away from her, from what she is trying to get him to do. He suggested quite detailed, prescriptive things for Justine, leaving Richard freer but told him he needed to find moments in the first exchange when he could 'sneak a look at Justine. A quick glance can be a way of saying the "thing" you don't want to say.' Throughout this phase of the work and the earlier stop/start reading there was considerable slippage in the pronouns and names used. Actors referred to their characters in both third person and first person, sometimes in the same sentence or, as here, when Neil referred to 'Justine' rather than 'Nina.' The duality of the theatre situation, the fact that it is Richard looking at Justine as well as Roland looking at Nina, is highly pertinent to what they find and what they show, as will be discussed in more detail later in this account.

Neil's interventions were not always to suggest things they should do but also to comment on the impact of what they had done. For instance, in one run, Richard rocked back on the chair legs, got up when Justine said 'block,' the word he could not bring himself to say, and moved across to the outer edge of the glow area, confronting her across this space. Neil's comment was 'It's like a gap they have to bridge.' He also loved the comic business Richard invented for Roland to assist his fake weeping, grabbing tissue after tissue and then whole handfuls of tissues from the box Nina holds out to him. His suggestions were enormously productive, especially for a highly skilled actor like Richard who would often take a suggestion and turn it into something extraordinary. Richard had been doing the big speech pacing around the whole stage but then Neil suggested he try it sitting down, 'It might be funny if such a spiel were launched from such a tight spot.' When he did this, his arms tightly folded across his chest, buttoned up, tense and angry with his feet twitching, it was extremely powerful, all the more so for being against audience expectations. Richard was surprised by Neil's suggestion that he wait until the reference to 'the stately leviathan' before getting up, but he did it and it worked brilliantly. His pacing around the space meant that he had reached the upstage corner for 'Warragamba Dam', which he 'placed' across the central block of audience with a flamboyant gesture. This also meant that his satirical reference to Nina's 'bouncing therapeutic bomb' was launched 'through the centre of the house', as Neil put it. This major speech received more work later in the process, refining the gestures that made it such a comic and dramatic *tour de force*, but the basic shape of it was established on this day.

Neil then said to Justine, 'He's getting a lot of direction' and began to work closely with her to find out what Nina is doing during this long rant. He approved of some of the things she had found, such as turning away slightly with an amused smile as Roland starts ranting, but as she said, 'there comes a point when it stops being entertaining'. Neil told her to stand on 'I'm not going to let you box me in', that she should 'match his aria in her own way'. All of this was worked out with run after run of the given fragment, the actor trying different things and Neil responding and/or suggesting more things to try. For instance, he suggested Justine pull back on the emotion for this speech, saying that Nina needed to be cool, that she had Roland's number and that she should 'absolutely meet him on intellectual energy level'. This was very pertinent advice as the character had been getting a bit shrill, sounding to my ears more like an aggrieved girlfriend or wife than a psychiatrist and it turned out to be prophetic of problems to come with the relationship between the two characters.

My reaction after watching a day of this work process was complete admiration for Neil's attention to detail, for the subtle and perceptive way he adjusted the timing of word and gesture, and his awareness of the potential of tiny details such as a glance or a half turn of the head. I was also in awe of the actors' ability to respond to Neil's suggestions, and to remember moves and gestures they had tried earlier in the session. They seemed to have a body memory of what had been tried because they wrote notes on their scripts only after numerous runs, trying different things.

I have already commented on the difference it makes for this stage of the work process when the actors are given a polished text to work with as compared to one they feel needs amendments. In the latter situation, they become extremely interventionist and suggest textual changes where with a more finished piece of writing, even one that poses performance problems, they will seek performance solutions rather than amending the text. This will become evident in the contrast between the blocking process involved in Scene 17 (the telephone call to Jake), a brilliantly written but difficult scene for the actor, and Scene 12 (the seduction of Steve Gooding), a scene that was constantly being rewritten and, as Kylie pointed out one day, received more rehearsal time than any other.

Richard and Neil began work on the blocking of the telephone call scene late in the afternoon of Day 11, but it was not possible to go very far that day because Richard did not have the speech 'down,' to use their very revealing phrase. The preposition suggests that learning the words is an almost visceral process, that the words have to be virtually ingested. Actors have different practices in respect of this process. Justine told me on Day 5 that she had not yet tried to learn her words and that she liked to begin work in the dark, doing little homework before rehearsals began or even in the first days. Her preference is to 'leave the part, the character and the journey to grow' gradually through the joint work process with the other actors. Russell, too, said on Day 6 that he does not like to learn the words before the blocking is in place because he does not like to 'get locked in too soon'. Richard's practice was different, however, and on Day 5 when it emerged that he had already learned a substantial amount of his huge part and the other actors were joking about him being 'so professional', he said 'if I was not off book by this stage of the rehearsal, I would be really worried', another spatial metaphor, drawing attention in this case to the constraining nature of trying to move when tied to a script. Richard's standing in the group and his centrality in every scene put enormous pressure on the other actors to match his practice, and Neil was surprisingly ruthless in obliging Russell to learn his words before he really wanted to do so.

Scene 17 - the telephone call

As this long monologue had to be done with the actor speaking into a mobile phone held to his ear, gestural possibilities were radically reduced. At the beginning of the speech, Richard was upstage, by the crash doors. Roland is ostensibly leaving the lecture room after the shattering scene with Daniel, so he slams the door from within Daniel's space but when he turns around, he is inside his own domestic space, on the phone to New York and at least two months have gone by (he has told Daniel he was about to go and visit his father in hospital, but his father has now died and been buried, and his mother has 'crashed and burnt' with her own cancer, dying six weeks after her husband). Neil wanted Richard to close the door sharply so that the audience would hear the sound but this was not possible as he is occupied in getting the mobile phone out of his pocket, so it was arranged that Josh would be there off stage to push the door closed. Neil was very particular about which of the two doors it should be and precisely where Josh should exert pressure (near the hinge rather than the door handle), the effect being created, as Neil saw it, was of 'the doors of hell closing' (Day 24).

When they began work (Day 12), the mood in the rehearsal room was quiet and intense. None of the other actors was there and Neil and Richard were totally focused on the task, with Matthew, Kylie and Josh in their normal, unobtrusive support roles. Richard said that he had about half the speech down and the rest was 'patchy' and they started with him simply reading the whole speech aloud. After that reading, he said 'there is something binding about sitting in one place for the whole thing, something very powerful'. They explored the possibility of working this discovery into the scene, with Neil suggesting he could be on his feet at the beginning, and 'place' the elements in the story of his mother's funeral (the lectern at which he was standing to give his eulogy, his mother's coffin, the aisle, the congregation), but then be sitting for the description of the tar pit, the moment in the play when Roland reveals the dark heart of his despair. The effect of 'placing' the elements of the funeral within the performance space is to dramatise the narrative, 'placing' the aisle of the church in the centre block of the auditorium transforms that part of the audience into the congregation, but the telephone functions at the same time to create the sense of another place, one that excludes the audience and is totally oriented towards the unseen Jake, whose reactions can only be surmised from what Roland says.

Richard paced slowly between the two chairs, creating a kind of figure of eight that Neil called 'the infinity walk' while he described the funeral and his own thoughts, they tried different moments when he could sit (when he comes out of the trance he has been in as he speaks to the congregation, when the minister leads him to the pew) and when he could stand again. After the description of the funeral, the speech has a sudden return to Jake that Richard found difficult to handle:

> Jake?
> No, no. The point, of it, no, not what I said, well, what I said was at least interesting, the point of –
> Jake?
> You there?

They tried to motivate the words 'Jake? You there?' as a dropout in reception for the mobile phone, but found this unconvincing and the second interpellation of Jake a distraction. Richard did in fact cut those three words much later in the process as he felt unable to make them 'work' (that is to say, become a meaningful part of the overall emotional trajectory of the speech). Otherwise there were no cuts or alterations made in this scene. For Neil, the great mystery of the play is the meaning of the 'No, no' and they never did decide precisely what Jake must have said to elicit this response. In the published text, Michael has cut most of this little exchange in which actor and audience know only what Roland says in response to what Jake must have said. In the end, the blocking they worked out had Richard in the upstage back corner, the darkest place on the stage, for Roland's admission that he is no longer able to write:

> But I can't be bothered. I have this really strong feeling, you see, that I'm meant to follow them. That they're waiting for me and that I'm meant to join them and that everything else is a waste of time, stopping me from going after them.

This is precisely where he was standing for the 'scorching' speech to Nina in Scene 3, which made a powerful symmetry. Neil suggested he 'look down "the aisle"' on 'I'm meant to join them', that is to say, to the part of the auditorium where the aisle was placed during the earlier description of his parents' wedding/funerals. In this way, the performance space itself was continually activated and rendered alive with the fiction, and the spatial echoes from earlier scenes created additional layers of meaning.

They worked for two hours, run after run, adjusting details, raising questions. When Guy arrived for his call, carrying a big box of pastries from the Bourke Street Bakery for morning tea, they interrupted the work to engage in an animated discussion of the merits of Persian feta and avocado or chocolate and beetroot muffins before returning again to the intense emotion of the speech and, for Richard, the concentrated act of memory involved. The interlude was a necessary respite, not an interruption, and it served the additional purpose of enhancing the group's sense of wellbeing, in particular perhaps the sense for Guy of his own place in that privileged group.

Some of Neil's suggestions to Richard concerned stress and emphasis ('the *next* horror stretch' rather than 'the next *horror* stretch'), some responded to what Richard was doing so as to deepen the emotion (for instance when he was in the upstage dark corner and turned to face downstage, Neil described this as 'scanning the platform of your life'). He did not give precise instructions, just a hint in a verb like 'use' or 'value' and this was all that was needed for Richard to do something wonderfully subtle and moving or funny or sarcastic or whatever he felt was needed. For instance, on the line about Roland's parents 'driving off to live their dream together in Como', all Neil said was 'use "dream together" and "Como"', and although I cannot describe exactly what Richard did, I know it brought out the pathos of the suburban dream and the quasi mystical quality that Como acquires in this play. Another time Neil said 'use the hardness of "body to be burned,"' and the result was a kind of bleak emptiness that I found quite wrenching. Sometimes, if he felt the character was becoming too emotional, Neil would pinpoint a word that he said needed to be 'dryer' and, again, this was all that was needed for Richard to rein in an incipient tendency to melodrama.

It was an extraordinary privilege to observe such a highly skilled actor and director grappling with powerful theatrical writing that nevertheless posed a very difficult acting task. Knowing the text almost as well as they did and focusing on every minute detail of Richard's performance, the experience provided moments of intense emotion as well as insights into the work process. I was struck anew by the embodied sensibility of the actor (Richard breaking off at a moment of high emotion to remark, 'This feels like a bit of a nowhere position'), and by the incremental way in which the scene's possibilities were explored, every run adding a new discovery, a detail to be incorporated or discarded. It came as something of a shock to realise that all this had happened before morning tea.

Blocking the Steve Gooding scene

Kylie was correct in her claim that this scene received more rehearsal time than any other, and they worked on it on at least eight separate occasions as well as continuing to refine and tweak it after every run of the play once they had moved into the theatre. It was virtually work-shopped from the ground up, with Michael accepting much of what the actors had improvised and writing additional dialogue to meet their needs.

Their first attempt at blocking the scene on Day 10 was high octane farce. The scene began with a school bag being thrown onto the stage, causing Roland to fall to the ground in a foetal crouch, saying 'Steve Gooding, oh no.' This was one of Richard's favourite lines and he said jokingly one day that all Russell's characters provoked the same response in him. Russell suggested a great many possibilities for the bullying (getting Roland in a head lock and running him at the wall, crushing his fingers in the crash doors) and there was a great deal of joc-ularity, underscored by a certain apprehension, about how to handle the masturbation scene. They were still not satisfied with the new version of the scene Michael had written after his visit to Sydney on Day 9 as it did not seem to them to have enough words to motivate and feed the violent action. Neil suggested a number of additions such as 'You can stick your fucken books up yer arse', 'Write that in yer pooftah notebook', 'I'm gonna break yer fingers. Try writing then' and 'I'll give ya medical reasons', and they indicate the direction in which Russell and Neil were taking the character of Steve Gooding.

On Day 16, when Michael was working with them, his first ques-tion on seeing what they had created was what had provoked this level of violence. The preceding scene with Nick in hospital has established that Roland is being bullied again now that his bodyguard is no longer there to protect him, but he felt there needed to be some explanation or provocation. He liked the line about 'writing in yer little poofter note-book' and thought that that required an actual notebook, and from there came the suggestion that Steve should manage to wrest the notebook from Roland. Eamon suggested that Gooding could read out something Roland had written about *The Play*, someone else suggested he could tear pages out, and Neil liked the idea of Gooding destroying the note-book, the symbolism of which is to keep the visions at bay, so Roland's action in unleashing the vision of Lynette McKenzie is vengeance as well as self protection. This work produced a basic structure for the scene,

Figure 10. Russell Dykstra as Steve Gooding in rehearsal
Photo: Heidrun Löhr

as summarised by Neil: 'a bang of violence at the top, then stuff with
the notebook, then the vision/ masturbation' but the actors could go no
further without more precisions from Michael.

Neil asked Michael if there was any possibility we could hear something of what Roland has been writing, Richard thought it might be his
observations of life around him, possibly some of the Mrs Norberry
scene that was no longer being used; Neil said there would need to be
some homoerotic trigger, such as the description of a rugby scrum with

boys with muddy legs. Ideas were being suggested all around the room and Michael seemed to be taking it all in but saying little. They queried whether Steve's anger would be triggered by a description of Lynette McKenzie, but Michael thought the horror would be greater if he found a description of his own body. They expected Michael to go away and rewrite the scene but he said he would do it there and then. He would give them three short character descriptions that Gooding could read out, one about some historical figure, one about Lynette and one about Gooding himself which would provoke 'I'm gunna kill you' and then Roland would produce Lynette. Richard made the important point that it would be good for Lynette to be mentioned in the notebook as the audience have not heard of her at this stage. Michael asked for the names of people in history who died young and I suggested Keats and Shelley, someone else said Rupert Brooke, which Michael pounced on as the boys would all have had to learn 'If I should die. . .'

Russell said 'let's mug it through', (a lovely bit of actors' jargon) and they did a very energetic version with the bag of books thrown on and off, Gooding tearing out each page, screwing it up and saying 'oops' each time, until he comes to the description of himself. They discussed how brave Roland is going to be in trying to get the notebook back, what he would do when Gooding comes to the page about himself. Richard spoke of the paralysis that comes with horror, the kind of slowing down or freezing, which led to Neil recounting his own experience of being assaulted and how he remembered shouting at the five people who were bashing him, 'Why are you doing this?' He then said that it was probably the same gang who bashed and killed a gay man at McKenzie's Point (the place Roland goes when he is 'skimming out') and there was a little silence in the room as everyone took in the reminder that violence against gay men and boys is an ongoing part of their lives, that it did not end in the 1970s, and that schoolyard homophobia can have traumatic consequences.

The next day, Michael was back in Brisbane but had emailed the revised text. They were delighted that he had incorporated so much of their invention, but still kept tinkering, reinstating lines he had cut that they felt were required for the logic of the action, and adding further colour. The material from Roland's notebook had references to Shelley, a Buddhist monk setting fire to himself (this was the period of opposition to the Vietnam War), Miss Beverly directing Roland's play (Neil proposed the phrase 'play practice' rather than '*Toy Symphony*'), and Steve Gooding himself (comments that indicate how much Roland has been watching him). Neil wanted 'Percy Bysshe Shelley' rather than simply 'Shelley' so that Gooding could mangle the pronunciation.

Richard queried whether Michael would object to this amount of further tinkering but Neil said he had told him he was happy for amendments and additions to the flashback scenes 'as they are not really his métier.' They worried about 'braindead' as an insult, wondering if it was in vogue in the 1970s, and eventually replaced it with 'total zombie.' Running the scene with these amendments, they concentrated on stage business, the notebook falling from Roland's pocket, Gooding seizing it and beginning to read, and they queried why Roland does not run away as soon as the notebook is taken. They had to wait for another rehearsal when a fight co-ordinator could be present to ensure that the moves could be safely performed, giving the requisite impression of violence.

Neil wanted Roland to give Steve a little push so that he would follow the vision of Lynette out down the vom but Richard always hated that and argued now that it did not fit with the end of the scene as it had been amended. Neil said 'that is just the script', which I thought revealed a great deal about the group's assumption of authorial agency in this scene, but eventually agreed that Richard need not actually push Steve off. On Day 18, they worked the scene again with the music for the apparition of Lynette, a kind of synthesised bossa nova, and they envisaged the scene as Lynette in her bedroom at home, brushing her hair, getting ready for bed, chewing gum, doing jazz-ballet-style high kicks over the back of a chair. When it emerged that Richard had not mentioned to Tess during his costume fitting the day before that he was going to have to be able to drop the notebook, Neil said 'this is a key costume problem for you'. Costume not only feeds the actor's process of creating the character, but must function in terms of the stage business as it evolves; in the end, the notebook was not in the back pocket of his trousers, as they had been thinking but in a shirt pocket that Tess incorporated into her design. This made it easy for him to drop the notebook while in his foetal crouch on Gooding's entrance.

The sarabande (Scenes 10 and 11)

The above descriptions might have given the impression that Neil's aesthetic judgement always prevailed and, although this was certainly the case most of the time, there were differences of opinion on some occasions and these, too, are very revealing of the nature of the work process. Of course, it was only Richard who had the experience and the standing to hold out against Neil for any length of time, and the occasions when it happened indicate the kind of give and take that are essential in any genuinely collective project. An excellent example was the time shift between Scenes 10 (Roland in Nina's consulting rooms in 2002) and 11 (Roland's visit to Nick in hospital thirty years earlier). There was a brief moment, dubbed by Neil 'the sarabande,' when the two timeframes seem to co-exist for a moment. Roland has been jousting with Nina, deferring the moment when he is going to tell her he is quitting the therapy, and she agrees to let him talk about Nick, the schoolfriend who died of leukaemia.

This is the new version of the beginning of the hospital scene that Michael sent them on Day 10, in which he included a brief description of Nick's background, explaining that 'in the 1970s, simply saying he was Latvian would have summoned all that up, but more is needed for today's audiences.' Also, the actors had always felt that for Nick to launch straight into his story of the dream was too abrupt.

NINA: You sure you don't want to talk about something else?
ROLAND: No. Not yet.
NINA: So . . . Nick.
ROLAND: Nick. He was older than me. He'd repeated a couple of years.
             His parents survived the war, they escaped the Russians.
             They lived in camps, they made it to Australia, lived in more
             camps and somehow they landed in the Sutherland Shire
             and settled down to an ordinary suburban life.
[Nick comes in, in hospital gown, pushing a drip]
NICK: This dream. Naked girls . . .

Michael liked the reinforcement this gave to the 'thematic thing in the play concerning suburbia' and Neil made a crucial improvement in replacing 'the Sutherland Shire' by 'Como', which Michael has retained in the printed text.

In keeping with Neil's desire to keep up the energy levels by having the beginning and end of scenes very tight, even overlapping, Guy was already visible, walking slowly towards the chairs from PS while Nina was saying 'So . . . Nick.' As Neil put it after their first attempt, 'We are not sure whether it is another visitation or a memory or whether we have gone back in time.' Nina was speaking from the 2002 reality and Roland seemed already to be back in 1972 but it was not clear from which time-frame he was speaking and for Neil, this was 'a very lovely moment'.

The next day, when they reworked the scene, Richard asked if he could defer saying 'Nick' until after Nina had exited (she goes down the vom). In his view, the moves of the three actors, Guy coming towards the chairs, Justine moving towards the vom and his own move towards

Guy were 'muddy'. Neil overrode Richard's objections, saying he loved the fact that Roland was in two realities simultaneously but, four days later, when they came back to the scene, Richard was adamant that he could not make the moment work in the way Neil wanted. He said 'I can't be in two realities. Either I am talking to Nina or to Nick, but not both at once.' From his perspective, clearly there was a whole shift of embodiment from adult to adolescent Roland. They tried it with Guy coming in from PS, Richard getting up and going towards him, and Justine leaving down the vom, but as Neil said, that 'just makes Justine's exit uninteresting'. They tried numerous alternatives and finally Neil gave in and said 'All right, Richard, let's try what you really want.' This was typical of the way differences of opinion between the two of them were handled: Richard would insist that what Neil wanted was not possible but, when Neil capitulated, would come half way to meet him. On this occasion they kept trying various possibilities in an exhaustive and exhausting process but at the end of the session Richard knew that he had not really made the moment work. Later that afternoon, after the actors had gone and Neil was packing up, I said that I had really liked the move he had called the sarabande on Friday and he said sadly 'Yes, but it no longer fits.'

They came back to the scene again on Day 17 with renewed vigour, did what they had tried at the end of the session a week earlier and this time made it work brilliantly. Nina spoke directly to Roland and her 'So . . . Nick' had a slightly interrogative lift, and Roland's 'Nick' was not a reply to her but was spoken with an internal focus, in a kind of reverie, as though he were summoning him up from the past. While telling Nina the background story, he was watching Nick limp slowly towards the chairs, pushing the intravenous drip stand. By the time Nick sat down, Nina had moved out to the vom, but Roland did not enter the 1970s reality until Nick began to speak. So Roland was looking back into the past from the present and the two realities did brush against each other for Neil's 'lovely moment' without Richard having to embody adolescent and adult simultaneously.

Nina's tears

There were occasions when one of the other actors queried one of Neil's suggestions, but he was always able to convince them and his judgement was nearly always impeccable. There was one moment, however, where I really wished that Justine had been able to prevail against him. The moment was the end of Act I, where Nina tries to persuade Roland not to abandon her therapy when he is still at risk of sliding back into depression and drug dependence. From the first reading on the first day, Richard gave Justine a little look when he said 'Don't be upset' and this began the suggestion of a relationship between the two that went beyond therapist and patient. The next day, when they read the earlier version of the scene to see whether it provided more explanation for Roland's reasons for abandoning the therapy, they found more scope for the idea that Nina could be falling in love with Roland, however improbable this might be ('good stuff for Justine to do', as Richard put it). On Day 18, when they were working the new version of the scene that Michael had sent, Neil said that he really disliked the new line 'there's so much more of you to understand, to bring to the light' and Justine agreed vehemently. No alternative was suggested, however, so Justine was left to struggle with this and the next one: 'No, I don't want to throw it away now, on what, another hurdle? Which might lead somewhere important?' Neil agreed this was a very lame line, but his advice was 'play the lameness'. This was hard enough for Justine, but matters were compounded when Neil wanted her to weep to justify Roland's 'Don't be upset.' Not just have her eyes well with tears but weep to the extent that she needed a tissue, and thus bring back the box of tissues with which the Nina/Roland relationship began. While there was a certain symmetry there, it always seemed to me to be totally bizarre behaviour for a professional psychotherapist and I did feel that Nina was being sacrificed to a bit of clever stagecraft, and that Justine's legitimate objections were not properly explored.

These descriptions provide insights into the sort of issues that arose during the detailed scene work, how differences of opinion were handled, how meaning is created through the careful mapping of word, gesture and movement, and how different the actors' process was in respect of scenes given to them in very different states of readiness. There was a significant range of inputs into the Gooding scene, from the physical theatre skills of Russell Dykstra, to Paul Charlier's music (based on his memories of the records his older sister used to play in the 1970s), Tess's costumes and the advice of the fight co-ordinator, and everyone in the room was enlisted in the task of suggesting words and phrases (even the university student present as an observer for a couple of days was dispatched to find out the name of the place where Shelley drowned), and this group involvement occurred when Michael was present as well as in his absence. In place of the quiet intensity, the mutual respect and trust between director and actor and their shared confidence in the script that was evident in the work on the monologue in Scene 17, the work process on Scene 12 was high energy, seemingly chaotic but in fact extremely controlled, and it involved a genuinely collaborative creative process. Neil, of course, was the lynchpin in all the work, helping Richard to find his way through an acting task about which he had grave doubts, finding the middle ground in the case of a serious difference of opinion, or orchestrating the ebullient creativity of the whole group.

Note

1   Neil said this during the rehearsals for *Gwen in Purgatory* when asked about a particular move by one of the actors. It is reported by Dino Dimitriadis in his casebook on the production, written as part of his honours degree in Performance Studies at the University of Sydney.

The sign systems come together (Days 15–19)

We are discovering the shape now. (Neil Armfield)

By Day 15 Neil and the actors had worked through the whole play, returning to certain scenes on several occasions as Michael sent new and amended versions. Neil explained that he would not normally have runs at this early stage, preferring to go back to the beginning of the play when each scene had been thoroughly explored and continue the process, deepening and refining the form they had found, but he had been obliged to have runs on the days Michael was able to be in Sydney in order to show him what they had been doing. The runs inevitably led to more textual changes and these, in turn, to the need to revisit the moves tentatively agreed upon. Returning to a scene that had already been blocked did not entail merely repeating what had been agreed in the earlier session as a means of imprinting it in their body memory. When Justine said that the last time they had worked on Scene 15, she had entered from PS, Neil explained that what had been done earlier had no particular status, and it became evident that his normal practice in the later sessions was to rethink the scene, going deeper and using the knowledge that had been accumulating through the blocking of other scenes and, in this case, the author's rewrites. In fact, this process was still going on right up to opening night and beyond, as will be seen in the notes Neil gave to the actors after performances he attended during the run.

A good example of the nature of the detail involved in this process of refinement is Richard's query about a line in the new version of the scene with the Headmaster that they received on Day 10. He thought Roland's question to the Headmaster about what he is going to do with the play scripts felt like exposition. So the end of the scene was amended and rather than

ROLAND: What'll you do with them?
HEADMASTER: Straight in the incinerator. All of them. Burnt.

it became

ROLAND: Please, Mr Devlin.
HEADMASTER: I shoved them straight in the school incinerator. All of them. Burnt.

The changes are small but are important for the characterisations they were evolving. The Headmaster becomes more crude, the act of destruction more decisive, and Roland's line gives a completely different view of his emotional disarray. As the scene developed, Richard took this aspect further, and the adolescent Roland seemed to wilt while Russell's gesture on 'Burnt' became more flamboyant.

The major work undertaken in the fourth week of rehearsals was this second phase of the blocking process, building on what had already been done. The actors' focus still seemed to be very much on minute details of interaction within the scene but Neil was already shaping the larger patterns that link scene to scene and thinking about the impact of music, sound and light in the creation of vital levels of performance meaning. He had from the beginning been at pains to pare back to the minimum the use of props and furniture (which had the effect that everything brought into that radically emptied space then became laden with meaning), but the impact of this only became really apparent in the latter stages of the process. This section documents how performance elements such as the set, furniture, props and entrances and exits were used to establish larger patterns and the function of these in the creation of meaning and effect. It also includes some consideration of the costumes, indicating the key role played by costume in the individual actor's process as well as in creating the overall 'look' of the production.

The chairs

Neil had said from the outset that he wanted minimal furniture in Ralph's bleak, 'nowhere' space, and on Day 2 when he announced he wanted to explore the possibility of doing the whole play with the same two chairs and nothing else, Ralph said this would be 'thrilling.' It was, however, only during the blocking process in Weeks 3 and 4 that the full impact of this decision began to become clear. As a design solution to the problem of constant shifts in fictional place and time and Neil's perceived need to keep up the tempo throughout, it was indeed thrilling. The two chairs were the shabby, hard, upright, metal framed sort many in the audience would remember from their own schooldays, and it had been decided that, at the outset, there would be just one of them, placed centre stage under the pale glow of the downlights from the shaft. As already suggested, this single chair, waiting for Roland as he comes quietly on to the stage has a slightly ominous effect, then Nina comes on, carrying her own chair and the box of tissues. In all the scenes located in her consulting rooms, she sat in the same chair; in the scene with the lawyer, he occupied the chair she had vacated; when Mrs Walkham did her slide show about Como, Richard moved his chair around so that he became a child in the class, sitting next to the projector and looking at the images that were partially visible on the front part of the stage ceiling. Both chairs were used in the classroom flashback scene, Roland still occupying the one he had been using in the preceding therapy session, and Justine, who does a lightning costume change in full view of the audience, transforming herself from Nina into Roland's classmate, Julie Pearson, used Nina's chair.

By this time it was apparent that as Roland occupies the same chair from scene to scene, it had become 'Roland's chair' and the semiotic force of that began to be discussed. On Day 10, when blocking the hospital scene, Neil said 'Do we like Nick sitting in Roland's chair?' and answered his own question in the affirmative but the next day he returned to the observation and commented that 'so far the only other character to sit on Roland's chair is Nick', then he added 'I am not sure yet what that means.' Later that day, however, they changed the blocking again and Nick sat in Nina's chair. It was not done to preserve Roland's chair but for pragmatic reasons to manage the flow of traffic but the same thing happened on other occasions too. On Day 13, when blocking the scene in the drug dealer's flat, Roland sits to make clear that he is not leaving without drugs, and Richard chose 'the other' chair. Neil said that the move would work better if he used 'Roland's chair' and I noted then that I was fascinated by the way they kept trying to find an opportunity for Roland to use the other chair or for another character to use his, as though they were resisting the semiotic force of it.

When they did a run for Michael on the afternoon of Day 13, I came into the room a little late from the lunch break and the stage was already prepared for the run. To my amazement, there was only one chair and I immediately jumped to the conclusion there had been a decision to run Act II with only one chair and began to consider the implications: only one chair because this is the act for personal revelations, whereas Act I is structured around the Roland/Nina couple. As soon as the run began, I realised that they were doing the whole play, not just Act II and that this was indeed the setting with which Act I begins. My mistake nevertheless indicates how powerfully the chairs were functioning even at that early stage and how their presence and position were getting loaded with important meaning. On Day 12, while they were working on a different scene, Neil remarked casually that he had been thinking that *The Play* could clear the stage of the school chairs and they could have smart bar stools for the final scene. He referred sardonically to the semiotics of such a change and I thought immediately that it could indicate Roland finally leaving childhood hauntings behind, or possibly abandoning the pure inventiveness of his childhood self, or that the chairs burned with the scorching of his mind and he is left with the meretricious reality of bars and celebrities. Both incidents reveal the complex meanings the chairs were able to convey in themselves but they also functioned within the blocking to make other significant connections. On Day 16, when they had been working on Scene 3, where Nina really probes Roland's feelings about the plagiarism case, Neil pointed out that when she said 'and that gave you satisfaction?' she was sitting exactly where the lawyer was sitting in the previous scene when he asks the same question.

Neil's reason for getting rid of the chairs after Scene 19, and having smart bar stools for the final scene was because he did not like the image of Roland and Daniel sitting down at their ease at this awkward moment of reconciliation. Ralph vetoed the change and proposed instead that the actors turn the chairs around, propping themselves on the backs in order to convey the impression of sitting on a high bar stool. Richard was unhappy with this as sitting in that way was extremely uncomfortable: all very well for a few minutes each evening, but very painful for hours at a time during the rehearsal work. Kylie said she would ask Shaun to provide some cushioning for the chair backs during the work sessions but it never happened. On Day 14, amidst a number of haemorrhoid jokes, they spent several hours on this scene. Richard suggested that the chairs could be removed at the end of *The Play*, and the two could do the final scene on their feet, but Neil said 'the chairs haven't finished their journey if they are simply removed'. I thought this comment showed great insight into the powerfully expressive role inanimate objects can play and it indicates a good deal about Neil's brilliant stagecraft. The actors were quite correct in their objections to handling drinks when there was no table to put the glasses on, especially when they had to have their hands free for the all-important handing over of the play script. Neil was adamant they had to make it work, and of course they did with consummate craft skill. Another little insight from Neil was that using the chair backs as stools 'makes it look like you're in a place, whereas if you're just standing, you're nowhere'. Working on the hospital scene on Day 15, both actors expressed some anxiety about there being too much business with the chairs. By this time, however, Neil was quite certain that 'the pattern of the show is that we use them' and in the event, his judgement was totally vindicated as even Richard admitted during the subscriber debrief session. He said then that he loved the way 'the whole play was structured around the movement in space of two chairs'.

Props

The space was radically emptied of furniture and this meant that any props that were mentioned in the dialogue (such as the stapler that Dr Maybloom obliges Roland to focus on when he fears he may otherwise summon up a vision) or were found to be necessary for the action (such as the box of tissues), had to be carried on and off by the actors and they became highly visible and meaningful. This was not a production in which the set contains multiple objects that can be used to motivate a line of dialogue or a moment of action and then revert to their former role of set dressing or 'reality effect' to use Barthes's term. It was remarkable how few objects did turn out to be really necessary. When the lawyer said 'think of the telephone book', that was all that was necessary for the audience to do the same. It was not necessary that he brandish actual directories, although they did spend a few minutes on Day 2 discussing how big the Sydney telephone directory was in 1994, and whether the white and yellow pages were in separate volumes.

A good example of a prop that became semiotically loaded is the soccer ball that Neil suggested (Day 8) Nick could be kicking around idly when he comes across Roland scribbling in his notebook behind the woodwork block. They discussed ways of motivating his presence (could he have come for a smoke, does he give Roland a drag?), in keeping with Neil's habit of filling out each moment, and creating back stories for the minor characters that will give colour and greater depth to their presence. Smoking was ruled out because, given that the next time the audience sees Nick he is in hospital, it might seem to be sending an inappropriate message about the evils of nicotine. Neil then suggested a soccer ball, as that would be in keeping with his migrant outsider status in the anglo rugby playing school. The stage managers immediately produced one and Guy used it to brillliant effect, kicking it on along the vom so that we see the ball before we see him, then kicking it around the stage for a bit, giving him the opportunity to sneak a few little looks at Roland before he speaks to him, even using it in his sex fantasy about the imagined person of Miss Beverly. The ball created a slight sense of anarchy that Neil liked, although it was a constant source of anxiety to Guy in case he lost control of the ball and it rolled into audience space. When Roland tells him he hides behind the woodwork block because Steve Gooding hits him whenever he sees him writing, Nick says 'Steve Gooding? Mr fucking Rugby Football?' and Guy used to give the soccer ball a vicious kick towards the OP wall, a gesture that told the whole story of his alienation from the dominant culture of the school.

People who have worked on other Armfield productions told me that he is well known for the extreme precision of his descriptions of the objects that will be used. He said that the pencil Mrs Walkham gives Roland should be red, about two thirds the length of a new pencil, round not hexagonal. As he described this pencil so that Kylie and Josh could get it for the next rehearsal, I wondered if he was remembering someone who wrote with just such a pencil, or whether the minute detail (that would not be noticed by nine tenths of the audience) was more to do with the body image he had of Roland writing. Nobody asked for an explanation. He was also very specific about how Mrs Walkham should treat her notebook before giving it to Roland: tear out the pages on which she had written things, putting them carefully in her handbag, not screwing them up as Monica did the first time she had all the props to deal with. Michael, who was present that day, said it would be lists of kids on detention but Neil said it would be shopping lists. I noted the point because it seemed to provide another tiny insight into Michael's darker memories of childhood and school, as compared with Neil's much sunnier view. Neil's Mrs Walkham would not resort to detention as punishment.

When they were rehearsing the scene with the drug dealer, it was necessary to find a container for the drugs that Tom finally agrees to sell to Roland. Josh produced a woman's handbag, one of several they had provided for Monica to choose from for the scene I have just been describing. This was clearly intended to be a stopgap until they heard what kind of bag Neil wanted, but he said he was quite happy for them to continue to use the old fashioned handbag. This was such an eccentric choice but, when people in the production meeting queried it, he said maybe it had been a bag that was snatched by a drug addict in a street robbery and that is why it has ended up in Tom's possession. In the following scene, however, Roland tips all the drugs, cigarette papers and paraphernalia out onto the floor, before lighting the cone and beginning to inhale. One day, Neil said happily that this moment thus referenced the moment in *Away* when Gwen tips out the contents of her handbag. As he had already commented that *Toy Symphony* is like a bonfire of all Michael's previous plays, I did wonder if the intertextual moment he had thus engineered was the reason for his choice of a woman's handbag or whether it had only occurred to him at that moment. It is doubtful whether many (any?) spectators picked up the reference, but it is nevertheless an example of the tissue of interconnected threads that marked this production, emerging from relationships between participants that go back so many years and involve so many other texts, productions and rehearsal processes.

Entrance and exit points

On Ralph's set for *Toy Symphony*, there were three possible entrance/exit points: the double crash doors on the upstage wall, the entrance from the wings on the PS side and the famous Belvoir vom, beloved of actors and spectators alike. The three entrance points form a triangle of lines of force. There is no entrance on the OP side of the stage. An actor entering from the PS has a long walk to reach the centre of the stage and is seen in profile by the PS block of spectators and full face by the other two; entering from the vom, the actor has his or her back to the central and OP blocks but is seen in profile from PS, and of course reaches the centre of the stage very quickly. As soon as the actor turns, he or she has command of the whole house; entering from the crash doors means the actor is facing the OP and central blocks, and is slightly in profile for the PS block. As mentioned earlier, when I first saw the set design I thought that Neil would use the crash doors for the spectacular entrances of the apparitions: Alexander the Great, Titus Oates, the medieval executioner and Chekhov. From the beginning of the blocking process, I was on the lookout for spatial factors that might be deployed to differentiate between these mythical figures, conjured by Roland, the flashbacks that represent the story he tells Nina about his past, and the comings and goings of characters in the fictional present.

This was not Neil's intention at all, and he used all the entrance points indiscriminately, not associating any of the off-stage spaces with a particular time, place or reality dimension. In fact, he quite consciously alternated the use of the entrances, on one occasion asking pointedly 'Have we brought a vision through here yet?' (Day 10) The choice of entrance and exit points seemed to be governed by pragmatic factors, such as the staging demands of the apparition (snow storm and blizzard for Titus Oates, flaming torch for the Executioner) and the degree and nature of the interaction with other characters on stage. Neil was, of course, always also concerned to ensure that the stage action had plenty to offer spectators wherever they were sitting in the fan-shaped auditorium and to make the best possible use of the multiple perspectives offered by the Belvoir stage. The experience for the audience in Act I was of one surprise after another, with no sense of where the next apparition was going to come from, nor whether it was going to be a memory flashback or a surreal fantasy figure. During some of the memory scenes, if she did not have to play a role in them, Justine would stand in the vom, a shadowy figure watching the story that Roland was ostensibly telling Nina. This helped to weave together the narrative of the past with its fallout in Roland's adult life and, although many in the audience could not see her because of the shape of the theatre, for those who glimpsed her standing in the dark passageway, it added another dimension to the scene being played out on stage.

The most frequent trajectory was for a character (vision or memory) to enter from the PS side and exit down the vom (Alexander, Executioner, Lynette, Chekhov, Dr Maybloom and Mrs Walkham in Act I), thus giving the audience in all three seating blocks a good view. Neil told me later that, for him, the vom functioned like a drain down which the apparitions and memory figures disappeared. Titus Oates, by contrast, entered from the vom and exited through the crash doors, doubtless because the most spectacular part of that apparition was his exit into the blizzard (Josh in the space behind the doors, throwing handfuls of artificial snow blown by a large fan, dramatic sound effects and Russell using his Lecoq mime training with gusto to force open the doors against the nonexistent wind). Miss Beverly entered through the crash doors, quite quietly but the moment was intense because of the reaction of the two boys and she did a half circuit of the stage along the OP wall, reciting her compilation of the most beautiful love poetry in the English language, and exited backwards down the vom, still reciting, still watched in awe by the lovestruck Nick. Mrs Walkham, too, in her Act II apparition, came in quietly through the crash doors and did a similar circuit along the OP wall but continued the trajectory around to sit in the 'other' chair to read D.H. Lawrence's description in *The Rainbow* of passing through Como.

Neil's tactic was to ensure that scenes began with high energy and colour in order to keep up the momentum of the action, a perception he had voiced after the first reading on Day 1 ('one of the tricks will be keeping it up to speed'). Actors thus had dramatic entrances rather than dramatic exits, although there were some exceptions, as shown in the audience applause that frequently marked Mrs Walkham's exit after her history lesson, and Titus Oates's heroic departure into the snowstorm. There was no pause between scenes and a marked feature of Michael's rather filmic dramaturgy in this play is that the interaction is frequently underway when a scene begins; this led Neil to get the actor to begin talking immediately, to talk while coming on, another factor militating against dramatic exits from the scene before. In Act I where time and place shift continuously, it is the incoming character who brings the new time and place, while the exiting character quietly takes the former time/ place with him or her. The production provided a number of delightful moments in which the realities coincided briefly (as already described for the sarabande between Scene 10 and 11), or seamlessly supplanted each other, or created a bizarre moment of confrontation. The high energy and speed helped ensure that the audience kept playing the game and did not have time to quibble about the leaps in spatial and temporal logic.

At the end of the poetry lesson, Mrs Walkham exits through the crash doors and Julie Pearson runs towards the PS exit, only to come face to face with Dr Maybloom striding into his consulting room, where the child Roland is already present. Justine used to stop in her tracks, hesitate for a second and then turn and run out along the vom in a lovely leggy kind of scamper that was perfect for the 10 year old Julie. When they first worked out this blocking on Day 17, Neil said it was a 'special moment where two realities collide' even though the disjunction is only spatial (primary school classroom becomes doctor's consulting room) but not temporal (both scenes take place when Roland is 10). The time shift in the next scene is even more bizarre in that it involves the use of an object. Dr Maybloom demands that Roland look at a stapler (in a more naturalistic staging this would presumably be on his desk but here it had to be placed on a little shelf in the wings in readiness for Russell to seize at the precise moment it is needed). Before exiting along the vom, he places it on the ground, demanding that Roland keep looking at it 'to force these horrid visions back down into the dark'. Roland is still sitting there, staring down fixedly in the next scene when Mrs Walkham comes by and asks him why he is staring at the ground. She then gives him the notebook and pencil and tells him to write when he thinks one of his 'special visitors' wants to appear. He begins to scribble and, before she exits down the vom, she gives a quizzical little look at the stapler, as much as to say 'more untidiness in the playground', picks it up and carries it off. Richard undergoes a bodily transformation, still writing in the same notebook, from scared 10 year old to a more assured teenager. So between Scenes 7 and 8, the place shifts from consulting room to school playground, and between Scenes 8 and 9, both place and time shift from primary school playground to four years later 'behind the woodwork block' at high school. Stapler, pencil and notebook provide a troubling material continuity while at the same time triumphantly displaying the power of theatre to transform anything into anything.

The most spectacular example of fantasy erupting into the real occurs with *The Play*. The creative process whereby this frenetic two-and-half minutes of stage action came into being will be described in more detail later in this account but the moment of the entrance needs to be mentioned here as it helps to elucidate the way Neil's staging of all the other entrances functioned in the overall experience of the play. At the end of the previous scene, Roland is sitting on the ground with the school case, and Mrs Walkham is standing behind him as he discovers the script and says dreamily 'This old play.' Then the music starts and the characters of *The Play* invade the space. They tried many different possibilities: coming in all together from one or other entrance, each coming in at a different entrance, the Mary Poppins figure of the Nanny appearing at the crash doors while Russell and Guy (as children) enter from the vom, and so on. My favourite version (which was rejected due to other pragmatic demands to do with bringing in the trolley with all the toy instruments) was when each of them appeared at a different entrance and stood there solemnly for a few seconds, waiting for the moment in the music when they would launch into action. It was reminiscent of the appearance of the characters in *Six Characters in Search of an Author*, one of the most magical moments in the theatre that never fails to send a shiver down the spine.

The complex and dangerous relationship between the real and the imaginary is an important part of the meaning Neil created in his production, and the spatial organisation of the action is one of the major ways the idea is made tangible. It was the choices made surrounding the entrance of *The Play* characters that suddenly revealed to me that, in Neil's blocking, the whole of the literal space is surrounded and permeated by imaginary/memory/fantasy spaces. The memory characters and the apparitions can erupt into the real from any of the entrance points, and disappear just as mysteriously via another. The idea of the interpenetration of the real world and the domains of memory, fantasy and imagination that emerged so strongly from Neil's use of the entrance/exits throughout the play seems to me to feed directly into Richard's perception, discussed at length later in this account, that the play is fundamentally about the artist's struggle with the sources of his own imagination.

Costumes

As has already been indicated, Tess Schofield, the costume designer who is another of Neil's long standing collaborators, had been unable to be present in the first week of rehearsals. This meant that the presentation of the costume designs, which would normally have occurred much earlier, perhaps even on the first day, did not take place until the beginning of the second week. Tess had done a great deal of work on the costumes and, when the whole cast assembled after lunch on Day 5, there was a buzz of excitement. This was clearly an important moment in the actors' creative process as the proposed costume is a major factor in assisting them to get a sense of the 'look' of their character, and this has a significant impact on the total embodiment they are bringing into being.

Tess had made a large sketch of each character in black ink on white paper and pinned swatches of material to the corner to show the colour palette. The sketches were beautifully done, very witty and astute and there was a good deal of laughter as she showed each one. The process brought home very strongly the amount of work Russell has to do: primary school principal, high school headmaster, copyright lawyer, drug dealer, Steve Gooding, Dr Maybloom and Chekhov as well as Titus Oates and at least one role in *The Play*. All Justine's roles, apart from Nina, were sexy young women (Lynette, Miss Beverly, the Nurse) or the child Julie Pearson and this is why Neil decided to swap one of her roles with Monica: Justine was to have the angry housewife, Mrs Norberry (Neil envisaged her with a tight perm), and Monica got the nurse. The later decision to cut Mrs Norberry meant that, after all, Justine's roles within the memory sequences were all young and/or sexy and this did definitely have an impact on the way the role of Nina developed.

Figure 11. Justine Clarke with costume designs in rehearsal room
Photo: Heidrun Löhr

The costume design for Miss Beverly made her a very strongly delineated hip 1970s schoolteacher, which provoked memories amongst the actors of attractive female high school teachers who used their sexuality to intimidate unruly boys. As Miss Beverly is now going to direct Roland's *Play*, they also began to fantasise about what kind of production it would have been. So the whole look of *The Play* could be affected by what has emerged about Miss Beverly from the costume design alone. The fat primary school principal in shorts and long socks, carrying his cane as a kind of tool of trade, provoked more laughter and it was evident there was a certain animus against headmasters. Often the character was defined by spectacles or wig, and Tess said she would be getting these as soon as possible so that the actors could begin to explore the embodiment that follows. Russell immediately changed Dr Maybloom's voice in response to Tess's choice of wig and spectacles.

The designs were pinned up on one of the walls and remained there throughout the process as a reminder. Tess provided rehearsal costumes for some of the characters to assist with the embodiment but the full costumes did not arrive until tech week when the production moved to the theatre. Seeing the costume designs was a very important stage in the actors' creative process, and the discussions made evident what a major interpretive role the costume designer plays. It was also a revelation of the fact that, although the rehearsals revolved so sub-stantially around Richard and the enormous role he has to play, the perspective from elsewhere in the creative process was very different. For the costume designer, there were nineteen characters in addition to Roland, as well as another three or four in *The Play*, and each one needed an elaborate costume even if the actor was going to be on stage for only a few minutes. The task for Tess in designing the costumes involved responding to the idea of the character conveyed by Michael's text as well as taking into account the real body of the actor playing the part, and then keeping in touch with the performance as it evolved in rehearsals so that the requirements of stage action and even substantial changes in interpretation could be incorporated into the costume where this might help the actor. The costume for Alexander the Great, with its moulded fibre glass body armour and shinguards, helmet, shield and sword for an apparition that would be on stage for two or three minutes was far more elaborate and involved a great deal more work and expense than Roland's costume that would be visible throughout the show. For Roland, Tess had to create something that was deliberately understated so as to be able to accommodate the shifts in time within the narrative.

Actors in other productions have told me how much they value the opportunity provided by costume fittings to discuss their characters, and this was the case on this production too. Throughout the rehearsal period, actors had to find time to go to the Wardrobe to discuss their costume requirements and for measurement and fitting sessions and, gradually over the weeks, Tess provided more and more elements of costume for use during the rehearsals, including a hospital gown for Nick, floral frock and lace up shoes for Mrs Walkham, a skirt with a pocket for the glasses and blouse with a little scarf for Nina so that she could practise the transformation from Nina to Julie Pearson, glasses and a white coat for Dr Maybloom, and so on. Costume did not just assist in creating the 'look' of the character but affected all aspects of the actor's bodily behaviour, type of walk, way of sitting, and so on, and thus had a major impact on characterisation. On Day 20, when they were working on the drug dealer scene, Neil suddenly exclaimed that Russell was wearing the wrong shoes. He was wearing the lawyer's brogues rather than Tom's sneakers and Neil interrupted the run, insist-ing that he go off and find the correct shoes as they 'will affect his whole demeanour and the kind of offers he makes will change'. This indicates that it is not just the individual characterisation that is affected but also the interaction that becomes possible with the other interlocutors on stage.

I had noticed that when Justine played Nina wearing her own clothes, usually jeans, her bodily movements were very free and casual. For instance, in an early work session on one of the therapy scenes, she sat with one leg curled under her on the chair, which seemed somewhat incongruous for a psychotherapist dealing with a difficult patient, although Neil made no comment. She and Richard also developed some business that involved her sitting on the floor next to him but as soon as Tess provided her with a skirt, all this kind of action was curtailed as the skirt constrained her behaviour. Tess's solution to the need for Nina to transform herself into Julie Pearson, a 10 year old child, in full view of the audience was ingenious but I think it compounded some of Justine's problems with the Nina character. She wore a quite short, navy blue, pleated skirt and a pale blue blouse with pin tucks and little puff sleeves that was apparently quite fashionable but could also double as school uniform; bare legs and flat black sandals of the sort that Tess's own GP wears (and that Justine said were so comfortable, she was going to buy them at the end of the show); a black and white scarf knotted inside the neck of the blouse that she pushed up to form an Alice band at the same time as she released her hair from the clip that held it up for Nina. The costume, particularly the rather short skirt, encouraged a kind of flouncing way of sitting that seemed inappropriate for Nina. Justine realised this and Tess agreed to let the hem of the skirt down a couple of inches, which was an improvement, but I thought the costume accentuated her youth and girlishness and thus made it more difficult for her to convey the idea of the highly skilled therapist with a razor sharp mind who forces Roland against his will to be honest.

The first time the actors got to wear their full costumes and to use all the props that had been obtained or made by Shaun, the company mechanist, was during the tech run and they made an enormous difference to the look and the energy. The wigs, especially, functioned to completely transform people's appearance. For Miss Beverly, Justine wore a voluptuous, long haired, dark wig, a silky mini dress with long sleeves in a bright orange, red and black paisley pattern and knee-high orange high-heeled boots. Damien reminded her that there would be a moving light on her so she would have to be extremely accurate about where she 'places' her lines (her recitation of a compilation of lines from famous love poems), Neil worried that the costume was too sexy and not ethereal enough as he wanted Miss Beverly to be both sexually alluring

Figure 12. Justine Clarke as Miss Beverly (dress rehearsal)
Photo: Heidrun Löhr

and pure, and Justine herself was preoccupied with the tricky business of finding the exit to the vom when she is walking backwards, gazing across the space into Nick's eyes. This combination of material and immaterial factors is typical of the issues the actors have to deal with.

Another character who was completely transformed by his costume was Steve Gooding, the school bully (see figure 10). Neil had wanted Russell to wear a dark wig as that is closer to his own hair colour but he was overruled by Tess and the general consensus in the rehearsal room for whom Steve Gooding had to be a typical 1970s 'surfie', with long blond hair. Tess had also given Russell a football jumper in Cronulla colours,[1] and short blue shorts (with padded buttocks to give the requisite muscular look), shin guards in his socks and gym shoes rather than studs. She had procured studs for him but it became evident in the rehearsal room that wearing studs on a polished floor was dangerous and would also constrain the kind of action he needed to do in the fight scene. It was then pointed out by someone with inside knowledge that footballers never wear their studs off the pitch, which is why they knot the laces and carry the boots around their necks. Russell had immediately experimented with that but the boots got in the way of the action they had worked out so the studs were abandoned. As soon as Russell came on to the stage for the first time in that costume, everyone present burst out laughing, and this happened night after night throughout the run. The character was instantly recognisable to Sydneysiders and the cocky strut that Russell developed and the way he flicked his hair back were elements of the characterisation that were a direct response to the costume.

Nick, the other 1970s schoolboy, did not wear a wig even though Tess had originally planned for the character to have the long hair of that period. Neil thought that because Guy had worn a wig for Tim Conigrave (the character he played in *Holding the Man*, the production immediately preceding *Toy Symphony* in the Belvoir season), it would be better for him to play both Nick and Daniel with his own closely shaven hair, part of the work of separating Tim from Daniel but also drawing attention to the deep connection for Roland between Nick and Daniel. This insight into the factors that enter into consideration in determining the look is interesting in that it acknowledges the context of the subscription season and that this production would be seen by many spectators in relation to the other productions of the season.

Every one of the twenty characters in the play, plus the four 'spookies' (Neil's term for the characters in *The Play*) had elaborate costumes, consisting of multiple elements as well as wigs and spectacles, and every detail had to be carefully chosen in line with the character and period as well as the actions the actor would be required to perform in that particular costume. The original design for each character was based on Tess's response to the script, but then as the actors developed their characters and major changes were made to script and interpretation, the costume also might need to change. The Wardrobe at Company B is a large, bright room just off the rehearsal space which makes it easy for actors to come for fittings and it reminded me of Matthias Langhoff's comment that in his ideal theatre, there would be glass partitions dividing wardrobe from rehearsal room so that the people making the costumes could see the actors and the action as they worked (Banu 2005, 271–2).

Attention to detail was the watchword. Even for a costume that would be seen for only a few minutes, everything had to be perfect, as was exemplified in the Mary Poppins look alike for the Alien Nanny. Here Tess was able to go to town with the details as Justine had virtually the whole of Act II to get dressed. The costume included a beautiful lacy high necked blouse that would be hardly seen under the jacket (but, as Tess said, 'if you don't get all the details right, it won't look right' and she was thinking of adding a lacy ruff at the neck), a mid-calf-length skirt that was flat across the front but accommodated a bustle at the back, a neat jacket with a velvet trim and dozens of buttons (but the actual fastening was with three buttons underneath this trim). The button boots Justine was using during rehearsals were not fussy enough for Tess and on Day 20 she was still trying to source a vintage pair on eBay. She had a basket with dozens of pairs of white gloves and chose a slightly off white pair as the hands must not look too glaring. The little flat hat with orange feather and red ribbons that Tess found in the wardrobe store turned out to have an interesting history of its own. The label inside indicated that it once belonged to the Elizabethan Theatre Trust and had been worn by one of the Street Women in the first production of Patrick White's *The Ham Funeral*;[2] Tess said she was planning to display it in a glass case somewhere at the end of the *Toy Symphony* run. She had also found a little black and white scarf that was presumably part of the Mary Poppins look and she offered it to Justine to take back to the rehearsals after one of her costume fittings, even though nothing Justine had so far done in the role required it or could really accommodate it. As Tess said, though, it could be the basis for some business that 'might lead to a delightful discovery'. In the event, the scarf was not used but the comment was a fascinating insight into the way both Tess and Justine knew that stage costume is so much more than just clothes.

Keeping track of all these details for each of the twenty-four costumes, elements to be made, other elements to be bought or sourced on eBay or elsewhere, other elements to be altered, perhaps with the assistance of the props department, was a substantial undertaking. Tess has developed an extremely efficient system with a computerised spreadsheet that assists in the task, informing her at a glance of the work to be completed and which member of her team was doing what, but even with this there was a moment of confusion during the technical rehearsals when it emerged that the Nanny's umbrella had been overlooked. As Ralph explained, this was due to some uncertainty as to whether it was the responsibility of the costume department or props (in fact it fell between the two in that it had to look exactly right for Mary Poppins but also played a vital part in the action of the dumbshow for which it required additional properties).

I was never entirely clear about the protocols that applied to the designers' work, what could simply be referred to the production manager and what had to be approved by Ralph, for example, or how much autonomy the designer had. On Day 20, when they worked on *The Play*, there had been some discussion about the risks for Guy in using Berocca (a vitamin supplement widely used in Australia, which turns bright yellow when dissolved in water) to produce the yellow vomit, especially as he had to swallow the residue, this being the least messy solution. Kylie warned that he would have to be careful about vitamin D intake during the run if he was intending to swallow that amount of Berocca every day and Ralph then suggested that they use 'an analogue foam' made from some material rather than the pseudorealistic

Berocco froth. As he said, 'Everything else is false so why have just that one literal thing?' Neil really liked the froth and insisted that they retain it but Ralph, while giving in, did mutter something about directorial intervention. This was a joke, which was the way they invariably handled differences, but it made me wonder about the role of the designers and the fine line they have to navigate in relation to both the actors and the director. It also makes it clear why, for Neil, the ideal arrangement is to have all the designers present in the rehearsal room as often as possible, participating in a genuinely collaborative process.

Sound and music

Paul Charlier, who has composed the music and designed the sound for many of Neil's productions over the years, was indeed often present in the room, cutting the music live as he watched what the actors were doing, and able to add an effect or sound pad (to use the term Matthew introduced) that would enhance the atmosphere briefly. Creating the music and soundscape for a dramatic production is a complex and subtle business as the sound is often working in an almost subliminal way on the spectators. Paul told me that ending a sound cue is the hardest part because 'if you are not careful it is like a fridge cutting out and the audience becomes aware of the sound because it has stopped' and he really dislikes that (26 March 2010). All the apparitions had dramatic and colourful sound effects, and the *The Toy Symphony* was referenced in musical effects at the beginning of the play and, of course, was central to the performance of *The Play*, but other moments required more subtle effects. Paul ended up rewriting the music for *The Play* five times as ideas about the content changed radically from one rehearsal to another. The music for Miss Beverly also had to be rewritten as she became a more romantic figure. The sound for all the apparitions, apart from Chekhov, had some basis in the 1960s, even the Medieval Executioner whose soundscape contained reference to a Ken Russell film in the choral music as well as bells tolling and fire crackling, and Alexander the Great whose music referenced the 'sword and sandal' movies popular in the 1960s.

Paul's original music for Miss Beverly (or Joy, as he always called her) drew on his memories of the records his older sister used to play at that time and, in its use of the sitar created the idea of a rather hippy young woman teacher. After he had played his suggestions for all the apparitions in the morning of Day 18, and was informed that Miss Beverly had now become a much more idealised figure, he went away to rework the music. That afternoon he played what he called 'a rolling texture rather than music' that would accompany the vision of Miss Beverly, and I wrote at the time that it was 'magic and holy and completely transformed the scene'. For Neil, however, it was still not holy enough and on Day 24, he asked Paul to make it 'a shimmering of starlight under her', so Miss Beverly was transformed from a sexy, comic and very physical apparition to a romantic dream. The sound pad for Chekhov began before his arrival and continued until the end of the play. As I noted when Paul first introduced it on Day 21, 'It's a kind of pressure, almost unnoticeable but definitely doing something, not music, not a realistic effect of any sort, just a kind of shaking in the air'. This really helped the actors in what always seemed to me a rather abrupt and difficult segue between Daniel accepting the gift of the script and the appearance of Chekhov.

Notwithstanding Paul's longstanding creative collaboration with Neil and his frequent presence in the rehearsal room, it seems that as with the other designers, the relationship between composer, director and actors is complex and delicate and requires tact as well as observance of unwritten rules. A story Paul told me illustrates this perfectly. He said that when he incorporated the sound of a clock striking into the music for the opening moments of the play, he had to decide how many times it would strike. It had to be more than once to ensure that spectators realised it was a clock but not too many times, and he chose three because, as he said, that is the time children get out of school. He never told Neil or the actors about his reasoning, however, because he said they tend to take such things literally and then either feel he is 'encroaching on their territory, interfering in the interpretive domain or second guessing what the director might do' (26 March 2010). Neil loved the three strokes but for him, as he told me much later, they functioned rather to recall the 'trois coups' that signal the beginning of a performance in the French theatre. Another comment made by Paul provides more insight into the different perspectives that might prevail among the different members of the creative team. The music and soundscape that is created for the production exists as an aesthetic totality for the composer while, for the actors it may be experienced rather as a series of fragments designed to assist this or that fictional or performative moment. Paul told me that he likes to go to preview performances of productions for which he has designed the sound and find a place to sit from which he cannot see the stage. This enables him to concentrate on the sound and it is on these occasions that he is best able to appreciate what he calls 'the tonal arches' that exist across the work as a whole, something of which the actors would probably be hardly aware.

Notes

1   Cronulla is a beachside suburb in southern Sydney and the football team that bears its name, the Cronulla Sutherland Sharks, regularly features in the finals of the National Rugby League competition.

2   The Elizabethan Theatre Trust's production of the play in Sydney in 1962 (directed by John Tasker) was the first fully professional production of White's masterpiece. It followed a controversial episode the year before when the play was twice rejected by the Board of Governors for inclusion in the Adelaide Festival, leading Tasker to mount a production with the Adelaide University Theatre Guild.

Runs and notes (Days 20–27)

> Having too many runs is the mark of a lazy
> director who has run out of ideas. (Neil Armfield, Day 18)

In the last seven days in the rehearsal room, substantial changes were still being made to the script, big decisions were taken, such as cutting the part of the Crazy Woman altogether, and major work was undertaken on *The Play*. This involved a significant expansion of Monica's role in playing all the instruments and making the sound effects to accompany the dumbshow. The highlight of the week was a number of runs of the whole play, each followed by extensive notes from Neil, but there were also sessions of work on particular scenes that were still being rewritten or needed further elaboration. The actors rehearsed on the Saturday of Week 5 (Day 25) and were then given a day off on the Monday when the production crew and designers began their marathon stint in the theatre to get the set, the lights and speakers installed, and Tess and her team were working overtime to get all the costumes finished. The final run in the rehearsal room, known as the Company Run, was on Day 27 and all the company staff were invited to attend, turning it into a rather special occasion, another tradition at Belvoir.

As has already been indicated, Neil's normal practice is to work carefully through the play with the actors, finding a spatial form for each scene and then to keep exploring the possibilities this process uncovers for as long as possible. This enables the actors to go even more deeply into the emotional and physical trajectories of their characters but, as they suggested from time to time, they also need the opportunity to consolidate what they have found. Running in real time what has been explored as fragments enables them to imprint in their body memory the sequence of actions, movements, gestures and thoughts involved. On a couple of occasions, the actors asked if they could do a run to put together what they had done (on Day 11, for example, and again on Day 18) and each time Neil demurred. He reassured them that there were going to be a good number of runs before they moved to the theatre and that, once there, there would be two dress rehearsals before the preview performances. He said, 'It's good to have a few runs but not too many. Just repeating things is not going to fix what is wrong and it won't help the work to grow' (Day 18). The sense of the work as a living organism, constantly growing and changing throughout the rehearsal process and beyond, is fundamental to Neil's practice, as will be discussed in more detail in the chapter devoted to his directorial method. Richard told me that Neil was 'notorious for having runs only on the last couple of days of rehearsal' (Day 15) and, while this may have been a bit of hyperbole, Neil did comment more than once on the disruption to his normal practice caused by the runs they were obliged to do in order to show Michael the work to date whenever he was able to be in Sydney.

In theatre parlance, the word 'run' is both a verb and a noun and, like so many other terms in current use in the rehearsal room, seems to refer to some rather different kinds of activity. The blocking and scene work involved performing a given fragment over and over again, trying different things each time, and each mini-performance was referred to as a run and followed by discussion and comment. My notes are full of phrases like 'another run' or 'they run it again.' Then there were the runs such as those requested by the actors on Days 11 and 18, which involved performance of a sequence of related scenes, once the moves and detailed analysis had been achieved, so as to consolidate for the actors what had been decided. Neil commented after one of the runs they had done for Michael that he would not normally give notes on a run done at that stage of the process (Day 19). The runs done in the last week in the rehearsal room were qualitatively different: the whole play was performed without interruption, including music and sound effects, Josh was no longer sitting at the prompt table with Kylie but actively undertaking his backstage role of assisting with costumes and props, and there was an in-house audience consisting of the designers and production crew. Then there were the line runs (when the actors sat, speaking their lines fast but, as I noted, somehow feeling the embodiment as they spoke, turning towards or away from the interlocutor as a ghostly indication of moves and doing sketchy, abbreviated hand gestures) and double speed runs (when they did the line run at double speed and their body movements were like those of sleepers twitching during rapid eye movement sleep). To cap it all, the sequence of performances in the theatre is also known as the 'run'. The significance of this terminological slippage is perhaps that, at every level of the process, what is involved is putting fragments together so that they make a greater unity. The connotations of physical movement in the word are also pertinent. Interestingly, the word used by French actors, 'filage', has a similar set of associative meanings: the literal meaning of 'filer' is to spin, as in spinning thread, that is, making continuous something that is discontinuous, and it also has a colloquial meaning of moving in a hurried manner.

There was a certain degree of ceremony involved in these runs of the entire play in the rehearsal room. Even as early as Day 9, when they performed Scenes 1 to 19 for Michael, the designers and production crew came to watch and Neil made a little speech to mark the occasion of 'the first run of the first production of this new Australian play'. When the company staff come up to watch the Company Run, this gives the actors the experience of performing for an audience that is both highly responsive and critically acute. In fact there were two runs attended by an in-house audience of company staff, one on Day 24 and one on the actual final day in the rehearsal room, Day 27. The energy levels were high on both occasions as the performances constitute a kind of validation for the company staff of their commitment to the company and, for the actors, there was the sense of reaching a definite milestone in their creative process. John Woodland, the company's artistic administrator, told me he loves to see the work at this stage, before it moves to the theatre and acquires all the additional trappings of set, costumes and lighting, because this is when the spectator experiences the actors' performances in their most direct, concentrated and pure form. Geoffrey Rush was present at the run on Day 24, Neil having cleared it with the actors beforehand, and his presence increased the emotional energy generated by the performance as everyone was keen to hear the reactions of such a highly skilled actor to the work as it was taking shape.[1]

Every run of a scene or segment was followed by a discussion in which Neil would give 'notes', that is to say, make his observations on minute details of what the actors were doing: moves, position in relation to the space or other characters, gesture, intonation, looks, what was working and what needed to be adjusted. There are unwritten rules about who may comment in what way and at what stage on details of the actors' performance, and giving notes is the director's prerogative.

Michael said after one run that he had masses of notes, but these were all about textual changes he wanted to make and he was in no danger of breaching what Monica referred to as 'the protocols' (see 'Preliminary Observations'). A run of the whole play necessitated a lengthy session for Neil to provide this kind of detailed feedback and the practice continued right up until opening night and, indeed, at intervals throughout the run of the show. During the last week in the rehearsal room and the transfer to the theatre, when the play was being run as a whole for dress rehearsals and preview performances, the note-giving sessions were a time consuming and clearly extremely important part of the process.

Reading though my notes on Neil's notes on the run on Day 24, I see that a significant number focus on words that were being swallowed or that had become so familiar that the actors were not giving them the full weight that would be needed for the audience and Neil often included valuable explanatory comments (for instance to Justine, 'make sure audience hear "afraid" in "what we're afraid of." It's the key to the play'). Other notes were designed to adjust details of tone or timing, but some involved larger changes (such as the shift in the nature of the sound pad required for Miss Beverly). A characteristic feature of Neil's notes was his openness to the idea that his advice might not work. This is an important element in his method of both empowering the actors and encouraging them to keep exploring. For instance, in referring to the fact that Roland says 'sad' five times in answer to Dr Maybloom, he asked Richard whether Roland 'floats into the zone each time or could he perhaps give the last one or two a bit of an edge? Show a little irritation with Maybloom?' Then he said 'I may be wrong.' Another note to Richard similarly indicated a possibility while leaving the actor's response open: 'when Nina lists the authors who have overcome writer's block, could you indicate in some way that you think it is sweet of her to include you in the pantheon of the greats? How you do that I leave to you.' He also gave precise advice, for instance in tweaking Nina's line 'So why are you here?' He had given a number of different notes on that line and here suggested to Justine that she might leave a slightly longer pause before the line. He told them Geoffrey Rush had said that 'Roland's speech is like a ten tonne weight and Nina's question is like a half ounce piece of brass that tips the scales back.' This seemed a wonderful description of the comic potential of that moment, but in spite of much adjustment and many notes, it never seemed to work in the way Geoffrey suggested, and never got a laugh in performance. When I spoke with Neil during the run, he said he was beginning to think that 'maybe it's not a laugh line' (20.11.2007).

Some of the notes led to substantial discussions and a decision to revisit the scene in question. A case in point was the hospital scene where Roland tells Nick what he has been doing with Steve Gooding. Neil and Richard had had a number of arguments about this scene, which had been significantly rewritten by Michael when Nick became a Latvian refugee rather than a cockney migrant. Phrases were removed and then reinstated as different visions of the relationship between the two boys were explored. The dialogue, as finally agreed after reworking the scene in the final week, is as follows:

ROLAND: 'Lynette, oooh Lynette.' It's like he's insane.
NICK: You made him crazy.
ROLAND: 'Oooh Lynette.' He lets me do anything to him.
NICK: You, what, suck his dick?
         [*Roland nods*]
ROLAND: Anything.
NICK: You total pervert. Fantastic!

The line 'you suck his dick?' had been cut when Michael was present on Day 22 and the energy in the scene revolved around the word 'anything'. Neil wanted the energy to shift on 'he lets me do anything to him' and Michael concurred. On Day 24, Neil told Richard he should be doing more with 'he lets me do anything to him' and they argued quite vehemently. For Richard, this was 'milking the moment' but Neil wanted to hint at the fact that there is 'a dark interesting shadowy area between Roland and Nick'. This was the reason he reinstated the 'you suck his dick?' line for the next run (and Michael has retained it in the published version). The addition certainly heightens the energy although, in my view, it also has the effect of accentuating the confusion over Roland's age when he wrote *The Play*. The naïve Roland who describes his play with such innocent fervour seems to be several years younger than the Roland who is having sex with Steve Gooding every day after school.

It seemed to me that the function of the 'notes' changed as the process progressed: in the early stages they were suggestions that the actors could think about, but later they became more precise and more directive. I asked the actors if, during the run of the production, a note was more akin to a criticism, whether it was a bad thing to get a lot of notes and their responses made it clear that that would be too simplistic a view. Neil certainly does not see his notes as criticisms but a story Russell told me raises some doubts about whether this is entirely the case from the actors' perspective. After the run had started, Neil had to spend a couple of weeks in Houston, preparing for an opera production he was to undertake in 2008. Russell told me that one night, when he thought Neil was still away, he saw him in the audience (sitting in the seat at the back of the auditorium that is known within the company as 'Neil's seat'). He said 'what made it worse was that when I spotted him, he had his head down, writing. That really threw me.' Russell might have been disconcerted by the sight of Neil writing because, at some level, actors do regard the director's notes as criticisms, or perhaps because it caused a momentary change of gear, making him think about what he had just been doing rather than simply living in the fictional moment. Whether or not a note is perceived as a criticism, however, what I observed was a collaborative process involving a group of artists who each take responsibility for their own part of the work, and are each involved in honing their own skills. The function of the director, through his notes to everybody involved, is to assist them to do this as powerfully as possible.

Cutting the crazy woman

A lot of ingenuity was expended on the Crazy Woman in the last few rehearsals as people realised that the play was stronger without the character but regretted losing the scene, especially as Monica was doing it in a wonderfully unhinged way that really added to the apocalyptic nature of the bushfire Roland describes for Nina. The actors had pointed out in their earliest readings of the play that the appearance of the Crazy Woman at the end of Act II suggested that Roland had already got his 'gift' back, especially because in that version he addressed her directly, saying 'welcome back,' and this raised questions about what was really going on in Act II. The work done by Michael to strengthen Scenes 10 and 15, makes clear that they constitute a single session between Roland and Nina, interrupted by all the high school memory scenes, and culminate in Roland notifying Nina of his decision to terminate the therapy. This is not because he has got his gift back but because the burning of Como has made him realise he no longer cares.

The scene with the Crazy Woman on the beach, listening to the account of the horrific bushfires on her transistor radio that originally ended Act I had been substantially cut over the weeks of the rehearsals, leading Monica to ask a bit anxiously whether it was due to the way she was doing the scene. Then, on Day 23, Neil assembled everyone and announced that Michael had proposed cutting the whole of the Crazy Woman, which he now saw as a stylistic anomaly. If she is perceived as one of Roland's apparitions, she will blunt the wonder of the Chekhov apparition that is the climax to Act II, and Michael thought it would be better to see the bushfires exclusively through Roland. Neil had already spoken privately to Monica about this and now asked for everyone's opinion. Some really liked the theatrical surprise of the scene, others agreed with Michael and felt it functioned more as a comment on the story than moving it on, in Monica's very apposite words an '*appoggiatura*' (a musical term for a decorative flourish that is not necessary to carry the overall line of the melody). The decision taken that day was that they would do a couple of runs in the theatre, one with the scene and one without, and make a definitive decision then.

On Day 25, they came up with a new solution by repositioning the appearance of the Crazy Woman. In this version, Scene 15 begins with Roland telling Nina about Nick's death and his sense of failure, she then says 'Tell me what's going through your mind' and, at that moment, the Crazy Woman comes on with her transistor radio and her mad description of the fires; Roland walks down stage parallel to her as she talks of the burning of Como, and she then exits down the vom, leaving him standing there. They cut all the dialogue between Nina and Roland in which she urges him to talk about the bushfires, picking up his speech where he says 'I spent my whole life explaining to people where I grew up.' I thought that this worked brilliantly, in that it was obvious that the Crazy Woman was part of his memory, like the lawyer or Mrs Walkham, and it was an extremely effective way to keep a sense of the apocalyptic nature of the fires and the burning of Como but to fold it seamlessly into Roland's decision to terminate the therapy. Some of the actors wanted to cut a bit more of the Crazy Woman's speech, in particular the reference to people being 'dead in a backyard swimming pool'. Both Richard and Guy thought that that felt like a seed for something the audience would expect to happen but in fact it goes nowhere. Neil was keen to keep it because it was such a powerful image (and in my view he was correct as, for anyone who actually lived through those fires, that is one of the most fearsome memories and it continues to haunt Sydneysiders). It is interesting that it was the actors here who were concerned more with narrative structure, and the director with the power of the image, and the whole session seemed to me to be a wonderful example of joint creativity at work.

Michael Gow, however, was not convinced by this reorganisation of the material and on Day 31, the morning after the first dress rehearsal, his decision to cut the Crazy Woman completely was announced. He thought that situating her scene where they had now put it would 'sabotage the moment where Roland realises, or tells Nina he has realised, that he felt nothing' when the fires destroyed Como. Monica took the decision in good part, saying that if it helped to clarify the emotional progression of the whole play and, incidentally shave some vital minutes off the first act, then she was happy. There was of course an underlying sense for her that the decision had been taken, in part, because of the way she was doing the scene, which shows just how vulnerable performers are, even when they are as experienced and professional as she was. In my view, however, it was because she was doing it so effectively that it took so long for them all to agree the scene should really be cut.

A good deal of time and energy in this last week was devoted to *The Play*, the subject of the next section. The process required for that work was very different and drew on different skills from those involved when director and actors seek to transform written dialogue into stage reality. Neil's brilliance as a director of scripted drama was evident throughout the weeks of the rehearsal process, his interventions assisting the actors to go more deeply into a particular exchange, transforming what had been a bit of a rant into something full of light and shade, tweaking and refining, pointing out where meaning needed further exploration. In the extensive notegiving sessions that followed the runs in the last two weeks, as well as the handwritten notes that were posted in the dressing room after performances he attended during the run of the play, it became clear to me that much of Neil's particular genius as a director resides in the nature, the quantity and the timing of his 'notes'. This point will be further developed in Part Two in the section specifically concerned with Neil's directorial method.

Note

1   Geoffrey Rush is a longtime member of the Belvoir 'family' and he and Neil Armfield have developed a unique collaborative process in which they rework and adapt a translated text, tailoring it to Rush's particular strengths as an actor before rehearsals with the rest of the cast and design team begin. Gogol's *Diary of a Madman* (1989 and again in 2010), Beaumarchais's *Marriage of Figaro* (1988) and Ionesco's *Exit the King* (2007) are examples of this process.

Creating *The Play*

We have together to work out what *The Play*
is as well as how to do it. (Neil Armfield, Day 14)

While requiring a lot of technical resources and creative ingenuity
from the actors and all the design and production staff, *The Play* was
not something to which Michael seemed to have devoted much attention. He knew the function he wanted it to fulfil in the overall dramatic
structure, but the details were extremely vague. When the actors had
read the synopsis during their stop/start reading work, Neil was still
referring to it as The Masque and said that he saw it as being 'beautiful and quite magical,' 'gentle' and 'naïve' (Day 3). The next day, when
Michael was present and the actors were describing some of their ideas
for how the flaming letters could work (see plot synopsis in 'The Starting
Point'), he said with some surprise 'I thought we had cut all that.' It is
true that in most of the earlier drafts, *The Play* has been reduced to a
single sentence, a final stage direction read aloud by Roland as he flicks
through the script but a late decision was clearly taken, perhaps by Neil,
to reinstate the longer synopsis of the action as it existed in the first draft
and this is what appears in the Rehearsal Draft. The actors were worried
from the outset that *The Play* is so obviously the work of a young child,
and yet it is supposed to be a production being put on by a class of sex-
obsessed teenagers. Michael's solution when this worry was raised with

him on Day 4, was that it should be made darker and more sinister in performance, which would run counter to Neil's idea of it being naïve and magical.

On Day 5, there was another discussion when they read it for Tess so that she could begin to plan the costumes. The version in use at that time included an astronaut (Kylie and Josh had already procured a space helmet) who would save the Nanny and take both her and the Boy into his rocket, so the basic message of *The Play* was that the nanny and the boy were being rescued from a world dominated by evil adults and escaping to a better place. Discussion focused on who would be playing which role, clearly important for Tess as she designed the costumes. Roland has to watch the play, which meant he would not be able to perform in it, so the three characters were attributed to Justine (Nanny), Guy (Boy) and Russell (Astronaut), which left Monica (Mrs Walkham) to play some of the toy instruments that Paul and Liam had been accumulating.

At the beginning of Week 3, Michael sent a new version which meant that much of the work that had been put in train would have to be radically altered. The Nanny has now become an evil alien who arrives in a rocket and imprisons the Boy, who is saved by a Detective. The Nanny attempts to leave in her rocket but is blown up by a bomb the detective has placed on board. There will be no flaming letters, so all the ideas for how to implement that idea were quietly dropped. Russell wanted to play the Evil Nanny but Neil was adamant that the role had to go to Justine, for whom Tess made a wonderfully detailed Mary Poppins costume that, as has been described, took her most of Act II to put on. While I loved Justine's alien Mary Poppins, I thought it would have made more sense for Russell to be the Evil Nanny as it would have made a better parallel with the rest of the play: Russell playing all the obtuse and destructive characters, Guy playing the Hero Boy and Justine the Detective who, like Nina, gets to the bottom of the trouble and liberates Hero Boy.

The first real attempt to work on *The Play* was a delirious session on Day 14, to which Paul brought the music he had composed and all the toy musical instruments he and Liam had been collecting, Liam produced a toy rocket made from toilet rolls and chopsticks in approved primary school manner and Ralph demonstrated how it could be made to 'explode' by being pulled apart. The actors displayed great comic inventiveness as well as revealing other unexpected skills: Russell is an accomplished conjurer, Justine does cartwheels and Monica's great musical ability and professional skill meant that Mrs Walkham's role increased exponentially. Neil had originally said that he had an image of Mrs Walkham laughing at the dumbshow while playing a triangle to accompany it, but when Monica's skills emerged, Paul and Michael Toisuta (his assistant) reworked the music and coached her in playing the full range of toy instruments. On Day 15, they showed Michael what they had created but he found it was still too folksy and cute, so Paul went off to make the music darker, and Ralph and Russell did more work on the bomb. On Day 19 they devoted another full session to exploring how something darker could be made out of the basic elements that were their obligatory starting point: the *Kindersinfonie* music (that, as Neil had said, 'made you laugh just listening to it'), the exuberant and absurd plot outline already given by Roland in the hospital scene with Nick, and the toy instruments, most of which are also comic. The problem was that, while Michael claimed to want something dark, perhaps along the lines of the satirical attack on middle class values that was the play his headmaster really did ban (as he told the actors on Day 14), a play drawing its inspiration from *The Maltese Falcon*, *The Night of the Living Dead* and *It Came From Outer Space*, what he had actually provided them with was nothing like that. It was also evident that the difference of opinion between Neil and Michael as to the nature of *The Play* was a part of some much more fundamental differences about memory and about the past that was being evoked in the rest of the play. These differences will be explored in more detail in Part Two.

The actors did their best, introducing details such as the Nanny using her umbrella as an instrument of torture, applying electrodes to the Boy's brain, lurid yellow vomit spewing from the Boy's mouth and the Detective engaging in karate-style combat with the Nanny. But the music defeated them all as it was so relentlessly cheerful and it set such a brisk pace to which all this activity had to be timed. Paul watched what they were doing and adjusted the music, writing in wonderfully weird noises Monica could make with the toy instruments to accompany the actions. The energy level was high and the final product was a genuinely group effort, incorporating ideas from everyone but it was definitely comic rather than sinister.

At the beginning of Week 5, *The Play* was still far from ready and required the active input of the actors, Paul and his assistant, Michael Toisuta, as well as Ralph and Liam in several extensive work sessions. They devoted several hours to it on Day 20 and again on Day 21, then they showed what they had done to Michael on his last visit to the rehearsal room (Day 22), Paul composed new music and Matthew Lutton led the work in the absence of Neil (Days 22 and 23). Each occasion they worked on *The Play*, I was struck by the wide range of skills they all brought to bear and the combination of sheer fun, inventiveness and

Figure 13. Russell Dykstra, Guy Edmonds, Justine Clarke in
The Play (dress rehearsal)
Photo: Heidrun Löhr

highly practical, professional expertise that characterised the process. Monica's musical ability meant that Mrs Walkham's role expanded from simply playing the triangle, as Neil had originally envisaged it, to taking responsibility for a wide range of bizarre instruments mounted on a trolley. While spectators would think this was the trolley on which she had brought the overhead projector for her slide show, in fact it had to be specially made. Guy (as an experienced percussionist), gave her advice on playing the drums, and later worked out all the percussion moves so that it would be simpler for her. Besides his unexpected skill as a conjurer, Russell drew on his physical theatre background to show Justine how to use the Nanny's umbrella (now the instrument with which she is seeking the reprogramme the Boy's brain) without actually injuring Guy's ear. The fact that they were all accomplished musicians and dancers meant that they could work very precisely to the music, timing the actions together with Monica's accompanying sound effects.

Monica was having great difficulty controlling the trolley while still playing the drum that was attached to one end, but once they moved into the theatre, Shaun Poustie and the ever-helpful production crew solved the problem by fixing a handle on to the drum and doing some major engineering to the way the wheels were mounted. No one at the time had any idea of Monica's cardiac condition although she did make a vague gesture towards her heart when apologising for not being able to skip one day. Richard was perhaps more aware than anyone else that she might be having difficulties as it was he who made the suggestion that, in the scene preceding *The Play*, Roland's old school case could have new hinges that would enable the lid to open flat and he could then put all the papers on the lid, thus obviating the need for Monica to bend down so far to pick them up from the floor. These are poignant memories a year after the shock of her sudden death, but even at the time and with no knowledge at all of her health problems, everyone was full of admiration for the utter professionalism of the way she dealt with the expansion of her role in *The Play* in the last week of rehearsals and of her gracious response when characters she was to play were excised (Mrs Norberry and the Crazy Woman).

On Day 23, when Monica noted the actors' moves on her music score, the list of actions for which she had to provide sound accompaniment was as follows:

Arrival of Nanny, floating down on umbrella in approved Mary Poppins style (toy xylophone)
Giving out poisoned lollies to dancing children (bell)
The Boy choking
Ray gun/umbrella used by Nanny to raise him and place him in chair (flex-a-thon)
Brain surgery with umbrella (ratchet)
Arrival of Detective (percussion)
Ray gunfight, karate kick for umbrella (flex-a-thon and cymbal)
Nanny KO in corner (drum)
Exit of Boy with umbrella (slide whistle)
Detective places the bombs
Nanny does cartwheels from back of stage to centre (drum and cymbal)
Karate kick to Detective (drum)
Rocket takes off (bull roarer) and explodes (big cymbal)

She then had to wheel the trolley in a complete circuit of the stage, still drumming, as the characters cleared the space, ending with a very loud drum beat. For Neil, this circuit functioned to cleanse as well as clear the space in preparation for the final reconciliation scene between Roland and Daniel. The list shows the dimension of the task for her as well as providing an indication of the action that had been worked out by the combined efforts of the whole company.

The bizarre instruments had to be variously shaken, blown or banged, and adding to the difficulty of the task was the tempo (the whole thing lasts only two and a half minutes), and the need for the sound

Figure 14. Monica Maughan playing the toy instruments (dress rehearsal)
Photo: Heidrun Löhr

cues to be timed precisely according to the recorded music as well as the actions being performed by the actors. This was a sudden increase in Monica's responsibilities and she did begin to look rather tired on some occasions. She told me on Day 24 that she had slept badly the previous night, going over and over the percussion cues in her head.

Neil's term for the characters in *The Play*, 'the spookies', drew attention to their very ambiguous status, not memory because the play was never performed, nor conjured apparition because Roland has lost the ability to produce apparitions. As Neil saw it, they are pure imagination but channelled through Roland's mind, the way he imagines the play might have been performed if it had not been banned. This does not really account for Mrs Walkham's involvement, so maybe Roland's fantasy version of the high school production is overlaid with memories of primary school plays in which Mrs Walkham was always present in the background, providing the musical accompaniment, and rockets were made of cardboard rolls and chopsticks. I have already mentioned the very important moment when 'the spookies' appear and how they invade the space but the actors also had to find a way to get rid of the school case and the handbag, still present from the previous scene. Complicating matters was the fact that Roland empties all the drugs and paraphernalia onto the floor and that the papers from the school case are also scattered.

A solution to packing up the drugs quickly, suggested at the production meeting in Week 4, was to have most of the sachets linked on a filament, leaving loose only the materials Richard actually has to handle. This facilitated picking up the whole lot with one gesture, and the school case was altered to enable the papers to be stacked on the lid rather than scattered on the floor, as has already been mentioned. But bag and case still had to be removed from the stage as they could not be there during the performance of Roland's imagined play. Ingenious solutions were proposed but it was Richard who suggested during the work session on Day 19 that if a filament could be attached to the case, it could be 'magically' pulled off down the vom (another job for Josh in the wings). Neil endorsed the proposal enthusiastically, saying it provided clear evidence of why Richard had been nominated for the AFI Best Director award, another example of Neil's generosity towards his collaborators that contributes so much to the sense of community that is a significant part of the Belvoir experience.[1] This was a very neat solution and it created what Neil called 'a sweet moment' before the Alien Nanny unleashes her evil on the world. While I loved the magical nature of it all and the way the case disappeared silently into the realm of mystery, I did think there was something wrong about the drugs, with all their connotations of self destructive behaviour and the slide into the tar pit, going off to the same place and bundled together with the school case and all that it had come to represent about creativity and hope. Richard did make a passing remark about this one day but such semiotic niceties were disregarded in the general relief at having found such a delightfully mysterious way of getting rid of the material elements from the previous scene.

Props such as the rocket and the bomb were very simple and home-made (and it was the umbrella that became both ray gun and brain laser), in keeping with the primary school aesthetic that was so dominant through Mrs Walkham's participation but they were used with great skill by highly professional performers. Russell was able to produce a large bomb that looked like the archetypal anarchists' bomb familiar to readers of comic books, then 'disappear' it up his backside when it was evidently too big for the model rocket on which he was supposed to place it, and through sleight of hand produce from his mouth a miniature version (made from a ping pong ball). Guy had to produce large amounts of bright yellow vomit (half a Berocca tablet) and some grotesque tremors as his brain was 're-programmed'. Once Justine's cartwheels were incorporated into the action, Tess added some startling red bloomers under the demure Mary Poppins skirt that were displayed to great effect, and her mime of the Alien Nanny being blown up, the rocket splitting into two halves in her hands, confetti (or sometimes red glitter) falling from above, strobe lighting together with Monica's crashing cymbal was a delight to behold. The overall effect was more Playschool than science fiction/horror film but that was entirely in keeping with Neil's vision even if not quite what Michael had been pushing for. And of course, it never did answer the question of how a work so obviously located within a primary school aesthetic could represent a memory of anything that would have been contemplated by Miss Beverly and her class of sport and sex obsessed teenagers.

Note

1   Richard Roxburgh won the 2007 Australian Film Institute award for Best Director for his film *Romulus my Father*, and Russell Dykstra won Best Supporting Actor for his work in the same film. The nominations had just been announced in October 2007, but the winners were not known until a couple of weeks later.

Technical production: a parallel universe

Creating a poem is itself a poem. (Paul Valéry 1922, *Cahiers* 8)

In addition to the rehearsal process involving the actors there was another whole production process under way that was dependent to a certain extent on what was transpiring in the rehearsal room but that had pre-dated the rehearsals by a significant margin. In Jim Hiley's account of the production of *Galileo* at the National Theatre in Britain, he reports that the production schedule at the National for a new play was twenty-two weeks, of which only the last seven involved the actors (Hiley 1981, 33). For *Toy Symphony*, too, Ralph Myers had been working for months on the set design and there had been many discussions with Liam Fraser, who would be overseeing the technical production for the show. Tess, too, had done a large amount of work on the costume designs before the actors assembled for the first day of rehearsals. The Wardrobe, located alongside the rehearsal room and presided over by Tess, was the centre of a work process that had its own budget, its own rhythm of work and its own kind of sociality. While Paul Charlier wrote most of the music during the course of the rehearsal period, he worked in his own studio and visited the rehearsal room from time to time and Damien Cooper, although he attended runs and contributed ideas to the combined effort involved in creating *The Play*, could only begin his intensive work with the lighting once the set was installed. So the technical production process was both spatially and temporally dispersed in relation to the actors' work. The so-called 'bump in' to the theatre when the set was installed, revealed another aspect of the parallel universe constituted by this production process in that there seemed to be a small army of workers involved, most of whom are not named in the credits list in the programme.

Production meetings were held throughout the rehearsal period for an hour a week, usually at 9am on Wednesdays, and they were a crucial part of the overall process. They were chaired by Liam Fraser, the production manager, and Neil and assistant director Matthew Lutton attended, together with the four designers (set, costume, sound and lighting), stage manager Kylie Mascord and her assistant Josh Sherrin, Tirian Rodwell (the costume co-ordinator) and Liam's assistants, Shaun Poustie (company mechanist) and Chris Mercer (technical manager). This was where all the practical details involved in getting the show together were discussed, options were presented to Neil, material changes emerging from the rehearsals and problems requiring physical solutions were put to the designers and production staff. While rehearsals were in progress, the set was being constructed in a workshop in a neighbouring suburb, supervised by Liam and Ralph, and costumes were being made/bought/procured, but Neil's imprimatur was essential for much of this work. Probably the best way to indicate the range of work occurring is to list the matters as I noted them at the first production meeting I attended in Week 2.

> Damien wants the ceiling overhang reduced for lighting purposes; he has a lighting black hole. Needs to know if the sightlines of spectators in what they call 'the pigeon seats' will be affected if they change the shape of the ceiling.
>
> Paul has a problem with placement of the speakers that have to be accommodated even though Ralph's design calls for blank walls. Can they be on pillars (but this would affect the actors' ability to walk along the wall), sunk into the walls, or visible and declaring themselves to be what they are? Ralph undertakes to revise his ceiling plan so that it will accommodate speakers and lighting positions.
>
> Will there be a rocket, and is it ascending or descending? The space above the ceiling is very constrained. Could the rocket be manoeuvred by visible strings? Could it come up from a trap door in the stage floor? Chris and Liam will get up into the ceiling and measure the space available.
>
> What material is being used for the ceiling? If it is gyprock, Paul says there will be consequences for acoustics.
>
> Tess is a week behind schedule with the costumes. Neil notifies her that Monica will play the nurse and Justine Mrs Norberry, thus completely

changing the costume requirements. Will Alexander need a shield and a spear? Ralph wants the shield to be shiny like a child's toy.

Tess asks if *The Play* is directed by Miss Beverly (hip 1970s English teacher) or by Roland (12 year old schoolboy) as this will affect the costumes. The Astronaut in *The Play* should bear some relationship to Alexander.

Neil warns that the nature of *The Play* could shift as he and Michael are still working out how it can function in relation to the Roland/Nick relationship.

They have found someone to spray paint the floor.

Will the crash doors open inwards or outwards or swing? The sound effects for the apparitions can come from off stage (from the vom and the crash doors because of the difficulties in placing speakers).

They need to get a fire permit for the Medival Executioner's torch.

Will they use paper snow (problem of litter) or a snow machine (noisy) for Titus Oates?

Can Mrs Walkham play the toy instruments and make all the bird song sounds in *The Play*? This would be comic and delightful but if *The Play* is going to be darker in tone, it may not be appropriate.

They are going to use an overhead projector for Mrs Walkham's slide show so Monica can be lit by the overhead projector.

Which budget is going to be used to pay the cost of the Russian coaching for Russell (a decision had been made earlier to get him to speak in Russian rather than miming to a recording for the Chekhov speech). Is this a rehearsal cost or a production cost?

By Week 4, the problems were compounded by ongoing uncertainty about the nature of *The Play* (Russell might have to be a child as well as the detective, so Tess had to be ready to create an additional costume), Neil warned that the current sweet tone was likely to change to something darker and Ralph mentioned the possibility of a silent film inpiration. Moreover, it was still not clear what form the rocket would take. Damien and Shaun asked whether pyrotechnics and smoke would be needed for the explosion and then roared with laughter when they heard that the rocket will be made from cardboard rolls. Liam showed his model and demonstrated how it can be pulled apart at the moment of explosion, prompting the suggestion that a puff of talc would be all that was needed for smoke. They were expecting to make a larger version but in the end Neil and the actors retained Liam's original model.

Liam was worried that the number of speakers and lights that would have to be hung in the ceiling space might cause overheating in the narrow space between stage ceiling and theatre roof. The placement of lights and speakers was the most serious matter discussed, Ralph defending the integrity of his black box and others joking that it would be good for a play where actors did not need to be heard or seen. In the end he agreed to a spotlight in the back wall that could be used to light people's faces when they are standing in the vom. There will need to be an operator for a cover spot who will stand at the back of the auditorium in what they referred to as the *Exit the King* position, clearly a reference to what had been done in that production, which had occurred earlier in the season. The opening high up on the OP side that can be used as an entrance (but not in *Toy Symphony*) is known as the *Keating* door as it was used in that show to memorable effect for the first entrance of the Paul Keating character.[1] This referencing of earlier productions seemed to me to function very interestingly to create a past and a sense of the working community, notwithstanding the transitory nature of the shows and the high turnover of staff in the production department.

Paul reported that he had sourced sound recordings of actual bush-fires from the ABC to use in the Crazy Woman scene but that it would be a cost. Neil said the scene could yet be cut completely, as indeed it was. This illustrates something of the frustration experienced by the designers and production staff, who use their ingenuity to source mate-rial and find solutions for problems only to be informed a few days later that everything has been changed. Liam told me later that the biggest problem from his perspective in trying to bring shows in on budget and on time was when people changed their minds and things had to be done more than once. He said the position of the speakers had to be changed six times and the spotlight in the back wall, referred to above, was installed but after the first preview performance it was decided to remove it because it shone in the eyes of spectators in the central block. The total cost for that light alone was $600.

The drinks for the final scene: Michael has said that Roland will not be drinking mineral water so that affects the kind of glass that should be used. Someone should go to Icebergs (the inspiration for the bar overlooking Bondi Beach where they thought Roland and Daniel would meet) and look at their glasses. Someone (Neil?) said they would be drinking vodka and lime and that Daniel would drink what Roland drinks (actually Guy asked for Daniel's drink to be whisky).

The trolley for Mrs Walkham's slide projector and the one for the musical instruments will be made in the workshop and there will need to be two as the specifications are different. The vibe is that the instru-ments are what Mrs Walkham has been able to find in the school music department and she has raided the rest of the school, hence the stands for the instruments could be test tube holders or retort stands from the science laboratories.

This was the world over which Liam presided, and the mixture of practical, interpretive and budgetary matters is typical of all the production meetings I attended. I was always struck by the combination of professional competence and playfulness involved. They were skilled semioticians in their different ways (even though they would probably not have used the term), fully aware of the implication of every design choice in relation to pop culture, high culture and period, aware too of the rules and regulations within which they had to operate, but extremely inventive and relishing the challenges posed by this play.

Chris Mercer was the technical manager and his task involved liaising closely with Ralph and Damien to implement their designs for set and lighting, Shaun Poustie's job was designated as production co-ordinator and he was responsible for everything required for props, set and even some elements of costume, and Tirian Rodwell (costume co-ordinator) was Tess's assistant while the costumes were being made/assembled and was then responsible for maintaining them in good order once the show was running. Liam Fraser's job as production manager was to co-ordinate all these strands of the work, working closely with the designers, obtaining the equipment they requested and trying to keep to the budget. During the intensive work and long hours of the bump in and then the meticulous work of the technical rehearsal when all the lighting and sound cues were finalised and entered into the computer program, it became evident to me that there were distinct groupings of people whose imaginative input into the show functioned differently, creating different socialities and channelling energy into the production in different ways.

I was made particularly aware of this when, at the third preview performance, I decided to stay in the auditorium rather than go down to the foyer and come back into the theatre with the audience. The actors were all in the dressing room preparing, Neil was in the foyer greeting sponsors, Kylie was in the bio box and everything was in readiness for the performance but the house was still in the hands of the technical crew. It was a delightful moment, marked by joking and laughter from Liam, Damien and Chris, who clearly enjoyed a level of intimacy that had not been evident when I had seen them in the rehearsal room. In my field notes that evening, I wrote that even though Neil was so friendly and open and inclusive, he was nevertheless the 'boss man,' belonging to an older generation and set apart from them as much by his age as by their respect for his artistry. The camaraderie I witnessed during those few minutes before Kylie called that she was 'opening the house' revealed something important about the hidden social life of the theatre and its function in the overall production process.

The bump in

Liam had told me that I could come to the theatre at about 4pm on Day 26 when I should be able to see the set virtually in place. When I got there, the whole theatre was a hive of activity but the set was far from being in place. Creating the false ceiling over the irregular shaped stage was like a huge jigsaw puzzle, with the wedge-shaped panels made to Chris Mercer's specifications from Ralph's design being installed under Chris's supervision. The walls of the stage space had already been painted black and the floor was covered with black material. At the same time, lighting crew were hanging lamps according to Damien's plan and another team of sound crew were installing speakers and equipment under the supervision of Paul and Michael Toisuta. According to the detailed plan drawn up by Liam, they intended to be ready for the paint crew to come at 7pm and the specialist spray painter who was to create the stippled glow at the centre of the space was booked for 9pm. Chris said that work in the theatre would not finish until 1am, that work would resume the next day at 9am, and they would do the whole thing again. Ralph told me that in fact it was dawn when he left the theatre so this was a highly stressful time for the design and production team. There were about twenty people working in the theatre, all quite young, and there was only one woman amongst that army of men. It was all very focused, quiet but extremely busy. Everyone seemed to know exactly what they had to do and they worked around the other crews in what looked to be a highly organised manner.

All the doors were open except for the big double doors through which the audience normally enters the auditorium. The 'Keating door' was open, as were doors at the end of the vom, and those at the top of the auditorium that lead to the corporate reception room and down stairs to the back of the foyer. The big delivery doors on the back wall that open on to the street were also open and the normally enclosed space of the auditorium felt as though it had been invaded. The theatre was revealed to be both a labyrinth and a place of work and it was a strange experience to be in the auditorium that I know so well in the midst of all this activity, with working lights on, ladders and scaffolds everywhere. At first it seemed to be a kind of transgression but I then realised that the work process possessed its own sort of performative magic, and that there was a certain kind of excitement in seeing the nuts and bolts of the illusion, the underpinnings the spectators never see, the immense amount of professional involvement that undergirds what they do see. This is 'the juju of craft' that Simon Callow finds such a thrilling part of the actor's experience of inhabiting the theatre building (Callow 1984, 182).

A few days later, I was sitting in the auditorium while the actors were in the dressing room getting ready for the first dress rehearsal. Someone called out from the auditorium 'Is Josh there?' and he answered immediately from somewhere backstage. What I wrote in my fieldnotes that night is as close as I can get even now to describing the impact this created of the interpenetration of theatre as work space and theatre as imaginary world: 'I love this sense that you never have in an actual performance of the theatre space as being so fragile, so surrounded by something else. All these exit doors that lead from the auditorium to backstage, to bio box, to green room and thus down two different stair cases to foyer or backstage. It is a labyrinth and people are so close in reality but in a different dimension, and the audience has no idea they are so close. The stage constitutes a whole world, an imaginary place, but it is a bubble, a fragile permeable space. If someone calls out for Liam or Josh and there is an answering call from somewhere off but so close, it so gives the lie to the enclosed nature of the fictional world. All around, from all sides there are people working, waiting for a cue, fixing things. The place is surrounded' (Day 30). Just how fragile is the imaginary world of the stage would become disastrously manifest on opening night, as will be recounted in the next section. On Day 30 though, what struck me was that Brecht's exhortation to the actors to reveal to the audience that what was going on was 'not magic/but work', could be turned on its head because what I was experiencing was the magic of work.

The move into the theatre was hard work for the production crew and there were a few glitches that added to the stress for Liam and his team, such as the mystery factor that kept triggering the theatre's fire alarm, requiring the building to be evacuated until the fire brigade could come and declare that there was no fire, thus causing production staff to lose valuable time they could ill afford, or the spray paint on the floor that had not dried properly and reduced the first run in the theatre to farce as actors' feet squelched or stuck to the floor. Notwithstanding these irritations and the fatigue caused by the long days and nights, the production crew, like the rest of the company were feeling buoyed by the sense the production was going to be a success.

When I interviewed Liam during the run, he told me that working with Neil was special in that he was so open and so ready to accept the contribution of actors and others. He said 'he is never willing to push in a certain direction but lets the actors create and explore more. He really tries things.' Of course, the downside to this, from the perspective of the production manager, is that things are often not locked down until they are in the theatre and then it may require a lot of overtime or extra staff to get things done in time, and this in turn causes budgets to blow out. Clearly this put additional pressure on Liam but it was worth it for the joy of being able to work 'in an atmosphere of such creativity where everyone is encouraged to contribute'. For the company staff, the work is never ending in that before one production is coming to an end, work is in full swing on the next. When I asked Liam what he thought had worked really well on the *Toy Symphony* production, he said rather sadly that the focus of his attention was so overwhelmingly with the present demands, attempting to satisfy the needs of the designers and the cast while thinking ahead to the next three shows, that he had no time to think about the show that had just finished. Then he paused and thought for a moment before saying, 'Your book is my legacy.' Actors and directors do sometimes express anxiety about the ephemerality of what they spend their lives creating, but Liam's comment was striking because it indicated in such a poignant way that the same kind of anxiety can afflict everyone involved, perhaps especially those who will never have their names displayed in lights outside the theatre.

Note

1   Ionesco's *Exit the King*, directed by Neil Armfield with Geoffrey Rush in the title role, was part of Belvoir's 2007 season. Neil's production of *Keating!* premiered at the Belvoir Street Theatre in 2006 before touring around the country throughout the next year.

In the theatre at last (Days 28–35)

You really have to stop inventing new stuff and let us
lock down what we have.
(Richard to Neil after the Company Run on Day 24)

As has just been described, the production staff and the designers, assisted by a small army of specialised workers, had worked day and night from the Monday of Week 6 to install the set and get everything ready for the actors, who moved into the theatre on the Wednesday of that week. At Belvoir there is a single shared dressing room in which, for this show, each actor was able to have their own mirror and bench space and there is a small cubicle for those who require more privacy for certain costume changes. There was a definite buzz of excitement as the actors moved in, taking possession of the dressing room, organising their costumes, wigs and make up in the optimum way and personalising the space that would be so central to their work and life for the next six weeks. Guy told me that the dressing room had already acquired a distinctly different feel from the preceding week when he was occupying it with the cast of *Holding the Man*. The dressing room is definitely the actors' space, and even with a communal dressing room there are unwritten rules about who can have access, as I found when I had unwittingly transgressed by dropping in unannounced after the show one night to deliver something to Richard. While the production staff have their work spaces around the backstage area and their work continues from production to production and even between productions, the actors occupy the theatre for a short period only and during that time, the dressing room is their particular space, a haven of security and the centre of their sociality.

For the first two days after the actors moved to the theatre, the centre of gravity shifted as the whole creative team worked through the play, establishing all the sound and light cues for the computerised program that Kylie would use to 'call' the show. This was the so-called 'tech run', and it was slow and meticulous work during which the actors were no longer the centre of Neil's attention. He is adamant that this is not the case so perhaps I should say rather that they no longer had his undivided attention and that the move into the theatre seemed to me to mark the beginning of some subtle shifts in the relationships between the participants. The production desk had been set up over two rows of seating in the central block of the auditorium and Kylie, Damien and Paul sat there, each with their laptop computers and a mass of electronic equipment and Neil sat either in the row in front of them so that he could turn around and talk quietly to them, or he stood in the aisle to watch and on occasion moved to different parts of the auditorium. When I spoke to Kylie many months later, she said of this phase of the work that 'it is not about the actors but it is about them' (Interview 2010), which encapsulates very neatly the paradoxical situation of the actors in relation to the rest of the design and production team.

There is a lot of repetition and the actors do a lot of waiting around during this phase of the work, but they must nevertheless be absolutely precise in their performance because, once the sound and light cues are entered into the computer program, the timing will be fixed for all the subsequent performances. A new iteration of the script, called the Tech Version and dated 6 November 2007, was distributed and the task was rendered more complicated as Neil was still tweaking moves and even changing some entry and exit points as he saw how the moves worked in the theatre. Paul Charlier, who has worked with Neil over many years, told me that it was Neil's practice 'to cut everyone a lot of slack during rehearsals' and then to crack down once they get to the theatre for tech week. This is the stage when 'he really shapes the work and can become very specific and directive' (26 March 2010).

On the second day there were two school students present in the auditorium, on work experience from their high schools and Neil called out an introduction before beginning work. Later in the day, during one of the moments when technical adjustments were being made and the actors on stage were just waiting, one of the students must have whistled. I had not noticed it but everybody in the theatre seemed to freeze and Neil called out 'who whistled?' The boy was told he must leave the theatre, turn around three times and knock at the stage door to be read-mitted. He was quite reluctant but Neil insisted and Josh escorted him out, still audibly grumbling about 'public shaming'. Neil's response was 'we are in the realm of the supernatural'. The incident reminded me that a few weeks earlier, when someone had whistled in the rehearsal room, Guy had told me that actors of his generation are sceptical about the old supersitions, such as saying 'the Scottish play' rather than *Macbeth* or not whistling in the theatre. I recount the story here because, although trivial in itself, it is nevertheless significant in what it reveals about the importance of this connection to a past tradition of practice for contem-porary performers, including those of Guy's generation, and the role such observances play in the formation of a sense of community. When Neil spoke of the realm of the supernatural he might have been referring to Roland's apparitions or to the fragile and mysterious enterprise on which they were all engaged, or perhaps to both as the one is a metaphor for the other.

There were two dress rehearsals (the evening of Day 30 and the afternoon of Day 31) and the first preview performance was the same evening (Saturday, 10 November 2007). That performance was a triumph, the audience was hooked from Roland's first big speech, they laughed and loved it and him, they gave Mrs Walkham a round of applause as she wheeled her trolley off after her slide show, there was a roar of laughter when Nick referred to 'Mr fucking rugby football' as he kicked his soccer ball around the stage, which was only eclipsed by the reaction when Steve Gooding ran on. That audience absolutely 'got' it and loved it. On the Sunday afternoon, the actors gathered in the Board Room at the company offices for Neil's notes and then went up the hill to the theatre for the second preview performance at 5pm. This performance, too, was very positively received, which energised the whole company and, in particular, lifted the spirits of the exhausted production crew. The third preview was for the sponsors and was less successful but the actors were not surprised. They told me the sponsor-ing companies take blocks of seats but then often do not use them, and the spectators who do attend are often somewhat unresponsive, creating what actors call 'a dry house'. When I spoke to Richard the next day, he told me how difficult it was to carry that enormous part for such a long time and to feel so little energy coming back to him.

Even though the play had been performed several times in the theatre for the preview audiences, the real focus of everyone's atten-tion was opening night, Wednesday 14 November 2007. The actors' call was for 2pm so that Neil could give them his notes from the preview performance the preceding day as well as run a couple of scenes that still needed adjustments and there would still be time for a substantial dinner break and rest before getting ready for the performance. Neil's notes were as pertinent and useful as before but I felt that the actors were really not paying attention in the way they had done in the past. Richard had not even brought a pen with him and had to borrow Russell's whenever he got a note. They were like athletes conserving their energies for a major competition or soldiers on the eve of a battle and it seemed that, in some intangible way, they were entering another dimension, one in which Neil was no longer the energising centre. Richard's warning to Neil concerning the actors' need to 'lock down' what they had done was given after the Company Run on Day 24, before they moved to the theatre, but I have used it as the epigraph to this chapter because it points to changes that took place during the transition from rehearsal room to theatre. On the face of it, these were entirely predictable, involving the need to move from the exploratory process of the rehearsal room to establishing a final form for the production and layering onto the actors' performances all the sign systems created by the design team during the technical rehearsals. Beneath the businesslike surface, however, the process involved a fascinating realignment of emotional energies and the socialities that underpin them, as will be discussed in more detail in the final chapter.

The opening night audience was a veritably star studded affair and the atmosphere in the foyer before the show was electric. It is significant that a large number of the celebrities attending the performance were actors and showbusiness people and, reflecting on this fact after the event, I think it reveals something important about the function of opening and closing night performances and the parties that follow. These rituals serve as a form of validation for all the participants, a celebration of what it is they do, and a reinforcement of the sense of community that will be discussed in more detail in my concluding chapter. This does not mean, however, that the opening night audience was uncritical or purely partisan. Far from it, for it was an audience of peers, experts in the art and craft of performance and, although they were there to support and celebrate the launch of a new work into the public sphere, they were also sitting in judgement. The newspaper critics writing their reviews the next day were part of the process of making the work public but the reactions of their peers, circulating through gossip and bush telegraph over the days that followed, probably mattered more to the participants.

The performance began really well, Roland's big speech got a number of laughs, Mrs Walkham's slide show was very well received and, even though Roland was in semi darkness, people loved his interventions. What struck me particularly on this night was the very special kind of silence that seemed to grip the audience in the scene with the copyright lawyer as soon as Roland began to speak of stealing the idea for a play. It was, as I wrote in my notes that night, 'a dropped pin silence, a kind of collective holding of breath'. That audience would have included a number of people who had lived through the *Sweet Phoebe* scandal and who would doubtless have taken sides even then. So the extraordinary silence and increased alertness was a response to the enormity of what Michael Gow was doing. Once the play moved into the memory scenes, it seemed that the territory was more familiar. The virtuosity and skill involved in actors switching roles, even the *coup de théâtre* of Alexander the Great's appearance were amusing but not mysterious to that audience. What received the biggest laugh was Mrs Walkham's reaction 'Well, 5a, wasn't that a big surprise!'

Everything was going well up to the first entrance of Nick when disaster struck: a woman in the audience collapsed. She was sitting in the central block of seats, fairly near the front, so the disruption was significant. Spectators alongside her moved into the aisle so she could lie down, front of house staff darted down the aisle to check on the situation and back up the steps to call an ambulance. The actors struggled to maintain focus but by the time an ambulance crew arrived with a stretcher, Richard was about to give his big speech about the bushfire destroying Como. At that stage Neil stood up (he had been sitting a couple of rows behind the woman) and stopped the show. The woman had recovered enough by then to be able to walk out, escorted by the ambulance crew onto the stage and out via the vom. The totally open nature of the Belvoir auditorium and the immediacy of the relation between actor and spectators meant that the event in Row D could not be disguised and probably the only person in the theatre who could not see it was Kylie in the bio box whose sightlines began at the front edge of the stage. The incident revealed a problem in the theatre's communications in that there was no telephone line from the front of house to the bio box. Kylie's only connection was to Josh in the backstage area and this explains why the performance was allowed to run for as long as it did.

It was a devastating blow. By the time Neil stopped the show, we were within five minutes of interval, the audience had virtually missed all the scenes with Nick, and the apparitions, the Steve Gooding scene and the scene with the Headmaster were all irretrievably diminished. Neil really wanted to go back to the first entrance of Nick but that would have added twenty-five minutes to the show and different people in the audience were calling out different moments ('the Headmaster', 'Steve Gooding', 'the bushfire'), but Richard and Justine had returned to the stage so Kylie called 'the bushfire' and the final scene of Act I resumed. In my view, the mood was broken and, unsurprisingly, the actors did not really manage to revive it. I noticed that in Act II Richard omitted quite large chunks of text and odd lines in places where he had never made a mistake before, which was evidence of how much the incident had unsettled him. The worst thing was that by taking the woman out along the vom, the mysterious and shadowy space of memory and fantasy was demystified, revealed as just an exit. In my notes that night I commented that what had most disturbed me was 'the revelation of the mechanics of theatre'. The thing that I had most loved about sitting in the auditorium during the work process, as I have described it in the previous section, was somehow horribly wrong when occurring in front of the audience. The fiction, rather than being totally powerful and all consuming was revealed as infinitely fragile. I did not want the juju of craft to be revealed to the audience, I wanted the fictional world to remain intact and the offstage to retain its mysterious connection to this fictional world.

Company members I spoke to afterwards admitted that some damage would have been done but they were on the whole remarkably sanguine. Indeed, Neil has told me that my description does not at all match his experience of the event. For him, the interruption and the need to backtrack and repeat a scene transformed the performance into a rehearsal and he felt the audience rose magnificently to the occasion. Other members of the company, too, said it was an understanding and knowledgeable audience and that, in fact, an incident of that sort usually makes audiences more supportive and demonstrative. In the event, the reviews were excellent and, as reported already, the production and individual actors received numerous awards so the damage was clearly not too great. It was perhaps the case that the audience rallied around and supported the cast after the interruption, but it is nevertheless also true that the experience of those vital scenes, almost a quarter of the play, was severely diminished for that particular audience, and this observation has been borne out by other spectators present that night to whom I have since spoken. The difference of opinion between Neil and me reveals a fascinating divergence between practitioner and spectator perspectives, and the whole incident was another reminder of the dangerous edge upon which live performance rests and that the real will always trump the fiction.

The run of the show thereafter was relatively uneventful, the actors were called upon to talk to audiences after certain shows (the schools' matinées and the subscriber briefing), and Neil attended performances from time to time, leaving pages of notes for the actors to consider the next day. I attended numerous performances, sometimes sitting in the auditorium and sometimes backstage. It was noticeable that audiences laughed very regularly at the same places, that there was usually a 'dropped pin silence' during the lawyer scene and that Mrs Walkham always received at least one round of applause, often one on each of her exits. In spite of Neil's reassurances to both Monica and Richard that the slide show scene was 'a gift', Monica told me when they first moved into the theatre that although she had really liked the scene when they first began work on it, she had come to hate it (Day 28). She said she had found it very difficult to learn the speech without knowing how many transparencies there would be and how much would be visible and that she was continually put off her stride by Roland's interjections. I noticed that she had marked in red on her script where he was going to interject, because she was really not comfortable with improvisation and 'winging it'. Interestingly, when I interviewed her during the course of the run, she then expressed some regret that there had been no subsequent development in the scene. She said that now she was comfortable with the equipment and the rhythm of the image changes, she would have been happy to do a bit more impromptu responding to Richard, but that he would have had to initiate this (4 December 2007). Presumably she never spoke to Richard about this so he kept carefully to the pattern of interjections they had rehearsed.

By contrast he and Justine developed a number of moments in his first big speech where he would pause briefly and she would be about to intervene, only to be cut off by the next sweep of rhetoric. Justine told me they were not rehearsed and she and Richard had never really talked about them. The first one happened by accident during a performance, and they took it from there. They were classic laugh moments, in fact imposed onto the scene, but functioning to draw attention to Nina's presence as the ostensible recipient of the rave and 'good stuff for Justine to do', to use Richard's words about another scene. It was also noticeable that he and Justine had some good fun in the classroom scene, firstly with Julie Pearson attempting to prompt Roland with the next line of the poem, then they both introduced some squeaking when Mrs Walkham says 'Quiet as mice', and before the end of the run I noticed that Roland was making little mouse ears as he ran back to his seat.

Observing the performance from a vantage point in the wings provided a totally different perspective on the actors' task. Viewed from the auditorium, the play is a *tour de force* by one actor, but from behind the scenes it is evident just how much work is being done by all the others. I sat where Josh suggested, in the little kitchen area that gave me a good view of the PS entrance and the passage down to the crash doors. The entrance via the vom was around to my left, past the dressing room. Josh had a table set up at both the vom and PS entrance points with the props required. The following account of Act I is taken verbatim from my fieldnotes.

Kylie gives the half hour, quarter hour and five minute calls, then she goes to the bio box, leaving Josh in charge backstage. At beginners' call, Richard and Justine go in readiness to PS entrance. Richard does a yoga stretch on the ground, then jumps to limber up. Josh has his headphones on and is in radio contact with Kylie. I can hear the audience and there is a buzz of expectation. [Other actors have told me they like to 'take the pulse of the house', that is to listen from backstage to the audience as they are coming in and especially to their responses in the opening scenes.] When Richard begins the long speech, Josh says quietly to me 'this is the boring bit', meaning that there is nothing for him to do for five minutes or so. Once the memory scenes begin, he will be dashing from OP to PS and be utterly focused on the job in hand.

Russell comes to the kitchen to get a biscuit, already wearing his Lawyer's suit and looking so smart that I didn't recognise him for a moment. Monica comes for a drink of water, already in costume and wig for Mrs Walkham. Before going on stage, she checks her appearance in the long mirror on the wall beside the PS entrance. She is already waiting in the wings during the Lawyer scene, well before her entrance. Josh doesn't get her trolley ready until the Nina scene. When Russell comes off as Lawyer, he dashes straight to the dressing room to change into Headmaster costume. As soon as Monica goes on with trolley, Josh goes around to the vom to be there to receive it when she comes off. Huge round of applause. Guy gets into Alexander costume in the dressing room but comes to collect sword and shield from Josh before entering. Guy, Monica and Russell all waiting in the wings during the 'baa lamb' scene. 'What is the next line' is cue for Guy to put his helmet on. At the end of the Alexander scene, Josh helps Russell with quick change into Maybloom, wig, white coat, hands him clipboard and pen (all these items are kept by Josh near the PS entrance and not in the dressing room). Guy gets into Executioner's costume in the dressing room then comes to collect hood, torch, gauntlets and axe from Josh. As soon as he goes on, Josh goes around to the crash doors to collect torch and get ready for the snow storm. Huge round of applause for Titus Oates. Russell then runs from the crash doors direct to the dressing room to get into the Steve Gooding costume.

Josh is ready with the hospital gown for Nick who has run around from the vom where he exits with the soccer ball that is then left on Josh's table on that side. Josh has the drip ready and Guy has to strip off all his clothes, while Josh is applying the bruise make up. He leaves all Nick's clothes lying on the ground as he has to get Miss Beverly dressed (wig, help with the boots that he has left unzipped in readiness, choker and radio mike). As soon as she goes on, Josh takes Nick's clothes back to the dressing room, puts away the Maybloom wig and gets Lynette's wig ready. Monica is already dressed as the nurse. As soon as Justine comes off as Miss Beverly, she has to change very quickly into Lynette. She already has Lynette's psychedelic underwear on under Miss Beverly's mini dress. Russell gets dressed as Steve Gooding in the dressing room. Everyone backstage is laughing as the huge audience reaction to Steve Gooding erupts. Guy is collecting cigarette and Coke can during Lynette's appearance. Russell then does a really fast change out of Steve Gooding into the Headmaster and Josh helps him with socks and they use slip on shoes for extra speed. There is a round of applause for Roland's description of his play, then Guy comes back to leave Coke can, cigarette and thongs (flip-flops) by the props table. Josh begins to tidy up various items of costume and props, takes shirt to laundry that will have to be washed that night because it got make up on it, takes shoes and socks from Russell as he comes off. Josh puts Daniel's black shirt, brown trousers and sandals ready for the quick change that will not occur until the end of Act II but he has a lot to do during the interval. He also gets the whisky glasses ready, puts the liquid in but not the ice cubes. Monica comes to put the kettle on during the final scene on Act I and there is very loud audience applause at the end of the act. Guy is already dressed in Daniel's T-shirt and baggy shorts before interval. All the actors come to the kitchen for a cup of tea during interval.

I have quoted this description at length because it reveals so graphically the high energy and high precision of what was going on backstage and provides insight into the very different demands made on the actors in this production.

The last performance was followed by another party in the foyer of the theatre and, again, the audience contained a number of showbusiness celebrities whose names I heard being whispered among audience members. Michael Gow arrived back in Sydney from Germany that evening but he only managed to get to the theatre for Act II as his plane was late. He was, however, able to take the final curtain call with the actors and on this occasion, they did beckon to Neil to come and share the applause, something they had not done on the opening night, to my surprise. While the party was an opportunity for all to unwind, not all the actors actually attended. My notes indicate that Richard did not come to either the opening night or the closing night parties and Kylie told me that he tends to avoid such occasions but that he was persuaded to put in a very brief appearance at the opening night party. It was said on the closing night that some of the celebrity spectators had gone backstage to see him in the dressing room so there was perhaps another party going on backstage, attended by a kind of A-list within the A-list. If this is so, it would only add to the aura and sense of privilege associated with the dressing room to which I have already referred.

At the same time that spectators, actors and company staff were drinking and socialising in the foyer bar, the production crew were dismantling the set and clearing out all traces of the production in readiness for the next one that would be bumped in even though this was not going to happen until after Christmas. There was a general sense of a job well done, and of satisfaction all round but the closing night party was less emotionally charged than the one on opening night. This was perhaps due to the fact that farewells and departures are part of the normal transitoriness of theatre, so this was business as usual, perhaps because it was Christmas and for everyone the demands of family and friends were coming to the fore, perhaps because the end is necessarily quieter than the beginning that launches the combined effort. But it was over and I realised as I left the theatre that none of the actors had asked me for any information about the book I would be writing. My academic project is, it seems, far removed from the rituals of recognition and celebration through which they find the validation they need, and these emanate substantially from within the world of the theatre. This point will be further elaborated in the final chapter.

PART TWO   Reflections after the
            event

Fact and fiction and the space between

When people say 'it must be autobiographical,' I say 'is it?'.
(Michael Gow, 2007)

In Michael Gow's play *Furious*, the central character is also called Roland Henning and there, too, he is a playwright who bears many similarities to Michael Gow himself. In one scene, Henning pressures Louise, who has written a doctoral thesis on his plays, to tell him how he does what he does.

ROLAND: Tell me! I need to know. What do I do? Describe it.
LOUISE: You take familiar lives, in a family context and . . . illuminate them? Transfigure them? . . . um, by . . . creating a comic surface – this is all just coming straight out of my thesis.
ROLAND: Go on!
LOUISE: Well . . . I suppose you create this comic surface, and through comedy and without totally resolving anything thematically . . . um, this comic mode, the comic framework, allows for a sense of renewal – (Gow 1994, 24).

Michael Gow does not simply take 'familiar lives, in a family context' but real lives, people he has known and incidents that have actually happened to him, and weaves them into a disturbing mix of the fantastic and the autobiographical. He both admits and denies that the Roland

Henning plays are autobiographical; for example, he told the actors in the Queensland Theatre Company/South Australian Theatre Company co-production of *Toy Symphony* (2009) that nearly everything in it was drawn from his own life but, when asked by Angela Bennie before the Company B production whether the play was autobiographical, he said 'Some of it, maybe; all writing is in a way' (Bennie 2007). Watching the rehearsal process for *Toy Symphony*, it was evident that the interpenetration of the real and the imagined, the factual and the lightly fictionalised was much more extreme and more interesting than this rather disingenuous reference to 'all writing' suggests. Michael told me during the rehearsals that he was currently reading J.M. Coetzee's latest novel, and loved the way the narrator is more obviously than ever Coetzee's alter ego, and he has also spoken in interviews of his fascination with the novels of Philip Roth and Kurt Vonnegut, where the distinction between author and character is similarly blurred. The interplay between his own life and that of certain characters that is a repeated element in his plays, and his ambivalent statements about these links, constitute a kind of elaborate tease. He told Angela Bennie that he chose the title *Toy Symphony* in part 'because Roland plays with some of the characters and others play with him. And the material of the play is playing with us and the whole thing, the objects of the play, they are objects I play with' (Bennie 2007).

Like other writers, Michael Gow might overhear the tag end of a conversation in the street and then build on that, weave it into a story, a situation, or use aspects of the lives of his friends and aquaintances in more or less recognisable ways to create fictional characters. As Mrs Walkham reminds Roland when she appears mysteriously in his apartment, D.H. Lawrence had done just this: 'he'd made enemies because he'd put people he knew in his books, he'd lost friends'. *Toy Symphony* is, however, far more overtly autobiographical than that kind of writing, and not just because of the connection between Roland's story of being accused of stealing an idea for a play and the real charge of plagiarism against Michael Gow that had rocked the Australian theatre world in 1994. The high school scenes, as they came into being during the work process in Week 2, are substantially drawn from Michael's own high school experiences, as he told the actors in numerous explanatory comments. The school's sporting hero did bully him, he said, and he did scandalise the school community by initiating a sexual relationship with that boy, which led to a cessation in the bullying but also eventually to the banning of a play he had written. He was protected from some of the bullying by the intervention of a boy who was an outsider in the school community. On Day 4, when Michael announced to the actors that he had decided to replace Nick Sharp, the cockney migrant, with Nikolajs Eglitis, son of Latvian refugees, he said it was because he was going back to the reality of what happened (even though the name Eglitis was plucked from a database). He said he imagined the character as 'a brooding hulk like Lennie Small in Steinbeck's *Of Mice and Men*', although Guy created a very different kind of character on the basis of the words Michael gives him, drawing this character from somewhere deep within himself.

The sporting hero of Michael's school did confess the sexual relationship to the PE teacher (himself a character in the play in some earlier versions, where he is called Mr Fielding), who reported it to the Headmaster. A play Michael had written was banned, but whether this was as retribution for what had been happening with the sporting hero or because of the transgressive nature of the play was never clear (on Day 4 he said that in the actual events on which he was drawing, the play was a satirical attack on middle class values, with the Mary Poppins-inspired nanny imprisoned in a basement and that that was why it was banned). His school band did play *The Toy Symphony* at a concert for the parents and speeded up the final movement in an aggressive and frenetic way that shocked the audience. Mr Devlin, the name given to the Headmaster, was actually the name of a maths teacher he had detested, although he recalled that the real headmaster in his day was a civilised man who gave the boys a day off in order to participate in one of the Vietnam Moratorium marches.

The primary school scenes are also peopled by figures he remembered from his own childhood experiences at Como West Public School; Mrs Walkham was a real teacher, remembered fondly by at least one spectator who came to the Company B production; Julie Pearson was really a child at the school (Michael identified her in the class photograph he brought to show the actors and at one stage said that she should be co-directing *The Play* with Roland); Dr Maybloom was really the name of the Gow family doctor, probably a second generation European migrant who had anglicised his name. Michael remembered him as 'very white' (which reminded me that there had been some protests in the USA at Hollywood's invariable representation of albinos as evil from associations for people with albinism). The scene with the child psychiatrist has some connection with Michael's own childhood (Neil told Richard that Michael had been sent to a child psychiatrist due to his 'overactive imagination;' it is also possible that there was another intervention after the Steve Gooding scandal, as something similar is recounted by one of the characters in *Furious*).

Richard asked Neil if he was himself the inspiration for Jake, the

friend who has moved to New York but who was responsible for the
dog incident in some way and who worries about Roland from afar. Neil
denied this but said he thought Jake was based on a real person, someone
known to several of them. There was some speculation about Tom, the
drug dealer from whom Roland gets his cocaine and whether he, too,
was based on a real person and if the incident depicted in Scene 18 did
happen. While there was no suggestion in any of the rehearsal room
discussions that Daniel was based on a real person, someone did tell
me many months later that the brutal dismissal of Daniel's hopes for an
acting career were uncomfortably close to an exchange he had himself
once had with Michael. The phrase 'learn to make a decent coffee' still
made him wince. Michael's motivation in presenting the character who
is his alter ego in such an unpleasant light was mentioned with some
perplexity on several occasions. The ruthless manner in which Roland
instructs the lawyer to 'nail a lid on' the woman who has accused him,
the cruelty of his attack on Daniel, and the sheer unpleasantness of the
blackmail with which he obliges Tom to continue to supply him with
the drugs are evidence of a deeply 'festered' character, as Richard put it
when they were working on the drug dealer scene on Day 3: 'He seems
to get off on doing it so cruelly, he doesn't have to turn it into a piece
of theatre.' However, they relished the scope provided for them by the
powerful writing in these scenes, 'Michael Gow at his absolute best' in
Richard's view (Interview 19 December 2007).

Neil commented one day on the way so much of the play references
moments, incidents and characters from Michael's earlier plays; he said,
'this play is like a bonfire of all his previous plays'. There are numerous
inconsistencies beneath the 'brazen self exposure' (Richard's term when
talking to spectators at the subscriber debrief) that seems to be involved
here, but in view of the extensive co-option of names, people and events
from his own life it seems that Neil's insight could be taken further. The
play, *Toy Symphony*, is like a bonfire of the author's life to date.

Monica told me that one night after the performance, when she came
into the foyer, a man who had been at the performance approached her.
He told her he had been a pupil at Como West Public School a few years
before Michael Gow, so had not known him then, but he did remember
Mrs Walkham, the character so memorably played by Monica. He also
remembered Julie Pearson and the Headmaster and he knew the famous
footballer on whom the Steve Gooding character was based. He also
told her he had written a local history of Como and thought that a good
deal of Mrs Walkham's slide show was taken from his book, including
the reference to D.H. Lawrence. While he did not seem particularly
perturbed by any of this, and was not asking for an acknowledgement of

Figure 15. Russell Dykstra, Monica Maughan (rehearsal room, Company B)
Photo: Heidrun Löhr

his book in the programme, he had been sufficiently stirred by the play
to want to speak to the actress who had incarnated (or reincarnated)
Mrs Walkham, and to hang around in the theatre for nearly an hour
in order to do so. This incident brings into focus some of the troubling
ethical issues raised by a working method that involves taking bits of
real people's lives and exaggerating or framing them within a certain
context, even if they are comically 'transfigured' along the way, even if
the outcome is 'renewal' or 'redemption'.

   Of course, it was not only Michael who was drawing on real people
and events in order to construct this work. Perhaps even more than
writers, actors use their own experiences and memories as well as their
observations of people around them in order to create the embodied
reality of the character the playwright's words suggest. I noticed that
Neil and the actors often referred to another actor's characteristic style,
or to the way a certain actor played a particular character, or to films,
or even to public figures with idiosyncratic gestures or vocal delivery in
order to describe the effect they were seeking. These references usually
provoked an anecdote or some gossip and much laughter. There was
also a good deal of personal story telling, some serious, some provoking
more laughter. Hilarity in rehearsal is by no means incompatible with

utterly serious purpose, however, and the anecdotes, the gossip and apparent digressions that were such a frequent occurrence functioned in part as a means of grounding the situation of the characters in the shared emotional life and memories of director and cast and in part as a means of constituting this shared emotional life. They also meant that certain people and incidents became part of the life of the rehearsal room.

During the *Toy Symphony* rehearsals, it was probably the scene with Steve Gooding that provoked the most of this kind of story telling, perhaps because the scene had to be virtually rewritten and, thus, required substantial input from the actors, but perhaps because memories were still strong of schoolyard homophobia and the contempt meted out to artistically and intellectually inclined boys in the sport-obsessed suburban culture of Sydney. Russell had a fund of schoolboy pejoratives used to describe homosexuals that caused great hilarity ('chocolate choo-cha boy' was the only one I managed to write down) as well as the ubiquitous 'fucken pooftah', and Neil remembered that 'cat' was a term of abuse in the 1970s and this has actually been retained by Michael in the published version of the play. Neil recalled that the sporting hero of his school would always miaow when he saw him in the playground. Anecdotes contributed from all around the room indicated that similar kinds of torment afflicted later generations: your shoes filled with sand and slung over something high, your tie 'microknotted' (this procedure had to be explained for people who went to different kinds of school: it involves forcing the tie knot up so tightly around a boy's neck that he cannot get it undone and feels that he is being strangled). Alan John, whose work as a composer was well known to all of them, was at the same school as Neil, who remembered 'the Fitness boys would wedge Alan John's bag so tightly in the rubbish bin that he couldn't get it out' (Day 16).

While the anecdotes provoked laughter, there was always an under-lying current of something deadly serious. The most chilling was the one Neil told (Day 10) about the choreographer Ross Coleman, who grew up in The Shire like Michael. He had been awarded a very prestigious dance scholarship while he was still at school and the headmaster had called him to the front at assembly to announce his award, and then said 'If any son of mine wanted to do ballet dancing, I would cut his feet off.' There was just silence in the room after Neil told that story, a kind of collective intake of breath and then a silence as people thought through that insight into what it must have been like, what it is still like, to grow up gay in our homophobic societies. The anger that fed into Michael's writing of the Headmaster and Steve Gooding scenes was given a light touch in the performance created by Neil and the actors but the darkness is still there, just beneath the surface, a trace remaining from all the ideas and stories evoked in the rehearsal process.

Not all the memories of school were negative. Mrs Walkham, the primary school teacher who nurtured Roland's creativity and believed in the life of the imagination (as well as the importance of acknowledging the authorship of poems one is reciting), and Miss Beverly who brought ideas of love and romance and the experience of beautiful language to football obsessed adolescents also triggered memories of school teachers who had been important. Neil remembered his own kindergarten teacher, Miss Bootle, with whom he had been in love, who got married when he was 6 but sent him a postcard while on her honeymoon, surely a sign of a dedicated teacher. The fact that Monica always got a round of applause on one of her exits as Mrs Walkham, and often on all three, can be attributed to the beautifully judged performance she gave but it was also an acknowledgement on the part of spectators of the role of the Mrs Walkhams in their own schooldays. As Neil said when he fielded questions from an audience of secondary school students, this is also a play about teachers, about the good ones (often English and Drama teachers) who do so much to open children's minds and imaginations, as well as about the bad ones who do the opposite. He told them one of the reasons he liked the play was because 'it took the lid off the bully boy/sport culture that is dominant in so many schools'.

For obvious reasons, JR was spoken about on numerous occasions during the rehearsal process and beyond (actors asking if she had been to see the production, expressing anxiety about her response). From the first day, when the actors asked Neil to provide background information to the *Sweet Phoebe* scandal, throughout the work sessions dealing with the scenes involving the copyright lawyer and Nina, as she probes Roland's reactions to his own behaviour in relation to the injunction, the real JR was evoked. Michael winced when he heard the actors use her name in relation to the character referred to in the play only as 'the woman'. They then established another soubriquet, the 'litigious friend', but it was rarely used. There was one line in Roland's self justification to the lawyer that I had thought ethically very dubious and had so far overcome my ethnographer's 'disciplinary detachment' to speak to Neil unofficially, querying whether the line could be cut. Roland says of the woman he claims is persecuting him, 'She doesn't have much of a grip on her life you see, she's got no real sense of purpose, okay? Like a lot of us.' It seemed to me that this statement was only tolerable if it included the 'like a lot of us' but that was a line Richard frequently omitted. In one note session, Neil had mentioned my anxiety about the implied criticism of JR and I then said how important it seemed to me that Richard not forget the line 'like a lot of us'. After one of the dress rehearsals, I said quietly that he had again forgotten that line and when he expressed surprise, three other people confirmed that he had indeed left it out. This suggests that everyone was listening for it, an indication of the extent to which JR hovered over the performance process, a troubling figure around whom many anxieties circulated.

JR was not, however, the only intangible presence haunting the rehearsal room. *Holding the Man*, the play in which Guy performed the leading role of Tim Conigrave, was running at the Belvoir Street Theatre throughout the rehearsal period of *Toy Symphony*. Tim Conigrave was an actor known to several of the cast and crew, and the play was based on his autobiographical memoir recounting his passionate, lifelong love affair with John Caleo that began when they were both at school, and ended with John's death from AIDS in 1992, and Tim's own death two years later. The play by Tommy Murphy is both heartwrenchingly sad and very comic, and Neil said one day he had seen it on at least ten occasions. It had been premiered by Griffin and had transferred to several other theatres, always with Guy in the role of Tim Conigrave. Neil's knowledge of Guy's performance (was this why he was cast in *Toy Symphony*?) and the potential spillover between Tim and the two roles Guy played in the Gow play, Nick Eglitis the doomed schoolboy, and Daniel, the serious young actor, explain why Neil should so often have referred to the other role ('That's a bit Tim.' 'Too cute, too Tim.') in his directions to Guy. It did seem to me, however, that these went beyond technical and craft matters, and that at some profound level the characters were linked, not only for Guy who embodied them all, but also for Neil.

Guy spoke on a number of occasions towards the end of the run of *Holding the Man* of the impact on him of channelling such strong emotional reactions from audiences. He told me that on one occasion, there was a group of schoolgirls weeping quietly, and he had been aware of other people in tears around the auditorium, but then at the end one of the girls 'really lost it and that unleashed it all over the auditorium' and his own emotion was so great that he was almost unable to complete the final speech. In the circumstances, it was inevitable that he brought Tim Conigrave with him and that Tim should, in his own way, have been almost as much of a presence in the room as JR. However, I do not recall Richard ever mentioning Tim and perhaps he never knew him, nor did he manage to get to see a performance of *Holding the Man* although he said a couple of times that it was his intention to do so. This is evidence of the selective haunting that can be at work in a process involving a number of people, each bringing their own artistic sensibility and their own life history to the work.

I first interviewed Neil about the play before rehearsals began and he told me that he had been immediately attracted by the 'ferocious energy' in the writing of certain scenes, such as the long speech about the creative cycle in the first scene. He said he was not sure what the play as a whole added up to at that time but knew he wanted to do it. In the months since he had first read the play, his mother had died and what now resonated most strongly with him was the darkness at the heart of the play, Michael's image of the tar pit and the whole idea of the chasm under the surface of life. Family is hugely important to Neil, both in reality (his parents were very much part of his life and part of the life of Company B, always there for opening nights and season launches, and supportive in many material ways) and in terms of his overall artistic and philosophical approach. The chasm under the surface of even the most happy and stable family life is, however, something he has known about since his schooldays. When he was 14, his mother developed cancer and was told by the doctors that she had only six months to live and his beloved elder brother was also diagnosed with leukaemia. Tragically, his brother died when Neil was still at school and, while his mother's cancer did in fact respond to treatment, his adolescence was overshadowed by grief and the fear that his mother would die. Michael's adolescence, too, was marked by the loss of a greatly loved friend, who died when both boys were still at school. This loss affected Michael deeply, and he has transposed it into fiction in his characteristic manner in *Away*, where the schoolboy Tom, the central character, is dying of leukaemia, and returned to it again with the character of Nick in *Toy Symphony*.

In addition to the shared experience of loss in their teenage years, both Neil and Michael came to the rehearsal room grieving the death of their mothers. Neil's mother had died only a year before, and Michael's parents had died within six weeks of each other three years earlier, a devastating experience he gives to Roland in the play. For both Neil and Michael, then, the death of Roland's mother and the account of the funerals in the powerful monologue in Scene 17, must have stirred memories and the sense of loss and grief. Tess Schofield, too, came to the rehearsals carrying a very recent experience of caring for someone dying of cancer and of the complex aftermath of death, and both Guy and Monica took time off in order to attend a funeral. It was not evident how close they were to the person who had died but it seemed that death and funerals and grieving were very much present in that room.

Mindful of Margaret Mead's exhortation to the ethnographer in the field to be aware 'that he himself, his own stability and well-being, are inextricably part of the observations he is making' (Mead 1973, 249), I should perhaps say a word about my own state at this time. My husband,

David, died on 14 October 2006, so the rehearsals for *Toy Symphony*
coincided with the first anniversary of his death, one of the hardest times
in the grieving process, as I now know. Having the daily requirement
to be present at the rehearsals and the nightly task of writing up the
day's notes helped me greatly but I did make a note that week that if I
allowed my thoughts to wander, they turned to David and my emotions
were very near the surface. The idea of the tar pit and Roland's anger at
doctors certainly resonated very powerfully with me at that time and it
may well be that my observation of the process was coloured by what
was most present to me in my own life. The line that Richard always
did very strongly and that always touched me on the raw was 'but even
as they sank they never gave up, never stopped struggling against pain
and fear and humiliation and doctors'. He would almost spit out the
word 'doctors' and on opening night, doubtless thrown off balance by
the disruption that had occurred in the auditorium, he actually said
'fucking doctors'. Michael rather liked the addition, so Richard kept it
and the moment got bigger and more angry. Later in the run, however,
Neil asked him to drop the adjective as he thought the original line
was stronger, and his judgement was, as usual, spot on. I thought that
when the moment got too big, it sounded as though Roland blamed the
doctors for his father's death, when the point is rather the wrenchingly
sad fact that, too often, doctors add to the humiliation and pain of the
dying process instead of alleviating it.

Many people were involved in the making of *Toy Symphony* and
many more were present in some way during the creative process that
brought twenty characters to life on the stage: the real people invoked
behind Michael Gow's fictions, including most powerfully JR, the memories of individuals and groups (like the Fitness brothers who tormented
Alan John) who fed the actors' process and Tess Schofield's acutely
observed costume designs, the people who were there by accident, as it
were, like Tim Conigrave, and the people who were silently there in the
minds and hearts of participants, deepening the emotional texture of
what was going on. If the fictional creation in the theatre is haunted by
real life, however, the reverse is also true. Richard's explanation on Day
1 for having worked in film and television for the last seven years was
that the experience of playing the central role in Patrick Marber's *Closer*
(Sydney Theatre Company, 2000) had put him off theatre. When I asked
him to elaborate on this later, he said that playing such a cold, shallow
character night after night throughout the whole run had been very
destructive to him personally.

Mark Seton's research into the experience of the actor has led
him to coin the term 'post dramatic stress' to describe the aftermath of

performance for actors who are playing deeply troubled characters. He claims that from the advent of 'method' acting onwards, 'actors have had to draw on their own emotions and experiences to deliver "lifelike" performances . . . of people being vulnerable and enacting trauma of various degrees but no-one [is] really tracking the fallout, what it does to actors' lives' (quote from Seton, in Morgan and Maddox 2010). Many actors would claim that cultivating detachment, maintaining barriers between the characters they play and their own emotional life is one of their professional skills. Jacques Lassalle clearly believes this and thinks that part of his job as director is to lead or push actors out of their comfort zone towards the shadowy terrain of the abject. Angela de Lorenzis quotes him as saying, 'Actors have the great privilege of being able to live their own abjection, because, with their formidable powers of exorcism, they are later washed clean of it' (De Lorenzis 2005, 330).

At the subscriber debrief session, a spectator asked Richard where he found in himself the 'lecherous lecturer' (in the terrible scene in which Roland attacks Daniel, demolishing him as a person and an artist). Richard said that it was in Michael's very powerful writing and he described the scene as 'dynamite.' While this is true, it is only part of the story and the experience of creating that scene and then performing it every night during the run, with the variations in emotional intensity that occurred, drew very heavily on the particular sensibilities of both actors. Guy recounted that on one occasion Roland's (Richard's?) ferocity was such that he found he had backed away not just to the edge of the stage, but up a couple of steps into the side aisle. He said it was such an extraordinary performance to which he had to respond, even to the point of 'smashing through the magic wall between stage and audience'. The performance varies in intensity from night to night, and this kind of energy cannot be produced at will (otherwise it results in what actors call 'pushing') but when it does happen, a good actor sharing the scene will respond accordingly. On some occasions, when Guy left the stage after that scene, he/Daniel was in tears, and it is this degree of variation that indicates how far away they were from merely repeating something learned, safe and removed from their own emotions. Each night was different, each night the dangerous edge was experienced differently, each night different demands were made on each of them. Guy did not know what he was in for on any given night because he did not know how ferocious Richard was going to be.

Richard told an interviewer that what made playing the role of Roland possible was that he was able to go home to his wife and eight-month old baby son at the end of it, evidently something he did not have when playing the role in *Closer* seven years earlier. He said:

With no-one to go home to it would be terribly different. I can easily imagine that because I've done it and it makes a time like this, where you're exploring the outer reaches of a person's terrible – albeit largely self-inflicted – drama, really kind of brutal on the soul. So just having my baby boy, it really kind of lifts you immediately to another place. (Morgan 2007, 14)

There is clearly a spillover from the fiction back into the actor's reality, and individual actors must find different ways to deal with it. Mark Seton's notion of 'post dramatic stress' is perhaps closer to the truth than Jacques Lassalle's optimistic faith in the actor's powers of recuperation, especially in the case of acting that goes deep, but both of them are pointing to the fascinating and dangerous space between fiction and reality with which actors, more than any other creative artists, must deal on a daily basis and in which the unwary can lose themselves.

Neil's play, Michael's play and Richard's play

I'm beginning to think it's a comedy (Michael Gow, Day 9)

Neil pointed out several times during rehearsal discussions and in interviews about his production that the background on which Michael Gow draws in the play is one he shares. He, too, is a child of the Sydney suburbs, was educated in the same state school system, and knows at first hand what it was like to come to a realisation of one's homosexuality in the sport-obsessed, homophobic culture of a 1960s high school. More profoundly, as has just been described, both men had experienced the deep sadness while still in their teens of losing someone very dear to them, and both came to the rehearsal process still grieving the death of their mothers. The shared background and life experiences are part of the reason that Neil was so immediately drawn to Michael's play, responding with uncharacteristic speed when his agent sent the script and including it in the season he was then planning. Eamon Flack said the shared background was what gave Neil 'an authoritative sense' in dealing with the material and I suggest that this sense developed into a quasi-authorial role in relation to the work as it was shaped during the course of the rehearsal process. As has been made abundantly clear in my account of this process, Neil intervened in decisive ways, not only to clarify the dramatic structure and the story line but also to add numerous details that function in particular to enhance the presence of the minor characters, softening the anger and the bitterness that runs through Michael's script, yet somehow deepening the overall experience. Textual amendments included the cuts and additions intended to clarify action and motivation that are a normal part of the workshopping process involved in bringing a new play to the stage, but there were also pure inventions that seemed to come from somewhere within Neil's own psyche. On more than one occasion, actors expressed some disquiet about the number and nature of the textual amendments, always to be reassured by Neil that Michael was happy with the direction the work was taking.

On the days when Michael was present in the rehearsal room during the first couple of weeks (Days 1, 4, 8 and 9), however, it became apparent that there were considerable differences between the two, particularly in relation to the scenes that recreate the childhood and high school memories. It was evident that Michael's view of the past was considerably darker than Neil's and that without Neil's comic touch the characters that people Roland's childhood and adolescence would have come across as a rather unpleasant lot: authoritarian headmasters, ignorant bullies, insensitive doctors, grotesque neighbours. In the early versions of the play, even Roland's friend Nick Sharp is another caricature, sex-obsessed to the point of what Richard referred to as 'priapism' (Day 7). Michael has said of the writing of the play that he had begun it many years earlier but had put it aside during the long years of his inability to write, finally coming back to it after the death of his parents. He had gone to stay completely alone at an isolated retreat in the Queensland rainforest and suddenly found himself able to write again, the whole play pouring out of him in an intensive three-week period while the rain poured down outside. He told Angela Bennie the experience 'was weird, it was like automatic writing. It was so exhilarating. It was terrifying' (Bennie 2007). Once the play had been accepted for production at Belvoir, he wrote several further drafts but as he commented to the actors 'the further it gets from the original, the crappier it gets' (Day 1). It should be noted, however, that notwithstanding my sense of the divergence between author and director in relation to the tone of the memory scenes, there were never any overt arguments between them during the rehearsal period.

The changes made by Neil and the actors, notably Richard and Russell, were always presented to Michael for his approval and nothing would have been included had he objected. Each change seems to be a small detail, often a matter of tone and colour rather than anything more substantial, but the cumulative impact of them all does shift the play in quite decisive ways. I can see from my field notes that as early as the third week of rehearsals I had already begun to speak of 'Neil's play' and to see it as something that differed markedly from 'Michael's play.' Neil's perception was that, in order to carry the interweaving of past and present in Act I, the play needed 'a buoyant comic energy' (Day 9) and much of his intervention throughout the process both in terms of structuring the action and in his idiosyncratic additions to the script was designed to enhance this aspect of the play. For Michael, as Neil admitted, the play 'had to go somewhere much darker'. It is significant that at the end of the second week of rehearsals, when Michael had seen the whole thing put together for the very first time, he commented that he was beginning to think that what he had written was a comedy. The admission was almost a throwaway remark, made as we were packing up at the end of the week, but I have used it as the epigraph to this chapter dealing with the different directions in which the three dominant artists wanted to take the material because it provides such a revealing insight into how open the process was. Neil's remark to the actors, 'Michael has been writing the play to discover what it is' (Day 2), resonates with Michael's own sense that the first draft was akin to automatic writing.

A few examples of the kind of differences I noted will indicate why I started to use the shorthand of 'Neil's play' and 'Michael's play.' In the middle of the fifth week, Michael spent a full day in the rehearsal room, watching the actors run scenes that he had rewritten or Neil and the actors had amended. When they were working on the scene between Roland and the child psychologist, they decided to cut a considerable amount of the doctor's speech about morbid fantasies because, as Michael very pertinently observed, it 'felt set up as social commentary'. Dr Maybloom originally said:

> Sometimes young people like yourself have what we call morbid fantasies, it's quite common and it's perfectly acceptable to have them. And they can be very powerful, very strong. Yours seem to be so strong they somehow become visible. But as exciting, as thrillling as these fantasies are, we do have to grow out of them. And sometimes, Roland, young people have trouble growing out of them. But if they don't, they can cause all sorts of problems when we grow up.

Michael's cuts streamlined this section of the speech:

> Sometimes young people have what are called morbid fantasies. And they can be very powerful, very exciting. But we do have to grow out of them because if we don't, they can cause all sorts of problems when we grow up.

In what was almost an aside, he added that he wanted to remove the doctor's admission that Roland's fantasies become visible because 'if Maybloom acknowledges they are real we will begin to like him'. This seemed to me to go to the heart of the difference in approach between Michael and Neil in that Michael was happy for the support characters to be grotesques, apparently wanted the audience to dislike them, whereas Neil's many interventions had the effect of humanising them, permitting them to become more likeable. In Michael's dark vision, the child Roland is oppressed by a number of malign authority figures, and only Mrs Walkham provides support, practical advice and kindness. Russell Dykstra's input was decisive in transforming these sinister bullies into buffoons, greatly aided of course by Tess Schofield's costume designs. Together with Neil's many other interventions, this produced a far sunnier view of the past, which was presumably Neil's intention when casting a powerful comic actor like Russell to play these roles.

A telling example of Neil's comic vision is his treatment of Mrs Walkham's slide show. While he did not change a word of the lesson and barely intervened in Monica Maughan's performance, he nevertheless set his own stamp on the scene by suggesting numerous places where Roland can be brought into the scene, call out, put his hand up because he knows what Mrs Walkham is going to say, get in first with some piece of information. He knows about the transit of Venus, he knows that sesqui centenary means 150 years, he is so eager to tell her that Ash Wednesday and Black Saturday refer to bushfires, that when she finally gets to that phrase in her prepared lesson, he says 'That's right!' Each time they worked on this scene, Neil came up with more suggestions (I think there were seven or eight by the end) and Richard exclaimed at one stage, 'You're turning him into a right little tosser' but he always did them brilliantly with a mix of childlike wonderment and excitement at his own knowledge. I did wonder whether Neil would remove one or two of the interruptions, especially in view of Richard's comment, but he never did and audiences loved the scene. After each one of his interventions, Richard would glance behind him, creating with that turn the rest of the class sitting there, the slightly defensive look on his face indicating perhaps that Roland knows that many of his classmates do regard him as a 'tosser'.

In Michael's script, there is no indication of what Roland is doing, or even whether he is still on stage. He could in fact stay in the present and join Nina in the shadowy space from which she watches the scene that is ostensibly being recounted to her by the adult Roland. Comparing the scene with the way it was performed in Geordie Brookman's 2009 production of the play for the South Australian Theatre Company, makes very evident the impact of Neil's treatment. Geordie Brookman, like Neil, had Roland become a child in the class for Mrs Walkham's lesson but he made him sit cross legged at the very front of the stage with his back to the audience, looking at the images that were projected on to a screen at the back of the stage. This had the effect of transforming the whole audience into members of Mrs Walkham's 5A class and the focus of audience attention inevitably became the images that were being projected. It was not possible to see what effect the lesson was having on Roland as the actor had his back to the audience and seemed to be simply looking at the slide show. In Neil's staging, the slides were barely visible but were perceived through Roland's excited response to them and to Mrs Walkham's commentary.

When Richard expressed anxiety about the number of Roland's interruptions, Neil said he was thinking about his own nephew, and followed up with an anecdote about Thomas, aged five, on his first day in kindergarten, saying to the teacher 'if there's anything I can do for you, just let me know'. Richard loved that story and, while pointing out that Roland is 10 and Neil's nephew was only 5, he did nevertheless seem to bring something of that innocence and trust into his performance. The interventions kept the level of excitement high throughout the scene as audiences responded to Roland's own interest and involvement, nearly every interruption getting a laugh and Monica usually received a round of applause as she exited. Although I saw Geordie Brookman's production only once, my impression was that in the absence of any interaction between Mrs Walkham and Roland, the scene rather lost momentum. The images that became the focus of audience attention were not sufficiently compelling and there was no indication of Roland's reactions. One of Richard's improvisations involved Roland yawning but Neil rejected that, saying that the scene shows Roland becoming aware that 'where he lived was a really interesting place', clearly a decisive moment in the evolution of the future playwright for whom Como will play such a significant role.

Casting the same actor to play both Nick Eglitis and Daniel permitted the past to resonate in the present in a number of subtle and unspoken ways and here, too, it seemed to me that Neil and Michael were taking the material in significantly different directions. The double casting was certainly part of Michael's plan for the support characters but from the many hints and suggestions that Neil made during the rehearsal process, it was evident that for him this was far more than a pragmatic solution to the problem of multiple small roles. It would have been possible to accentuate the differences between the two characters and, indeed, in Tess's costume designs they look so different that spectators might not have picked up that they were played by the same actor. Nick was to have long hair as was normal for schoolboys in the 1970s and it was Neil who vetoed the wig, ostensibly to make a distinct break with Guy's role in *Holding the Man* in which wigs played such a large part (Day 13). A more important reason was that, as he had said in some of the earliest rehearsals, he wanted spectators to see the link between the two characters, to see that when Roland looks at Daniel, he sees 'someone who reminds him of someone he was once in love with' (Day 3). When Michael was asked by Neil the next day whether Roland and Daniel are going to fall in love, he answered with a categorical 'No' but gave no further explanation, nor did anyone press him for one. Neil had already made clear that, for him, at the centre of the play is 'a striving for lost innocence' (Day 1), and a major element of this is the way we are led to see Nick, the boy who died, in Daniel, the young actor who is instrumental in bringing about Roland's redemption. When Neil originally proposed this interpretation, Nick was still the randy English schoolboy but the later transformation of the character into the more complex and romantically inclined Nick Eglitis made Neil's version of events even more compelling.

There was no doubt in Neil's mind that Roland was halfway in love with Nick even though the latter is clearly not gay, and 'his' Roland is haunted by what never had the opportunity to come into being. He was equally certain that in the final scene, as Roland watches Daniel explain how he has made sense of the gratuitous cruelty inflicted on him, he 'is beginning to fall in love with Daniel' (Day 9) in part because of the way he reminds him of Nick. Neil returned to this point in a note after a later run, when he said specifically, 'Roland should be fallling in love with Daniel during the speech' (Day 14). The way the relationships between Roland, Nick, Steve Gooding and Daniel were created in performance involved powerful and ultimately decisive input from the actors, particularly Richard, as will be discussed in more detail below, but for Neil, it was extremely significant that the play 'begins with Roland alone but when it ends he is with someone'. He made this point in one of his notes after the full run of the play they did on Day 19, and glossed it with the further comment: 'The play is about Roland coming to terms with his demons and beginning to become human.' The character's redemption comes through the return of his mysterious gift but, for Neil, it was important that the way this occurs involves both the relationship with Daniel and the rediscovery and passing on of the precious manuscript. In keeping with Michael's much bleaker view of the human condition, however, he never gave any encouragement to the idea that Roland might find a fulfilling relationship.

Rehearsal is concerned with a plethora of tiny details, each one of which adds a touch of colour or tweaks a moment, but like a single brush stroke in a huge canvas, might seem too insignificant to be described in detail. Like each brush stroke, however, each detail has a vital part to play in the whole. A wrong detail, like a touch of colour in the wrong place, can have a disastrous impact. A little exchange between Neil and Michael that occurred on Day 15 will illustrate this point. The whole cast had been working intensively together with Michael on the sequence of high school memory scenes and, just before the tea break, Michael pondered aloud whether, when Nick recounts his dream of naked women to Roland, he should include Miss Beverly among them, indeed 'should they all be Miss Beverly but not?' His reason was a structual one: Roland produces the vision of Miss Beverly to calm Nick when he begins railing against the hospital, so this earlier mention of her in relation to the dream would explain why she is the figure Roland 'pulls out'. Neil immediately objected to the idea, saying that 'Miss Beverly is not a porn queen'. In his view, she had become 'something holier' with the transformation of Nick Sharp into Nick Eglitis. Michael was perhaps still thinking of the Nick Sharp versions of the scene in which, after Miss Beverly exits, Nick demands to see her in the shower, or naked. Neil's instinct here was unerring and he seemed to be as much author as inter-preter of the work. Miss Beverly is Nick's dream (or Roland's interpreta-tion of Nick's dream) and the way she is presented reveals something about both boys and their relationship to each other, all of which adds poignancy to the fact of Nick's early death. Neil's note to Justine that she be 'both sexy and non-material' (Day 29), his insistence to Paul that the music be rewritten to make it less comic and his careful choreography of the moves of the two boys in relation to the apparition (described in more detail below) all worked to create an aura of romance very dif-ferent from what might have happened had Michael's suggestion been followed. Michael fully endorsed the idea of 'pure love' Neil was at pains to create and, by the end of the rehearsal on Day 15, was able to say quite categorically 'Miss Beverly is not a porno dream' as though he had never toyed with any other possibility.

The area in which the divergence between Neil and Michael appeared to be most acute was *The Play*. In the first draft, this is described in some detail in a long stage direction and Michael clearly intended it to be performed in some way. In later drafts, however, there is no performance of the lost/remembered/imagined play, simply the material presence of the script that Roland flicks through, reading aloud only the final stage direction, 'As the rocket leaves the Earth and the stars come out, the toys in the bedroom play Haydn's *Toy Symphony*.'

I have already shown how *The Play* took shape only in the latter stages of the rehearsal process and how both Michael and to an extent even Neil seemed happy to leave the initiative to the actors and design team in determining the actual content. It was intriguing that, while the performance of the play-within-the-play, whatever form it took, was going to require significant expense and a good deal of ingenuity and while it was to fulfil some important functions in the overall dynamic of the play, its content should remain so fluid. As the dynamic became clearer, so the demands on the as-yet-to-be-created play became correspondingly more complex. Written by Roland as a gift that he hoped would help Nick get better (so does Nick have a role in it, is there a character who represents Nick?), banned and destroyed as punishment for Roland's seduction of Steve Gooding (is the play itself shocking, scandalous, subversive or is the banning simply spite on the part of the Headmaster?), retrieved when Roland is at his lowest ebb and instrumental in rekindling his creativity and human decency (does it provide some evidence of the playwright to come?), *The Play* when it finally materialises has a lot of expectations to meet.

The naïve scenario that formed part of the script the actors were given at the start of the rehearsal process located it clearly within a primary school aesthetic, as did the active involvement of Mrs Walkham in the rediscovery of the script. *The Play* could thus be seen to represent the unfettered imagination and creativity of Roland's childhood, and this fitted perfectly with Neil's vision of the overall dynamic in which it is this reminder of his ability to create that holds him back from the tar pit. Neil told me later that he thought Mrs Walkham's line 'She knew it was precious' was a decisive moment in Roland's realisation that he does have a precious gift and that it should not be thrown away wantonly. For Neil, *The Play* would be a whimsical evocation of the kind of fantasy world the child Roland might have imagined and the fact that he originally referred to it as a masque indicates the genre he had in mind. It would be a pastorale, it was Roland's gift to his dying friend, depicting escape from a cruel world to a better place, and there was no problem if, in its realisation, there was an overt reference to the homespun aesthetic of primary school productions. The logical flaw, as pointed out by the actors after the first reading, is that Roland is no longer at primary school when he meets Nick, and the play as described is hardly something that would find favour with 15 and 16 year olds. Michael, too, when he saw the improvised version that formed part of the first run of the whole play, performed for him on Day 9, objected to the whimsy and sent a radically revised version of the scenario at the beginning of Week 3. What had been the story of a boy escaping in a space rocket became the story of a boy captured by an evil force that comes from outer space and masquerades as Mary Poppins.

When the actors performed this version for Michael in the run they did on Day 15, he was still dissatisfied, wanting it to be much darker, less 'faux naïf', and he advised them curtly to 'kill the skipping'. A reference for the tone he wanted it to achieve was Barrie Kosky's *Es Brent* (the second part of the *Exile* trilogy performed by his Gilgul Company). The impediment to doing this was the necessary dominance in performance of the chirpy and comically repetitive music of *The Toy Symphony*, even though Paul undertook to produce a darker version of the music but, as I wrote at the time, 'this is really a huge problem because it goes to the heart of the difference of emphasis between Neil's world view and Michael's. Neil was happy for the masque to be pastorale, comic, folksy and that was certainly the message of the music.' Something else hangs on the way *The Play* is realised for it is the culmination of all the other mysterious apparitions and thus has an impact on how the idea of theatrical creation is viewed. Neil's frequent resort to the explanation of 'magic realism' when asked about the apparitions, indicates his desire to keep it on a very lighthearted level while Michael was clearly drawn to showing the roots of Roland's (or his own?) creativity coming from a much darker and more murky place, as Dr Maybloom had in fact foreseen many years earlier.

Given the importance of *The Play* in relation to the central theme of artistic creativity and in bringing about a positive resolution for the hero, it was somewhat surprising that the author was prepared to hand over responsibility for the content to director and actors to the extent that he did. In the absence of a fully worked out script from Michael, it might indeed have been more prudent to revert to the option adopted in those earlier drafts in which there is no performance and Roland simply reads aloud the final stage direction. Thinking about the likely impact of that option, however, makes clear just how important a role the performance of the play-within-the-play fulfils in the overall dynamic of the production. It constitutes a joyful celebration of the power of theatre, bringing to a climax all the other scenes of apparitions, rekindling the comic energy of the first act that has spiralled down into despair as Roland lays waste to every relationship and finds himself increasingly alone, and it clears the way for the final moral resolution. The play would indeed have been impoverished without it. It is a measure of the theatricality it celebrates, and of the utterly delightful way in which Neil and his team were able to marshall all the elements of performance in a frenetic two-and-a-half minute extravaganza, that audiences seemed oblivious to the logical inconsistencies involved. Notwithstanding attempts to accommodate Michael's desire for the content to be darker and more satirical, *The Play* as performed belongs fairly and squarely at the heart of Neil's world view.

Playwright and director are not the only authorial forces in the theatre. Observation of the rehearsal process in many productions has shown me that actors, in creating their own characters, necessarily have an impact upon the creation of the characters with whom they interact and can thus be seen to play a significant part in the authoring as well as the realisation of the theatre work. The centrality of the character of Roland in this play, his presence in every scene and the fact that the other characters exist only in relation to him meant that Richard Roxburgh found himself intervening decisively in ways that affected far more than his own character and went to the heart of what the play ended up being about. It was perhaps because none of the other actors had such a massive role, or perhaps because of Richard's undoubted authority and longstanding collaborative relationship with Neil, but I noted that his interpretation and the direction in which he wanted to take the role became more and more compelling in determining the performance outcome. In the last couple of weeks of the rehearsal, it seemed to me that in addition to 'Neil's play' and 'Michael's play', there was also 'Richard's play' and this became even more marked during the run as the production settled into its mature form.

Looking back at the process, Neil was adamant that he recalled no sense in which Richard had resisted exploring Roland's homosexuality. My notes are, however, full of moments when Neil gave hints as to what he saw as the relationship between Roland and Nick or Daniel or even Steve Gooding, always urging greater awareness of the erotic undertow, and these were often either not acted upon or were specifically rejected by Richard. On the second day of the stop/start reading, Neil said he 'would love the sexuality to be more tender, more visceral' and this referred to Roland's relations with Nick and Steve Gooding as well as Daniel. He said 'it's all there but it's not felt or fecund'. I have already quoted his very revealing comment that when Roland looks at Daniel, 'he sees someone who reminds him of someone he was once in love with' (Day 3) but Richard never actively explored the idea that Roland was in love with Nick. For him, Roland and Nick are 'more like mates' and he said categorically that there is 'no sexual relationship between them' (Day 5). There are of course many forms of love, not all of them sexual, but Neil continued to push for some acknowledgement that the attraction between these two boys has an erotic dimension. As he put it, 'there is a dark interesting shadowy area between Nick and Roland' (Day 24). After the Company Run at the end of Week 5, he said he realised they needed to do more work on the moment he had called the sarabande (discussed in the chapter on scene work) and said quite specifically that he wanted Roland to be 'in a deep sad dream of love about Nick' at that moment. It was, however, Richard's view of the relationship that prevailed and Guy followed Richard's lead, as he was bound to do within the dynamic of the performance. When I interviewed Guy during the season, he told me that he saw the relationship between them as brotherly affection and that 'Nick is like a big brother to Roland' (Interview 27 November 2007).

For the two actors, both of them straight, there never seemed to be any doubt about Nick's sexuality, notwithstanding the many hints dropped by Neil concerning the 'shadowy area' he hoped they would explore and this applied even more so to the murky relations between Roland and Steve Gooding, another ostensibly straight character. When Richard queried why Roland has stopped visiting Nick in hospital ('I didn't go to the hospital for two weeks'), Neil suggested that perhaps he 'feels some guilt from the fact that he may be enjoying what he is doing with Steve Gooding' (Day 11) and in a later rehearsal (Day 18), he wondered aloud whether Nick should 'notice' that Roland says he visits Steve Gooding 'in his room' after school (that is to say, does Nick perhaps feel some jealousy at what Roland is doing with Gooding, in spite of the fact that his own sexual fantasies concern Miss Beverly?). Neil also had many suggestions about how the penis showing in the hospital scene should be handled, telling Guy that Nick should laugh at Roland's embarrassment 'because you know he likes it', which was really an indirect note for Richard (Day 10). Richard always resisted playing up that moment, or 'milking it' as he put it, and he actually groaned when Neil referred to it again in his notes on the run from Day 24, suggesting that he could giggle or have some other reponse when Nick says 'It's okay, you can look.' Neil reassured him, saying 'that moment is gold, believe me'. Overall, what Neil wanted to achieve in the three scenes involving Nick was to build up a heart wrenching sense of loss and regret for what had never been and he intervened to micro-manage the performance more decisively in these scenes than elsewhere. My observation at the time was that 'it is Neil who is driving all this, none of the details are initiated by Richard and perhaps Guy is too shy in the circumstances to do much initiating, even though in character terms he is supposed to be two years older than Roland' (Day 27). Neil told me when I interviewed him later, that he would have liked to expand the 'moment of quiet togetherness' between Nick and Roland in the hospital and that he sensed 'in the play a deep longing for that figure to be there', for the 'relationship that never occurred' to be present in some form (Interview 20 November 2007).

The moment Neil was referring to occurs just after the apparition of

Figure 16. Richard Roxburgh, Guy Edmonds: the 'amazing moment'
(dress rehearsal)
Photo: Heidrun Löhr

Miss Beverly has exited and before the Nurse bustles in to send Roland
home and take Nick back to the ward. On Day 9, when they worked on
the version of the scene Michael had sent during the week, Neil said
there was an opportunity for 'something amazing' at that moment.
Michael, who was present, pounced on this slightly apprehensively and
Neil explained that, as this is the first time Roland has conjured someone
contemporary, it must be a 'gobsmackingly wonderful moment for him'
and that there could be some realisation between the two boys of just
how wonderful it is. He suggested that instead of going straight into
the 'what if I never get out of here' speech Michael had placed there,
Nick could perhaps acknowledge that the vision had been produced for
him, saying something like 'you did that for me'. Richard thought that
sounded 'a bit sappy' so they tried 'You did that?' 'Yes'. 'Thank you'.
Neil also wanted some gesture of affection in that moment of quietness,
either for Nick to put his arm around Roland or for the two to stand
quite close and for Nick to lean his head on Roland's. In my notes of that
day's work, written up that evening, there is the following comment: 'I
think Neil had in mind a sort of recognition of love between the boys,
and that is the amazing moment he wanted. In fact Michael's reworked
script does not really do this but the performance does when Nick puts
his head against Roland's and the two are standing very close before

the Nurse comes in' (Day 9). And I followed this with a query: 'So is this moment something from Neil's play or from Michael's?' On Day 11, they worked on the scene again, with Nick putting his arm around Roland as they both watch Miss Beverly's slow exit but Richard objected to the head touching on the grounds that it was too sentimental and Neil accepted that judgement.

Michael's revised script takes up and elaborates Neil's idea of the 'gobsmacking' realisation of what Roland has achieved:

NICK:	Fucking amazing.
ROLAND:	Yeah.
NICK:	You can do real people now.
ROLAND:	Yeah.
NICK:	Living people.
ROLAND:	Yeah.

The exchange is followed by a stage direction '*Silence*', so Michael has left a space for director and actors to decide whether the relationship between the two boys might come to the fore in some way during that silence, as Neil had wanted, or whether the focus remains the excitement of the vision and Roland's increasing mastery over his gift. Michael and Richard seemed to be on the same wavelength here, preferring to emphasise Roland's experience as creator rather than Nick's as receiver of the vision and this is perhaps what caused Neil to think there was a missed opportunity in terms of deepening the relationship.

With Steve Gooding, too, notwithstanding the high farce of the way the scene was played, Neil wanted to explore some very shadowy and troubling areas of the relationship. In his notes on the run they did on Day 19, he said that what was now needed was 'the furtive sense of Roland's adolescent fantasy being fed by Steve Gooding' and he commented that the way the scene was written (substantially, it must be said, as a result of Neil's own input and the improvisations of the cast) might mean that they would have to 'invest' it to some extent to achieve this result. He had commented days earlier on 'the deep ambivalence' he saw at the heart of the scene between Roland and Steve Gooding (Day 9), and in the course of that discussion had mentioned the 'self loathing' that leads some homosexual men to fall in love with heterosexual men, setting themselves up to be rejected, while others are attracted to people they know will beat them up. Richard was not comfortable with this line of argument and Neil acknowledged that 'it is not overtly part of this play but it is present'. Two days later, he returned to the idea, suggesting to Richard that in the Headmaster's disgust at what has been revealed about the seduction of Steve Gooding, 'there is some humiliation for Roland' (Day 11). He said 'self loathing is part of being homosexual' and, he called it 'a dark secret' that he thought should be present in some way. As he put it, 'it would be great to pull that little string'. Richard certainly responded to this suggestion and, while the Headmaster ranted, Roland would sit huddled on his chair in mute misery; the reaction grew in intensity during the run and Roland actually seemed to be reduced to tears on some occasions, which created something very different from the bravado that had characterised Michael Gow's behaviour in the event from his own schooldays on which he claimed to be drawing in this scene, at least as he described it on Day 4.

When they first worked on Scene 16 (Roland's attack on Daniel) in the stop/start reading, what emerged most strongly for Neil was 'the sexuality that underpins things, the unspoken things, the fear' (Day 3) and he often expressed his admiration for Michael's skill 'in cruising sexual tension', which he saw exemplified in this scene in particular. Richard, while acknowledging the sexual energy in the scene, said 'Beyond anything else it is cruel. A kind of cruel provocation' (Day 3) and this was the way he performed it. Neil pointed to numerous moments when he could look at Daniel, notice how good looking he is, give some indication of possible attraction but in Richard's view, this is 'predatory gamesmanship' not seduction (Day 12) and he played the scene with anger and contempt and a kind of desperate self disgust.

There are two moments when Daniel tries to challenge Roland. On the first occasion, the exchange is:

DANIEL: What do you get out of this?
ROLAND: As much as I can.

And on the second it is:

DANIEL: Yeah and you get –
ROLAND: I get something unexpected, unforeseen, something crazy. Something to write about. Something. To write about.

In the rehearsal on Day 12, Neil's advice to Richard was to 'enjoy "As much as I can"', which I took to mean he wanted Roland to show some pleasure in the idea of having sex with Daniel but this was almost entirely lacking in the way Richard was taking the scene. Neil also suggested that the 'something crazy' should be more 'gentle and wonderful rather than scornful'. Neil's input throughout this work session was finding ways for the scene to become more erotically charged and less nasty than Richard was inclined to make it. For Richard, however, Daniel was simply collateral damage in the scene which was overwhelmingly about Roland's despair at his inability to write, and the anger and desperation he loaded on to 'something to write about' became increasingly intense as his performance evolved during the run of the play. Neil acknowledged the validity of this interpretation and, with characteristic grace, told Richard that he had realised his advice about the 'something crazy' was completely wrong (Day 12). When advising Guy to 'receive all the cruelty of the "suck me off" stuff', he added 'it is rather a cruel scene' and Richard came in very strongly, saying categorically 'it is a hideous and brutal scene'. This was quite a revealing indication of the way Neil's perception of the erotic potential of the exchange was leading him to downplay the cruelty that Richard saw as central and wished to accentuate. He commented more than once on the powerful writing in the scene and clearly relished the opportunities it gave him as an actor.

On Day 15, Michael was present and had prepared a revised version of Daniel's long speech which clarified his motives in agreeing to meet Roland (Scene 21). Neil thought that, even though Daniel now says he has agreed to the meeting only because he wants to thank Roland for the insight into being an actor he has derived from their earlier confrontation, there should be evidence of mixed motives on Daniel's part, some acknowledgement that at some level there is a sexual exchange going on. When they ran the new text for the first time, the performance from both of them was beautifully judged, and in my notes I commented in particular on Richard's reactions: 'RR's facial expressions as he listens to Daniel are really stunning. Subtle reactions, a wince, a nod, a quick glance. We really see his disgust at the memory of his own action' (Day 15). What we did not see then or at any time thereafter, was any sense that he was physically attracted to Daniel. They worked in meticulous detail on the timing and gestures involved in handing over the precious play script, creating around the physical object a kind of force field that Neil called 'the zone'. The object became a tangible sign of repentance and reconciliation, and what was at stake in the scene as it evolved was the rekindling of Roland's creativity far more than any possible future relationship between him and Daniel. This focus fitted neatly with the emphasis Richard had given to Roland throughout, his delight in the power of his own imagination at each one of the apparitions, coming to a climax with the imagined performance. 'Richard's play' was substantially about the artist's struggle to create, the murky depths from which inspiration comes, the damage that is done to the artist himself as well as to those who surround him. When we spoke during the play's run, I was not surprised that he did not have much to say when I asked him about playing a gay man as it had not loomed large in his performance. He acknowledged that Roland Henning's homosexuality 'informs who he becomes as an adult' and that 'the pain of his early experiences contributes to his isolation', but this seemed almost incidental compared with the issue that really sparked his interest and that he saw as the central issue of the play, namely 'how do you navigate a life as a creative soul and how can you nurse this creativity without it destroying you or being destroyed' (Interview, 21 December 2007).

The scene that seemed to me to move the play decisively towards Richard's preferred emphasis was Roland's conjuring of Miss Beverly for Nick when he visits him in hospital. From their earliest readings, they noted that this was where Roland moved from classical to suburban inspiration (originally there were two apparitions in the hospital scene, the suburban housewife as well as Miss Beverly), and commented that he 'is getting power over his gift' (Day 3). The idea was thus planted early in the process that the scene is as much about Roland's agency in creating the vision as about feeding Nick's desire for romance. Richard's analysis was that, although Roland produces the vision as a means of distracting Nick from his self-destructive behaviour, he 'is still surprised himself by the manifestation. It opens up a new world for him' (Day 9). When Neil told Richard that Roland should be focusing on Nick's reaction, Richard immediately pointed out that 'producing this vision is a big moment for Roland too' (Day 10). They experimented with a number of different ways of blocking the scene, with different entry and exit points for Miss Beverly, and physical juxtaposition of the three characters. On one occasion when Neil had told Richard and Guy not to move but to let Justine do her circuit around the stage, following her with their eyes, Richard commented immediately that he felt he had become caught in the magnetic field created by the locked gaze of the other two, and he mimed a frantic attempt to free himself by climbing over a rope (Day 10). Removing Roland from this force field made it easier for the scene to be blocked in such a way that Nick gazes intently at Miss Beverly, who returns his gaze, while Roland watches Nick.

This blocking produced what Richard later called 'a wonderful Cyrano moment' when Roland is looking at Nick and Miss Beverly passes behind him so that Nick is looking through him at her. He said 'so Roland receives the love and passion he would have craved but it is actually going to Miss Beverly' (Day 15). I was amazed to hear him say that as it was the first time he acknowledged that there was that sort of dimension to the relationship between Roland and Nick and, as has been shown already, that was not at all what he and Guy ended up producing. I thought the scene was extremely affecting when performed in this

Figure 17. Guy Edmonds, Richard Roxburgh: watching Miss Beverly
(rehearsal Day 9)
Photo: Heidrun Löhr

Figure 18. Guy Edmonds, Richard Roxburgh: watching Miss Beverly
(dress rehearsal)
Photo: Heidrun Löhr

way but the Cyrano moment was lost when they reworked the blocking, having Justine enter from the crash doors and do a half circuit of the stage, exiting down the vom. There seems to have been a gradual shift of emphasis in the way Richard handled the scene, but by the time the production had moved into the theatre, I noted that his invariable practice was to watch Miss Beverly as she moved around the space, hardly glancing at Nick at all. The scene was still a poignant evocation of Nick's romantic yearnings but the power of Richard's stage presence ensured that audiences were also kept aware of Roland's amazement and wonder at his own ability to conjure the apparition. In the subsequent development of the production, this became more marked, and it fed neatly into Richard's preferred understanding of the action. A comment I wrote after seeing the performance on 6 December spells this out: 'I have noticed for some time now that Roland does not look at Nick during the Miss Beverly scene but only at his own wonderful creation. In all the apparitions, his full attention is on the wonder of what he is able to do' (6 December 2007).

As the production developed over the course of the run, the apparitions still functioned within the dramatic narrative of the past as part of Roland's relationships with other people (protection against violence in the case of Alexander the Great and Lynette McKenzie, or as a gift

Figure 19. Guy Edmonds (Alexander the Great), Richard Roxburgh
(dress rehearsal)
Photo: Heidrun Löhr

to Nick in the case of Titus Oates and Miss Beverly, or mischievous self assertion in the case of the Medieval Executioner), but Richard increasingly played all the scenes so that the emphasis was on the mysterious power of Roland's creative genius. This certainly helped to make a more coherent connection between the two acts where the magic realism of Act I slides rather uncomfortably into a darker form of psychological introspection in Act II. Richard's focus made thematic sense of the anarchy of the first act and its re-emergence in the frenetic energy of *The Play* and the appearance of Chekhov, who 'just turns up' as Daniel puts it, the choice of phrase neatly making the connection with Alexander the Great all those years before. It did seem to me at the time, however, that what was happening was more than a shift of emphasis and that it amounted to a major restatement of the play's central theme. 'Richard's play' was much more about the difficulty of being an artist than about the corrosive effects of unresolved trauma or the anguish of growing up gay in the 1970s, and he confirmed this in the comment I have already quoted, namely that the central issue of the play was 'how to navigate life as a creative soul' (Interview 21 December 2007).

A stark contrast with the rehearsal tensions over the extent to which Roland's homosexuality would be manifested in his relations with Nick, Steve Gooding and Daniel was the way his relationship with Nina, his psychotherapist, was teased out and developed. Neil told me that, while in some shows the sexuality of the actor might be an issue, this was absolutely not the case with *Toy Symphony* and that he had not even thought about it when casting the play. I am sure that he and the actors would be adamant that gender relations within the rehearsal room played no part whatever in the creation of the fictional world of the play but it was nevertheless evident that Richard and Justine found it very easy to pick up on little moments when they could hint at a mutual attraction between Roland and Nina, however unlikely or inappropriate this might be.

It was already apparent in the earliest readings and was accentuated when they retrieved an earlier draft of the scene in which Roland tells Nina he is going to give up the therapy. They were all struck by the way the relationship with Nina was 'beautifully realised' in the scene and Neil commented that he had 'picked up from the way they read it the sense that she has enjoyed the challenge of Roland's therapy and is perhaps a little in love with him' (Day 2). These early readings contained hints of the performance to come, constituted by little pauses, glances and bodily orientation to each other, so Neil's point about 'the way they read it' is highly pertinent. There was something beyond the actual words that was created in the interaction between the two.

That afternoon, they began the process of the stop/start reading, and returned to the beginning of the play. Perhaps under the influence of what had been discovered in the abandoned scene, they now started to see the seeds of this warmer relationship in the first therapy session. Richard said that Nina calls Roland's bluff and by the end of the scene he has to admit that she has won, and Neil again picked up that 'she is beginning to be attracted to him' (Day 2). He reported the next day on his phone call to Michael, who had expressed interest in the idea that Nina could be attracted to Roland (Day 3). This, it seemed, was not something he had been aware of when writing the play but he was happy for them to explore the possibility. By the end of the first week, when Michael spent a day with the actors, the issue was no longer even in question. When Russell asked Michael if Nina is going to fall in love with Roland, it was Justine who jumped in with an answer, 'On some level, yes' (Day 4). The speed and certainty of this response were somewhat surprising, especially given the fact that the character simply disappears at the end of Act I, having fulfilled her functional role of permitting Roland to relive some childhood experiences. Actors are adept at finding some individuality in even the most purely functional roles and Neil, too, displayed great comic ingenuity in assisting this process. In this case, however, it was not simply Justine exploring a slightly underwritten character but for Richard, too, there was the discovery that the attraction between Nina and Roland seemed to be mutual, notwithstanding the fact that Roland is gay. On Day 16, when they worked on the scene where she gets him to talk about the damage done by the obligation to analyse his own process, they were sitting side by side on the floor for her speech about the creative act being like sleepwalking. Neil said it looked cramped but both actors said they liked the physical proximity and Richard added 'there is a kind of tenderness between them'. In my notes on the session, I said 'Neil encourages the warmth between the two characters that seems to come so easily to them both' (Day 16).

Much later in the process, when they had decided that the two scenes (10 and 15 in my numbering) between Nina and Roland are in fact a single therapy session separated by the whole high school memory section, Michael sent some new text for the beginning of Scene 10.

NINA: How was the week?
ROLAND: The week was very . . . interesting.
NINA: Unbelievable, yes. I nearly called you. I didn't of course, but . . .
            [Pause] So. Do you want to talk about what happened?

The exchange sets up the premise that the two scenes represent a single session, in which he will first talk about Nick and his high school memories, and then the bushfires and his decision to terminate the therapy. Richard pointed out that Nina's admission 'is a little bit of a tease for the audience. It makes it seem that something has been going on' (Day 27), perhaps that in her involvement with this client she is overstepping the bounds of professional care. That idea had already been floated during their work on the very emotional scene when Roland acknowledges scorching his brain in the attempt to defend himself against the plagiarism charge. The exchange was:

ROLAND   So, she's shut me up after all. Maybe for good.
NINA: I don't believe that.
ROLAND: You haven't asked me if I feel guilty.

For Neil, Nina's unguarded retort was a giveaway, a personal opinion she should not have disclosed, and the fact that she momentarily loses control of the session and it is Roland who moves things on to the next topic, supports this insight. In performance Roland would give her a quick glance, indicating he had noticed her slip.

From details such as these, actors find the undercurrents that enable them to create complex emotional situations and, in the case of the relationship between Nina and Roland, the work was greatly helped by the real warmth that characterised the relationship in the rehearsal room between Richard and Justine. She told me that she had first worked with Richard when she was only 16 and he still called her Clarky, the nickname he had given her back then. The ease with which the actors found the potential for something deeper and warmer in the relationship between patient and therapist was perhaps a factor in Neil pushing it as far as he did. I have already described my reservations about Nina's tears and the box of tissues and it still seems to me that this was an error of judgement that compounded the problems that Justine was having with the scene in which her emotion was more that of a jilted lover than the anxiety of a cool professional foreseeing the shipwreck ahead for her client.

***

The Company B production of *Toy Symphony* bore the unmistakeable imprint of Neil Armfield's direction and yet, as I have argued in this chapter, Richard Roxburgh, too, had a profound influence on the outcome. I have said that Neil's input was quasi-authorial and, in a similar vein, I think it can be said that Richard's was quasi-directorial. In a play structured around such a hugely dominant central character, it was perhaps inevitable that the actor playing that role would have a decisive impact on all the other actors as their characters have no existence outside their relationship to his. In Neil's production, even Mrs Walkham's slide show is experienced through Roland's response to it. Neil refined and shaped the material to find the comedy where others might have produced something much darker, more raw and angry, notably in the heavy reliance on actual people and events taken from the author's own life. In his turn, Richard was selective in his response to Neil's direction, focusing on what he saw as the central theme, namely the pain and deep joy of being a creative artist, and leaving somewhat understated any exploration of the character's homosexuality.

In my second interview with Neil, we spoke about the huge difference between the finished work and the starting point but he nevertheless demurred when I asked if his role really amounted to that of co-author. While admitting how much work had been done in rehearsal to clarify the narrative line, the emotional and dramatic logic and to establish the moral point, he insisted that 'the structure they found was there all the time' but that there had to be 'a stripping away of the extraneous in order to find it' (Interview 20 November 2007). He referred to Michelangelo's famous comment about the sculpture being present in the block of stone and his task being to chip away everything that is not the statue. The analogy is not precise because Michael Gow's role was far more than supplying the raw material, and indeed he was also a vital player in the process of stripping away the extraneous, but it points to the collaborative nature of the process involved in theatrical production more generally. Just as the sculptor needs the block of stone and the block of stone will remain just that without the eye and skill of the sculptor, so the artists involved in theatrical production are dependent on each other. None of the artists involved can exercise their art independently of the others, each makes a decisive contribution that nevertheless demands the contribution of all the others in order for it to have the impact it does.

In the case of *Toy Symphony*, the collaboration went even deeper in that the play was being written through the process of bringing it to the stage. While I have spoken of 'Neil's play', 'Michael's play' and 'Richard's play', what I have really shown is the complexity of creative agency in action. The three artists most responsible for the outcome contributed their different skills and insights to explore the tangle of possibilities represented by Michael's 'crazy, colourful fur-ball' of a script, as Richard described it when talking to subscribers (19 December 2007). The openness of the rehearsal process, Neil's particular gift to his fellow artists, meant that differences of emphasis and interpretation were not suppressed but permitted to remain in a creative tension with each other, providing 'mutual enrichment' as Neil put it (Interview 20 November 2007), and rendering the resulting work more complex.

The director's process

Theatre is a collective dream: it can and should be. (Neil Armfield, 2009)

The previous chapter ends with a reference to the nature of the rehearsal process being Neil's particular gift to his fellow artists and this chapter is an attempt to explore some of the complexities of the role of director in a genuinely collaborative creative process. 'So you're going to tell us how Neil does it' was the response of one journalist in the euphoria of the party after the final performance of *Toy Symphony* when someone told him that I was writing a book about the rehearsal process. For this highly experienced theatre goer, the production he had just seen bore the unmistakable hallmark of Neil Armfield's directorial magic, and he had no doubt that the quality of Michael Gow's writing and even the remarkable *tour de force* of Richard Roxburgh's acting in the demanding central role were somehow secondary to whatever it was that Neil had 'done'. Many people use the word 'magic' in relation to Neil's productions and, indeed, I find that I have used it myself on more than one occasion in my fieldnotes as I attempted to describe the transformation that his interventions had brought about in an actor's performance of a particular speech or exchange. While evidence about Neil's characteristic directorial approach is scattered throughout this book, this chapter draws some of the threads together in order to focus more particularly on the work process that leads to the 'magical' results so admired by spectators and critics, and on the artistry involved in stimulating the creativity of others at the same time as shaping a coherent work of art from the flood of possibilities produced by the group.

Re-reading the entire corpus of my fieldnotes, from the first day of rehearsals to the last night of the season, with their countless references to what Neil said and what Neil did, and attempting to extrapolate from all these details an outline of his working method, I think it is possible to speak of two sets of interrelated factors, one set that refers more to the production itself and the other to the nature of his relationship with his collaborators, in particular the actors. In the first set, there is his hands-on approach to the text, his comic inventiveness in relation to both stage business and the text, the sensitivity and spirit of fun which he brought to the support characters, endowing with hints of narrative depth and emotional interest what might in lesser hands have been rather cartoon-ish sketches, his almost embodied knowledge of the Belvoir stage and the relationship between fictional space and audience reality it makes possible, and his phenomenal attention to detail. Then there is the other set of factors, the way he relates to the actors, designers and production team, his sensibility in relation to, and ability to juggle, the very different needs of the five actors with whom he was working on this production, his ability to deepen and enrich their performances so that they each felt they were going further in their art, and the atmosphere of shared purpose and creative energy that predominated in the rehearsal room and in the theatre. It is not easy to say precisely how this atmosphere is created but there is no doubt that it is a direct result of Neil's leadership and management style nor that it plays a crucial part in creating a sense of commitment to the work they are all involved in bringing into being and a willingness on each participant's part to go the extra mile. Eamon Flack thinks that, for actors, 'it's the spirit of Neil's engagement with them that is as important, or perhaps even more important than the detail of the production' (Interview 18 May 2010). This is a valuable insight and it suggests that features of the life of the rehearsal room that may not seem to be directly relevant to the making of the work are in fact central both to the making of that work and to something larger of which that particular work is only a part (this point will be further elaborated in the final chapter).

The director's task

The creative process for the director on a particular production has a characteristic shape made up of four very different phases. There is the period of great creativity constituted by the rehearsals, followed by the shorter but even more intense practical phase involved in transferring the work to the theatre, fine-tuning the technical requirements for sound and lighting and making adjustments in response to the reality of set, costumes, props and preview audiences. Upstream of this intensive work, however, there is a much longer period of more intermittent reflection, pondering the nature of the production to come, applying for funding and making decisions about casting and design that will have a determining impact on the later work. Then there is a final phase that occurs when the production is up and running although this is greatly truncated or even nonexistent for some directors as they might by then be deeply involved in work on another production, possibly in another city or even in another country.

Participant-observation is, by its nature, ill equipped to deal with the first phase of the director's work process, which might extend over many months, even years, and consist of intermittent bursts of activity. I had no access to this phase of Neil's work in relation to *Toy Symphony* but have pieced together some of its elements based on things that were mentioned during the rehearsals and in interviews. Neil told me that his involvement with the play began when his agent sent him a copy of the script one day early in 2006. He told me that he was not sure 'what it all added up to' at that stage but was struck by the 'dazzling confidence in the writing'. In the intervening months the play 'sat' with him, he thought about casting, read the whole thing aloud with Richard Roxburgh and discussed the possible look of it with Ralph Myers. Perhaps more important were the events in his own life that led him to a greater sensitivity to the dark undercurrents in the play. The death of his mother at the end of 2006 constituted a rupture at the heart of the family life that is so important to him and certainly led to a renewed appreciation of Michael's transposition into the fiction of his own experience of losing both his parents within six weeks of each other. Before rehearsals began, he told me that the tar pit image resonated very strongly for him and that he had become more and more fascinated by Michael's idea of the chasm that is present under the surface of a person's life.

The decisions he made about casting and the choice of collaborators for the all important design functions indicate something about the way his ideas about the play were beginning to take shape. The fact that he was determined to get Russell Dykstra for the multiple male support roles indicates an awareness of the comic potential of those scenes, notwithstanding his sensitivity to the darkness in the play and, even though Monica Maughan was apparently not his first choice for the role of Mrs Walkham, it was an inspired bit of casting. Roland's strongest memory of his primary school teacher was her voice, and the strength and warmth of Monica's beautiful voice allowed every spectator somehow to share that 'memory'. Richard's availability and willingness to take on the enormous central role were probably critical in Neil's decision to programme the play in the 2007 season, and certainly Richard's involvement came prior to all the others. It was not known at this time that *Holding the Man* would be transferring to Belvoir and would be the production immediately preceding *Toy Symphony*,[1] but it is likely that the production was a factor in Neil's choice of Guy Edmonds to play the two roles of Nick and Daniel, and it is even possible that it points towards the way Neil envisaged the function of those two roles. Guy's sensitive portrayal of Tim Conigrave, both in the ebullience of his love for John Caleo and in its tragic aftermath, seemed to me an indication of Neil's perception that that dimension could potentially develop in the relations between Roland and one or other (or both) of the two characters. Neil's decision to have only one actress, rather than the two suggested by Michael, to take the roles of Nina and the nurses and other young women who form part of Roland's teenage memories was motivated by his desire to make 'a good night's work' for the actress in question. His choice of Justine Clarke may have been affected in part by his desire to bring her into the Belvoir 'family', which was a point he emphasised when introducing her on the first day of rehearsals. He said then that it was quite surprising that she had not to date appeared in a Company B production. These two points indicate concerns that are not limited to what the actor can bring to the production but also what the production can do for the actor and suggest something more about why Neil is so greatly loved and respected by his actors.

Central to the work Neil was doing in the preliminary phase were of course his many discussions with Michael Gow about the script and about changes he felt needed to be made. He discussed the script on numerous occasions with Eamon, his literary manager, in order to clarify his own thinking and then took these ideas to Michael. As indicated already, this process had led to at least four draft versions of the script before rehearsals began. Equally important were the discussions with the designers, from which more can be deduced about the direction of Neil's thoughts as they were taking shape. The comic potential is very clearly evident in Tess's costume designs for the memory characters, while the darkness at the heart of Roland's creativity is most evident in Ralph's set and in their joint decision to rely on Damien Cooper's characteristically dramatic shafts of light, haze and moody shadows rather than 'placing' the action in any literal way. Paul Charlier's first task as composer and sound designer was to research the background to *The Toy Symphony*, thought by them all at that stage to be the work of Haydn, but Neil and Paul had clearly discussed the potential impact of the light-hearted children's music accompanying some very dark memories.

At Company B, the rehearsal phase of the production process lasts five weeks and, as Neil recalled one day, it was only after he took over as artistic director that the company began to allocate five weeks for work in the rehearsal room, followed by one week in the theatre. He reminded Richard that they had rehearsed *Hamlet* (in 1994) in four weeks as that was the company practice at the time, although the two of them had had a week alone together prior to the rehearsals proper in which they worked intensively on the play. The word that comes most insistently to mind as I look back at the *Toy Symphony* rehearsals is openness, and by this I mean both the kind of egalitarian inclusiveness that embraced everyone involved in the project but, more importantly, an openmindedness about the work in progress. The word should not be taken to mean that the work was unstructured (on the contrary, there was the security of a routine and a timeframe), but that what was going on was an exploration, a process of discovery, not simply 'getting up' yet another production. When the rehearsals began, no one knew quite what was going to emerge at the other end, not Neil, not the actors, and certainly not Michael who was making discoveries about his play throughout the process. Neil's inclusiveness meant that everyone was involved in the exhilaration of this search even though it was sometimes not clear where it was leading. One day towards the end of Week 4, when major changes were being made, some of which seemed to make things even more confusing, I mentioned to Justine that I was still very unclear about what the play was really doing and where it was going. I was surprised by the energetic way she concurred, saying 'we are too', referring I assumed to the group of actors (Russell, Monica and herself) who regularly ate lunch together in the kitchen. While they had obviously discussed some of their perplexities, her comment did not convey any anxiety, rather a cheerful confidence that Neil, Michael and Richard would find their way through the tangle of possibilities.

Part of Neil's practice of keeping his options open, of not getting bogged down in a fixed form and settled interpretation until the last possible minute is his reluctance to do runs until late in the process, as has already been mentioned. The practice is very revealing of his sense that the work is an organic phenomenon, that it continues to grow and evolve throughout the rehearsal process and beyond and can take surprising turns. While this can cause difficulties for the designers, who may be required to make considerable changes late in the piece, and it probably adds to the actors' stress levels, it is fundamental to his creative practice. Given that Michael's play was still incomplete when rehearsals began, Neil was the ideal director for it because his exploratory process was precisely what was needed to assist the work to find its final form. In this, he was greatly aided by the fact that he understood at a very deep level what Michael's play was about, and because he had the experience and authority to intervene quite decisively.

The final phase of the director's process occurs during the run of the production and, as already indicated, there are many directors who regard their work as finished once the play has opened. This is not the case with Neil, however, and his involvement continues throughout the run as he attends performances from time to time and continues to give notes to actors and crew, not just pointing to things that need tweaking to maintain their effectiveness but also finding new things, new dimensions to explore. When I went to the dressing room on 28 November, two weeks into the run, there were several pages of handwritten notes pinned to the wall, Neil's observations on the performance he had seen the day before. Richard expressed some exasperation at the quantity of notes and at the sense that Neil was still changing things, and a few days later he told members of the schools' audience that any production by Neil 'is like a painting that is never finished' (a phrase that met with Neil's entire approbation). He was perhaps remembering his experience in Neil's production of *Hamlet* in 1994, when he told a journalist a week before the play opened that Neil's habit of changing things right up to and, indeed, after opening night was in fact a help to him in the enormous task he had in each performance: 'it makes you feel . . . that it's an ever-changing thing that's not an absolute, so there's no sense of this great immutable mountain that you have to scale every night' (Morgan 2007, 14).

Kylie would pin the most recent set of notes on top of the earlier sets and Neil had asked that they be given to me at the end of the production's run but when I got them they were all muddled up and, as they are not dated, it is not possible to say exactly which performances prompted them. There are typically about ten to twelve pages of notes per performance, with about eight to nine items per page, which constitutes a great deal of detail and explains why for Richard, with the enormous role that he had, there was too much detail to take on board immediately although he told me that he did attempt over the next few performances to respond to them all. Guy's practice was to copy down the notes that referred to him and work through them systematically before the next performance.

The following examples illustrate the way Neil was still adding things and intervening to deepen the performances. A note for Monica some time during the first two weeks of the run said: 'Maybe darker, almost a chuckle, wiser on "but oh, so unlike."' The moment referred to is the scene when Mrs Walkham reads D.H. Lawrence's description of Como to Roland as the latter seeks oblivion in drugs: 'a bit like Lake Como, but oh, so unlike'. Because Monica was such a consummate actress, she used this note beautifully and I have a vivid memory still of the way she would hold the 'oh' slightly, of the rhythm this gave the line and the affection and ironic inflection in her voice on 'so unlike' that opened up a whole reverie about colonial place naming, like and unlike, Lake Como and Como New South Wales, the exotic and the suburban.

A note to Justine led to the creation of a delightful bit of comic business that I was surprised to discover had not been part of the scene much earlier. The note reads, 'Juz: maybe repeat the title block gesture as you say the title of the poem.' This referred to Justine as Julie Pearson in the poetry lesson, selected by Mrs Walkham to recite for the Headmaster. The scene begins with a burst of energy as Justine transforms herself from Nina, the cool professional psychotherapist, into a 10 year old child, turning a neck scarf into an Alice band and fishing out little round spectacles from her skirt pocket as she runs upstage to join the class.

MRS WALKHAM: You begin, Julie Pearson.
JULIE PEARSON: Oh to be in –
MRS WALKHAM: Uh!
JULIE PEARSON: 'Home Thoughts from Abroad' by Robert Browning.
                 Oh to be in England now that April's there . . .

Julie begins her recitation in a high pitched gabble but Mrs Walkham, stopping her immediately, gestures to mime the presence of the title on the printed page, thus reminding her to state the title and poet's name. Neil's suggestion that Justine should echo the gesture is an example of his impeccable comic sense and it enhanced the comedy of the moment and was a real winner with audiences who were immediately captivated by Julie Pearson, an eager little girl doing her best, trying to remember what she had practised but overwhelmed by the responsibility of reciting for the Headmaster. In Geordie Brookman's production of the play, Julie Pearson croaked the lines in a petrified way which threw the emphasis to the cane held ominously in the Headmaster's hands, a perfectly valid interpretation but one which removed the sense of warmth in the relationship between Mrs Walkham and her class that was such a feature of Neil's production and of course created a very different kind of memory of primary school.

Although Neil went away for two weeks during the run of the play, the kind of hands-on involvement he had during the weeks he was in Sydney meant that for the actors there was no sense that they were just repeating what had been rehearsed weeks before. The actors themselves introduced comic business and the production evolved throughout the run as some of its potentialities were realised more fully and others were let go. I have never seen a production as frequently as this one and, although I did note that energy levels varied (this was especially noticeable on one Sunday matinee), I did not get the impression that the performances ever settled into a totally familiar or routine form. The importance of Neil's ongoing presence was, however, perhaps less in its effect of keeping the actors on their toes and more in what it revealed about 'the spirit of his engagement' with them, to use Eamon's phrase.

The Swedish director, Vilgot Sjomon, once said in an interview that the reason he preferred making films to directing plays was that he found it painful to have to withdraw from the work on opening night and hand it over to the actors:

> What I find painful in the theatre is the process of leaving – I mean the director gradually pulling back, slowly giving over more and more to the actors, until on opening night you're cut free. I can hardly stand this. I understand the actors love it. (Sjomon 1966, 102–5)

It is evident that Neil does not ever withdraw, but remains deeply involved, attending performances from time to time, continuing to give notes and keen to find the opportunity to develop certain aspects further. This may be particularly so in the case of his productions for Company B where, given his role as artistic director, he has responsibility for the whole season of which the given production is a part but, as he explained to me when I asked about this aspect of the process, he regards his work as a gift to the actors and he loves seeing what they achieve with it. There is a profound generosity here and it is fundamental to Neil's process and the relationship he has with his actors.

Working with the actors

For the first week to ten days of work on this production, Neil's attention was substantially devoted to the text, clarifying the storyline and the dramatic structure, making changes in response to what the actors were showing him, responding to the changes Michael was making. During the next two to three weeks, although textual changes were still being made, many as a result of Neil's suggestions, his energies were more focused on the actors' performances, with their discoveries about the characters and relationships they were bringing into being, and with creating a spatial form for the work. In the last two weeks, especially once they began doing runs of the whole play, his concern was the production as a whole, bringing together all the semiotic systems that would contribute to the overall experience, finding and shaping the bigger patterns. It was during the middle phase of the work that his skill in working with actors was demonstrated over and over again, not least in the seemingly effortless way he met the very different needs of the five actors in this production.

From Monica, who had been a professional actress for fifty years, to Guy, who was in his 20s and not long out of drama school, from Richard with his classic NIDA training to Russell with his comic skills honed at the Lecoq School in Paris, the differences in background, experience and approach were considerable. This meant that the five actors needed and wanted very different kinds of guidance and stimulation from the director and that their working methods and practices were different. The differences did not reside simply in questions such as the stage in the process at which the actor wanted to get his or her lines 'down' that has already been mentioned, but also in more fundamental matters such as whether they preferred to approach their character from the outside, as it were, creating an embodiment that revealed the persona, or whether the persona came into being first, acquiring voice and embodiment along the way. These differences impact on the type of directorial intervention that is of most assistance to the actor.

Neil's preference is clearly to intervene a great deal in the actors' performances, providing detailed advice on everything from moves, use of objects and gesture to intonation and thought processes, but he also knew when to let well alone. He hardly intervened at all in Monica's delivery of Mrs Walkham's slide show, apart from organising the place of entrance, exit and the business involved in plugging in and unplugging the projector. On the first occasion she did the scene (Day 2), he let her go through the whole thing without stopping her once. She asked whether it was 'too posh' or 'too condescending' and he just smiled and said 'it's sitting in a really nice place' then went on to talk about his own much loved kindergarten teacher, Miss Bootle, and how much he would have liked a similar lesson about Concord when he was at primary school there. The point of the anecdote was not a digression but a way of deepening everyone's understanding of the

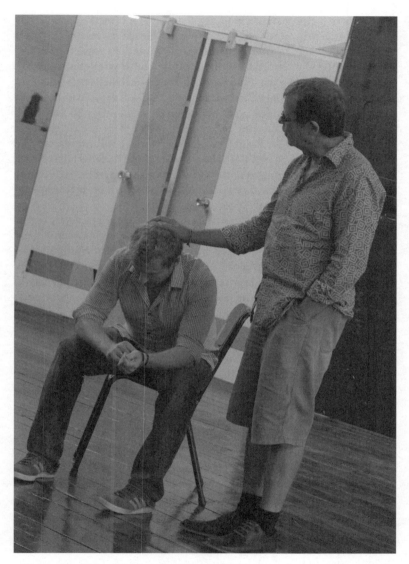

Figure 20. Richard Roxburgh, Neil Armfield (rehearsal room, Company B)
Photo: Heidrun Löhr

function of the scene. Similarly, when Richard and Justine first began to work on the opening scene, he observed 'there is a high level of comedy in this scene and the problem will be to keep it fresh so I'll try not to interfere too much'. Another feature of his directorial interaction with his actors is his preparedness to say that a given direction was wrong and to change his mind in relation to what he sees developing. This is an important element in the openness, the sense that what they are all engaged in together is a process of discovery. The actors are not puppets being manipulated by the all-knowing director to achieve a pre-planned outcome. He rarely congratulated them and it was very late in the piece before I heard him say that a run was good (it was on Day 20 at the end of a long session devoted to yet another iteration of the drug dealer scene, and at the end Neil said 'that was very very good' and I noted that that was the first time I had heard him say anything like that). Normally, the closest thing to congratulation was a phrase like 'that has got to a very sweet place', which, while encouraging the actors, nevertheless suggested there was still a way to go.

His sensitivity to the different needs of his actors is perfectly exemplified in the various sessions devoted to the two scenes between Roland and Daniel. Here he was working with Richard, the star of the show, a highly skilled actor with whom he has worked on many occasions, and Guy, a young actor at the beginning of his professional career, eager to learn and doubtless somewhat awed by the task involved in working so closely with artists of the calibre of both Neil and Richard. As indicated, Neil clearly likes to intervene a great deal, but while Guy was keen to co-operate, Richard dislikes what he sees as micro-management, preferring to find his own way to the desired outcome.

I have already mentioned the difference of opinion between Richard and Neil concerning Roland's attitude to Daniel in the scene after the lecture. Once Neil accepted Richard's interpretation that Roland knew perfectly well that Daniel was not offering sex and that he was playing the scene as 'predatory gamesmanship' (Day 12), he restricted his subsequent suggestions to Richard to practical matters of blocking, sharpening and enhancing the interpretation that had come from Richard, no longer trying to change it. He knew when he could trust Richard to find a solution by himself as had been demonstrated on many occasions earlier in the process. For example, on Day 11 when they were working on the last scene in Act I, Neil said 'Can we get that better?' in reference to the line 'And I felt nothing' that Richard had always seen as a crucial turning point in his character's journey. Richard's response was simply, 'It will be' and Neil nodded and said no more. In working on the Daniel scenes, Richard commented one day that a given line had been 'over-noted' but that he would think about it; Neil took the point, saying reassuringly 'that'll fix it up then' and moved on to something else. The kind of notes that fed Richard's creative process were those that gave him an acting challenge, and Neil certainly provided a good deal of this in these scenes. For instance, when Daniel cuts Roland's apology short and tells him to 'shut up and listen', all the latter has to respond with is the single word 'Yes.' Neil's note after the run on Day 22 was 'Just gather as much dignity as you can on "Yes,"' and Richard commented how much he preferred a note like that to one telling him what to do with his hands. Another similar kind of note was on 'It's just this thing I wrote', when he is persuading Daniel to accept the gift of the *Toy Symphony* script. Neil said 'Put some darkness on "this thing."' The point is to devalue the script slightly but with the sense of mocking yourself as a writer.' It was not just Richard who received notes of this sort. After the dress rehearsal, one of the notes for Guy referred to the moment in the scene when Daniel is importuning Roland and the latter turns on him and asks 'Why did you follow me?' The note was 'just allow the atmosphere to prickle a little. Feel the ground move under you,' a great note for a good actor to work with.

While Guy is a skilled and sensitive actor, he is much less experienced than Richard and really benefitted from the kind of detailed input Neil gave him, sharpening and deepening his portrayal of Daniel, pulling him back from over-emotionalising certain moments (after one of his rather high flown explanations for Daniel's state of mind, Neil simply said 'whew', which was all that was needed for Guy to take a much more grounded approach to that moment). Beside the warnings about 'weighting' or 'squeezing' a moment, there was also advice that helped Guy in his realisation of some beautifully judged emotion. After one run, Neil said 'I'm not getting "reeling"' (the word Daniel uses to describe the effect Roland's cruelty had on him). I had not really noticed what Guy had done the first time, but the next time they ran it, the moment was transformed, the whole back story seemed to be there in that word, constituting a kind of reproach that would have been utterly mortifying for Roland. In my notes I wrote 'when the actors are so good, Neil doesn't have to more than hint that something is getting swallowed up or glossed over, and they produce something stunning'.

Most fascinating to watch was the way Neil assisted Guy to explore the differences between Daniel and the character of Tim Conigrave he was still performing every night. Neil talked of 'getting rid of Tim', pointing out that Daniel is a much more solemn character (on another day he said 'Daniel is a serious, dark young man'). He pointed to Guy's rather 'flip' way of saying a certain line as 'part of what I call the Tim thing', and suggested that Daniel's line 'If I was honest, I suppose . . . now I'm here . . . advice? No. Insight. Maybe I'd like some insight, into it all, theatre, acting?' should be done seriously, avoiding the hint of coyness that was coming into 'insight' (perhaps as a response to Michael's question

Figure 21. Guy Edmonds, Neil Armfield (rehearsal room, Company B)
Photo: Heidrun Löhr

marks), and the rather detached way he was saying 'I suppose.' Subtle details such as these assisted Guy in creating the sense of a young man who is serious in the pursuit of his chosen profession and in his admiration for the great writer (which of course makes his dismay all the more acute when Roland turns the tables with a crude sexual demand). On a line in the final scene, Neil said 'this went a bit Tim. There was a kind of cute quality. There is a tendency in Tim to sweetly understate but Daniel doesn't do this.' It was only possible for Neil to assist Guy to disentangle these two characters because he had watched many performances of *Holding the Man* with such attention and because he engaged imaginatively with both characters. Neil's coaching of this gifted young actor in going deeper into finding the differences rather than getting trapped in repeating the same character sharpened Guy's performance of them both, to the extent that David Berthold, the director of *Holding the Man,* had commented on the development of his portrayal of Tim Conigrave over the period of the *Toy Symphony* rehearsals. Guy told me later that the experience of working on *Toy Symphony* under Neil's direction had been part rehearsal and part master class and that what he had learned 'now informs the way I read'.

The kind of vocabulary that Neil used in his notes and comments to the actors is highly revealing. He would say things like 'explore' that word, 'travel with that', 'go further with that', 'you're wasting that';

typical interventions required the actor to 'use', 'value', 'weight', or 'hit', a given word or phrase. In this way, although the moment or word was indicated with absolute precision, the initiative remained with the actor to find a way of responding, to see where the process of exploring, valuing or using the word took them. And the actors did respond with great sensitivity and skill. One of the great delights for me as I watched the repeated runs of fragments of scenes, was the transformation that Neil's hints brought about, as will be illustrated by the following examples, drawn from different phases of the rehearsal process.

In one of the earliest work sessions on the opening scene (Day 5), Neil made quite explicit suggestions to Justine, encouraging her to lay weight on words like 'destructive', 'fear', 'pressure' and the phrase 'for whatever reason' in her line 'For some reason, you currently believe, for whatever reason, you *believe* you can't write.' By teasing out the force and emotional colour of these words, he was giving Justine some clues as to delivery but then he said 'Maybe this is a note for Richard' by which he meant that these words could be starting something for Roland, could 'start shaking things loose a bit'. This exchange between Nina and Roland is the very beginning of the play and by that time in the rehearsal process, I had heard the actors read the scene a number of times, but with Neil's intervention it started to break open, his suggestions indicating something of what would be lost if the actors skated too glibly over the surface, seeing the words merely as psychologist's jargon. Another note involving a character's response carried even more serious implications. In the scene with the lawyer, where Roland makes the important admission that he had indeed stolen the woman's idea, Neil said 'I want to feel a kick from the lawyer when Roland says "but I did"' (Day 16). Russell had the tendency to rush in with his response 'We know now that you did not,' but Neil's advice was extremely important in order for the audience to realise how important the admission is, and what a quandary it creates for the lawyer.

Some interventions were purely physical, such, as asking Guy in the hospital scene exactly where on Nick's spine the needle was pushed in (Day 10). Guy put his finger on the lower part of his spine and Neil said 'Just feel something of that.' The next time they ran the scene, Guy's body tensed slightly as he said 'It fucking hurts' and it lifted the moment to a new level. It was done very subtly by Guy and is an excellent example of the way Neil adds little touch to little touch, colouring the moment, creating something that is layered and complex.

In the scene between Roland and Tom, the drug dealer, there is a turning point in the relations between the two when Tom receives a brief phone call from his son, Josh. Before the call, he has been refusing to supply Roland with any more drugs but as soon as he realises his ex-wife and son are on their way, he wants to get rid of Roland as soon as possible, which gives Roland the upper hand to extract the drugs he wants. After the last run in the rehearsal room (Day 27), Neil commented that 'we had lost the change of temperature on Josh', that is to say that the cause of the shift in power relations between the two men was not being made clear. He suggested that rather than replacing the mobile phone in his pocket after receiving the call, Russell should continue to hold it. He said 'Keep Josh in your hand – that will help.' The note was typical of the way Neil thinks and of what he makes possible for the actors and for attentive spectators.

Working with Neil means this kind of watchful attention to the implications of every word, every intonation, every gesture. On stage everything conveys meaning, there is no such thing as an innocent gesture and this is particularly the case when actors are handling props or elements of the set. The production used very few props, but Neil was alert to every nuance of meaning that was being conveyed, as Guy discovered when they were working on the hospital scenes on Day 10. The blocking they were developing had Nick exiting behind the nurse, wheeling his intravenous drip and turning to urge Roland to stand up to Steve Gooding:

NICK: Fight him. Do something to him. Promise.
ROLAND: I promise.

He had been pushing the drip stand with his right hand, but when he turned back to Roland, it was blocking his way. Guy's solution was a deft manoeuvre slightly earlier whereby he changed hands just before the turn but Neil pounced on this immediately, exclaiming 'by what law of logic or motivation did that happen?' The pragmatic solution was unacceptable; where every move, gesture and word is meaningful, and the way they are mapped together creates yet more meaning, then it all has to be precisely calculated. In the end, their solution was for the nurse to wheel the drip stand because Nick has in any case disconnected the cannula from his hand and pushed the stand away when he has his outburst about wanting to get out of hospital.

Another example of this kind of detailed mapping of word and gesture, also involving Guy, occurred on Day 14 when they were working on the first scene between Daniel and Roland. Daniel wears glasses, part of the image of him as a serious student, and Guy was exploring a number of gestures, such as pushing the glasses further up the bridge of his nose, taking them off and so on. The moment in the scene was Roland's three offers to persuade Daniel to take a plunge and go with him, the two characters were confronting each other across the space and Guy must have taken his glasses off at some stage during the aggressive speech that is directed at Daniel. I had not noticed this as my attention was on the extraordinary performance Richard was giving but Neil misses nothing. He told Guy to keep the glasses on, saying 'If you take them off it makes it seem you might be shifting ground, beginning to give in to him.' This observation was typical of the detailed semiotics involved in their process and of Neil's sharpness in interpretation.

Neil is well known among actors for making apparently outlandish, odd or quirky suggestions for actions or gestures and the extraordinary thing is that they are extremely effective even though it is not always easy to say why. An example of this is Russell's look off as Dr Maybloom warns Roland of the serious consequences of having morbid fantasies. Roland is sitting in 'his' chair, Maybloom is standing next to him as he says 'we do have to grow out of them because if we don't, they can cause all sorts of problems when we grow up. Social problems, mental problems, what we call marital problems.' Neil told Russell to look briefly back over his shoulder towards the PS side through which he had entered when he said 'what we call marital problems'. His explanation was 'maybe he is having a bit of an extra-marital fling with Joyce, the receptionist'. This is a perfect example of the way Neil crafted back stories to fill out the situation of the support characters but there was no way the spectators could know at that stage in the scene that Maybloom even had a receptionist. Joyce is not mentioned until later in the scene when he calls her on the intercom to send the police. The remarkable thing is that this slightly furtive look and the smug, pursed lips with which Russell said 'marital problems' almost always got a laugh from audiences. I cannot explain why this is so and Russell told me that during the run, Neil had suggested another gesture that he could try. This was looking down at his finger nails as he said the words, but after experimenting with that a few times and not getting any response from the audience, he reverted to the furtive look towards the absent Joyce, which continued to provoke laughter.

According to Michael, 'marital problems' is psychologists' code for homosexuality and the moment is thus a forerunner to other assaults on Roland's sexuality that he has to withstand as he grows up. In Neil's production, Maybloom's intervention focused more on suppressing Roland's extraordinary creative ability but the other dimension was not absent. Neil said 'we can't afford to let this scene tilt into comedy' (Day 17) and restrained Russell from some of the energetic scribbling with which he had been punctuating statements he was eliciting from Roland, such as that what he most liked in *The Iliad* were the battles where 'the heroes are really strong and fearless and they're nearly nude except for their armour which is blinding'. It would have been very easy to produce a caricature of a psychologist here and easy to exploit the comic potential, but by restraining this impulse and showing that Roland was surrounded by people who genuinely cared about his welfare, it accentuated the predicament of growing up gay in a society that sees homosexuality as an illness or a crime. It was Richard, not Neil, who suggested the word 'nude' where Michael had written 'naked' and there was something irresistibly comic about the way he said the line that audiences loved. This is another example of the collaborative nature of the creative process that led to the production.

Another example of one of Neil's quirky but extremely effective directions was for the moment when Daniel is asking Roland for advice to help him in his work as an actor.

DANIEL: Some . . . yes. Clue. Hint?
ROLAND: And you think I'd have that?
DANIEL: Yes. You would. Definitely.

Guy is standing towards the PS side of the stage and Richard is up against the OP wall and Neil's suggestion was that when Daniel says 'You would. Definitely' he should point at Roland. Guy used to do this with his arm outstretched in quite a big gesture and, although I have no idea why, nor what the gesture really indicated, it always produced a reaction from the audience, perhaps amusement at the character's confidence and trust, perhaps at his chutzpah in continuing to put pressure on the great writer.

Neil's long experience of working for the asymmetrical Belvoir stage means that he has a deep body knowledge of the space, awareness of the different perspectives on the action available from the three blocks of audience seating and the potential power of the different entrance/exit points. I was rather surprised at first to note that he sat in the same place every day during the blocking rehearsals, his place by Kylie's table translating to a position in the front row of the central block of audience seating close to where the vomitory opens on to the stage (see figure 3). He did not move around to sit in different positions in order to experience the performances from the perspective of the different audience blocks, as other directors I have observed have done but it soon became evident that he did not need to move around because the space, with all its idiosyncrasies, was hardwired into his brain. He would remind the actors when the blocking they had devised would mean one of them had

Figure 22. Guy Edmonds, Russell Dykstra (Chekhov) (dress rehearsal)
Photo: Heidrun Löhr

his or her back to one of the blocks of audience for a considerable period
(such as Nina during Roland's long tirade in the first scene or Nick,
sitting on the same chair for the second hospital scene while Roland exu-
berantly describes the play he has written). In these cases, where it was
not possible for the actor to move, his or her position on the chair was
tweaked slightly to give the PS block of audience at least a profile view
of the actor. Russell's entrance as Chekhov in the final apparition was
from the PS side, and his trajectory was to walk up to Daniel, perched on
his bar stool beside Roland at centre stage, then exit down the vom. He
shook Daniel's hand as he spoke in Russian to him, then patted him on
the shoulder before exiting. Neil asked him to focus on Daniel but not to
shake his hand (perhaps because this raised issues about the corporeal-
ity of the apparitions) but later in the session (Day 15) he reinstated the
pat on the shoulder because it enabled Russell to turn slightly towards
the PS block of spectators who would otherwise have seen the Chekhov
figure only from behind.

I noted at the time that the Belvoir Theatre was Neil's instrument
and that he played it like a virtuoso musician, knowing from long
experience how best to exploit its particular features. It must be admitted, however, that once I had seen the whole production from many
different spots in the auditorium, it did seem to me that the optimum
audience position was in fact the central block from which Neil had

Figure 23. Neil Armfield (rehearsal room, Company B)
Photo: Heidrun Löhr

actually done the blocking. His spatial sense and memory for detail are
both extraordinary, as the following anecdote will illustrate. On Day 23,
when they were working on the final scene in Act I where Nina prompts
Roland to talk of the terrible bushfires that have destroyed Como that
week, Neil pointed out to Richard that he should have been just behind
Nina's chair when she said 'ash' ('Terrible weekend. The air filled with
ash, burnt leaves'). Richard was pacing around the stage during this
interchange and claimed that he had been walking at exactly the same
speed as usual, so the mystery remained until someone noticed that the
chairs had been wrongly set at the beginning of the scene and that Nina's
chair was a foot or so away from its normal position. This is a perfect
example of Neil's accuracy and recall and also of the way the words and
movements are mapped together in a poetic whole for him. Actors, too,
have extremely accurate recall and a kind of body knowledge of their
position both on the physical stage and in the fictional world but the fact
that neither Richard nor Justine seemed to be aware that anything was
amiss on this occasion suggests how subtle was the kind of patterning
Neil was creating.

Another example of Neil's alertness to this kind of patterning was
his comment on Day 6 when Richard and Russell were working on the
lawyer scene. Richard was pacing around the stage while Russell was
seated and the all-important admission of plagiarism, 'But I did', was

spoken by Richard from the upstage corner. Neil suggested that he do this with his back to the audience because it made Roland seem more guilty and would make it possible for the lawyer to roll his eyes or react in some other way. When they ran the scene again, Richard continued his pacing during the exchange that follows the admission and when he got to the confirmation 'And I'm admitting I did, okay, I'm confessing to you that I did that', Neil pointed out happily that he was in the exact spot he had been in when he made the first admission. Whether this was conscious or unconscious on Richard's part, it was perfect timing and, through Neil's acute observation, became part of the structure of the scene.

Shaping the text: director as author

Neil's role in the major restructuring and modification of the script has been described already and Michael, too, was making changes right up until the preview performances, both as a result of Neil's comments and in response to the work he saw being done by the actors. The impact of Neil's cuts was usually to sharpen the moment, remove anything that smacked of exposition, and ensure that the progression of ideas and the emotional logic of the action was clear, and they were always accepted by Michael with a good grace. Having written a 'crazy fur-ball of a play', Michael was in fact always more than ready to pare it back and to cut words if the point was already apparent in what the actor was doing. That sort of intervention is what might be expected from a good director working with a relatively unfinished script, but Neil's inventiveness did not stop at pruning and shaping. As has already been indicated, he was extraordinarily adept at suggesting additions and alternative, usually more colourful, words or phrases that would help the actor create a sense of the personality of one of the support characters or slightly change the emotional temperature of a given moment, and Michael has retained a significant number of these in the published text.

The three additions that Neil made to Justine's part in the first scene give a good idea of the level of detail involved and of the range of functions that his interventions served. After the *tour de force* of the writer's block tirade, Nina is beginning to pin Roland down as to why he is seeking her help, and he talks of his friend Jake's involvement in the plagiarism scandal:

He introduced me to this woman who was babysitting a dog that belonged
to friends of hers. She's a friend, was a friend of Jake's. The dog went
missing, ran away, got stolen and she went crazy trying to find it again.

This is quite a long speech and Neil suggested that Nina should quietly
interpolate 'A dog?' after 'friends of hers.' In the published text, Michael
has retained the interpolation and added a stage direction for Roland:
'he looks at her for a moment, then goes on,' which may be an indication
of his approval of the way Justine and Richard handled the moment in
performance. The slight double take Richard did when interrupted had
a definite comic potential and the actors could certainly have played this
up but I do not think that that was Neil's intention. He gave Justine notes
on several occasions on how to say the word ('dryer', 'less surprised',
'remove the question mark') that suggested to me he saw the interpolation as being an opportunity for Nina to assert her presence very subtly,
more to punctuate Roland's glib flow of self justification than to draw
attention to the dog as such. Of course, it does also do the latter and
the absurdity of the story is emphasised by the dryness of Nina's query.
Another suggestion was that Nina add 'No wonder Jake's worried about
you' to the speech where she begins to confront Roland about his drug
habit. The absent Jake, Roland's only friend, was an aspect of the play that
Neil found rather haunting and why he was keen to retain the long telephone call scene notwithstanding Richard's technical objections to it. He
said he loved the idea that all we know of Jake is that he worries, and the
sentence he has added here functions to strengthen that idea for the audience. The third addition is to Nina's series of questions to Roland concerning his drug habit. She says: 'I assume some amphetamine, or coke
is it? Worse?' It was Neil who added 'worse?' as the climax of the series
of unanswered questions and it usually provoked a laugh from the audience. The laugh was probably a response to Roland's gesture of irritation
at the suggestion he could have sunk even lower than speed and coke,
as audiences were usually already extremely sympathetic to Roland/
Richard by this stage, having laughed on numerous occasions during
the writer's block speech, often crowning it with a round of applause. I
think, however, that Neil's intention was not to provoke a laugh but to
elicit a response from Roland that would motivate Nina's next line, 'At
this point, at any point, you can leave', thus adding to the sense that she
is calling his bluff. The three additions all have a bearing on the character
of Nina and provide material for the actress to use, strengthening the idea
that she 'has got Roland's number,' as Neil put it one day.

Some of Neil's suggestions accentuated the comic potential of a
moment: 'How convenient' (Scene 5) and 'Not particularly' (Scene

21) were little interpolations for Roland, of which Richard took full advantage to develop the self irony that was one of the character's more attractive features, or 'upon request' added to one of Tom's pretentious claims, the bureaucratic language heightening the absurdity of his belief that he is a valued service provider. In others, the humour is in the word itself, words like 'dandy' or 'plummet' owing much to Neil's brand of whimsical humour. A slightly bizarre suggestion was that the nurse should say 'quick sticks' when urging Nick to go back to his bed in the ward. It was another typical Neil suggestion, giving a slightly idiosyncratic touch to the nurse they had decided, after a ten-minute discussion, was called Sister Shirley, but it did not meet with much enthusiasm from Michael, and Neil later cut it. Giving the nurse a name, even though it would never be used in the dialogue, was not a frivolous distraction but a means of crafting the back story that would assist Monica to find the character's 'voice' and a kind of individuality even though she is only on stage for a couple of minutes and has no more than a few sentences to say.

More outrageous than any of these suggestions, was Neil's addition to Roland's long, bitterly angry speech to Tom, telling him he is giving up the struggle and is seeking annihilation in the drugs he is trying to obtain. After Roland says 'I've had it', Neil suggested he add 'pussy's bow, darling'. Richard used to say it with a ferocious parody of campness and a kind of self loathing that Neil had tried on other occasions to introduce into Roland's responses. Michael joked when he first saw the run of that scene that he would include the words in the published text but add a stage direction that the phrase should only be used if done in exactly the way Richard Roxburgh had done it in the Belvoir production. It was in this speech that Neil also made one of his characteristically quirky suggestions for a move: Roland avoids Tom's attempts to get him to leave by sitting down, apparently intending to stay put until given the drugs he has come to obtain. Neil asked Richard whether his move to the chair could be a skip. The suggestion seemed so outlandish that at first I did not think Neil could be serious and Richard, too, was sceptical. The first few times he did it almost under protest but what he eventually produced was a kind of scooting walk that got him to the chair in a few long strides, usually producing an amused response from the audience, the apparent playfulness adding a chilling note to his deadly serious purpose.

I had heard from other people that Neil could be extremely proactive in making changes to a play script during the rehearsal process and I asked Eamon Flack whether the sort of preparedness to intervene that had occurred with *Toy Symphony*, proposing additions as well as cutting and shaping, had been more or less than he had observed on other productions. He said that he had noticed in all Neil's work 'a need to claim the play' and that this applied to his productions of classics or other well known plays, and not just to new Australian works. Eamon has been literary manager at Company B since 2004 so has been in the privileged position of observing the work of Neil's most mature period. He made the very perceptive point that Neil needed 'to incorporate elements of his own dreamings' in the works he directed, which is very much what is going on with his interventions in Mrs Walkham's slide show scene or even the naming of Sister Shirley and his desire for her to say 'quick sticks'.

Creating community: the heart of the matter

Neil's rehearsals are hard work but at the same time very pleasurable for all the participants. From the first day onwards, the atmosphere in the *Toy Symphony* rehearsal room was purposeful but also relaxed and even sociable. Neil was at the centre, setting the tone, totally in control of the work process even though the impression he gave was more like someone presiding over a social event in his own home than running a work place. Indeed, a concomitant of the discourse of family that pervades his practice is the notion of home, and it is not just Neil who regards Belvoir and Company B as home. In more than one of the interviews he gave before the show opened, Richard Roxburgh referred to Belvoir as home (*Sydney Morning Herald*, 9 November 2007) or, more specifically, as his creative home (ABC, Talking Heads, 2007) and I think this is true for a significant number of Sydney theatre artists. For Neil, the term is both figurative and literal, and it is typical of his sense of humour that the only furniture in his office, apart from his desk, is a large, comfortable, chintz covered settee, striking an incongruously domestic note in that busy work environment. In rehearsal, he was affable and chatty, told wonderfully indiscreet stories, took a personal interest in each member of the group and, if he was under pressure from the numerous commitments involved in running the company, he never let it show. I was reminded more than once of what Antoine Vitez said about his own working process: 'The only way I can live my life in the theatre is in an atmosphere of continual good humour. Concord.' (Vitez 1985, 152) On one occasion Neil brought his dog, Kevon, to the rehearsal. Richard looked wonderingly at Kevon, who was then extremely old and quite deaf, and said "when we were doing *Hamlet*, Kevon was just a pup." The comment was another example of the way time is measured for them all by reference to the productions they have made and it functioned as a reminder of how long Richard has been associated with Neil and Company B but it seems to me that it did more than that. In itself just a passing remark, it conveyed something of the homely, familial nature of the relationships Neil establishes with the people who work with him.

Tensions can run high in the theatre, especially as deadlines approach or if there are differences of creative opinion or if the director's demands are impossible to meet within the timeframe or budget. Some directors are notorious for their outbursts and destructive behaviour towards their collaborators, and it is said that Tadeusz Kantor, for example, could on occasion give way to 'homeric rages' (Meyer-Plantureux 2005, 205). Working with a director like Kantor, the actors and other collaborators must feel that their own creativity is entirely subordinated to that of the great man and that their task is simply to fulfil his vision. With Neil, although it is evident that he is a major artist and each of his productions is an expression of his own dreaming, as Eamon put it, his great skill is to harness the creative energies of everyone in the room, not just for the purpose of making the work but also to enhance the craft skills and artistry of the individual participants. The rehearsal process I observed made it abundantly clear why, for so many actors, it is during the rehearsal period that they feel most creatively alive and why they regard Neil Armfield with such admiration and respect. Justine told me that, although most of her acting work these days is for film and television, she tries to manage her commitments so that she can do one theatrical production every year. Unless she does this, she said that she finds her acting begins to lose depth because the actor's process in film and television involves very little rehearsal and it is only through the intensive collaborative work of theatrical rehearsal that she can nurture and develop her acting skills. Theatre historian Odette Aslan, writing about French theatre practice, claims that while rehearsal used to be regarded as a chore, it is now commonly experienced by actors to be the most complex and profoundly satisfying phase of their work. It is the nightly performance that has become repetition, while rehearsal (the French word for rehearsal is *répétition*) is a far more demanding and exhilarating process of exploration and discovery (Aslan 2005, 25).

Relationships between the artists in the rehearsal room played a crucial part in creating the positive atmosphere and here, as in everything else, it was Neil who set the tone. Richard's prestige and standing in the profession and his longstanding friendship meant that he could treat Neil with a degree of mockery that would have been entirely inappropriate from some of the others, but it was equally evident that Neil enjoyed that kind of banter and teasing. As I have shown already, he intervened hugely in the actors' process, making countless suggestions, sharpening and honing the performances he elicited, providing material that fed the creation of characters even where the playwright had given little to go on. He was unfailingly kind and polite to them all, especially Monica, whom he treated with the deference due to an elder of the tribe, and he was mortifed when he thought he had hurt her feelings on one occasion. He had worked a lot with Russell but never with Justine, which might have been a factor in the very different way he treated them, but this might also have been part of his response to their very different practices. Justine begins in a low key way, as she told me, 'just letting it sit and gradually take shape through the joint work with the other actors' (Day 5). Later on she told me that she does not normally 'find her character' during the rehearsals but during the preview week, when all the work comes together (Day 32). Russell seems to take a diametrically opposed approach, starting with a big, somewhat 'over the top' physicalisation and gradually pulling it back and refining it. It sometimes seemed to me that Neil adopted a rather schoolmasterly tone in his dealings with Russell but, whatever the dynamics of their working partnership, it is clearly a highly effective one, as evidenced by the outstanding work Russell did in the production, work that won him two prizes for Best Supporting Actor (Sydney Theatre Award 2007, Helpmann Award 2008), and equally clearly it is a relationship based on mutual respect and admiration for each other's artistry.

For the production crew, on whom must fall the high pressure of completing complex technical and practical work in very short timeframes, the story is perhaps not quite so rosy. Returning to the theatre a year after the *Toy Symphony* experience, I found that nearly all the production staff, including Kylie, the stage manager, had moved on, either to jobs in other theatres or out of the industry all together. I asked whether this level of attrition was normal and was assured that it was. The high turnover is caused in part by the low pay scales in theatre compared with rates of pay for people with similar qualifications and skills working in the corporate sector or in film or television. Christine Sammers, who had prepared a report for the Board of Directors on working conditions in the company, told me that she thought burnout was another factor and that, in addition to the problems of low pay, production staff frequently felt that there was just too much work to do and that they were unable to do it to the level that would have given them total job satisfaction. Of course, this is also a result of tight finances in that a single individual must do work that in a more lavishly funded theatre would be shared by several, and it does mean that production staff are often obliged to work under great pressure. Christine told me that staff working at Belvoir are deeply committed to the company and are prepared to work long hours, but exhaustion clearly does also take its toll.

The designers, too, may have problems when major decisions are not made until very late in the process or when the direction of the work changes radically. Paul Charlier was certainly confronted with a hugely increased work load when the lighthearted, frivolous music he had prepared for *The Play* had to be rethought in Week 4 and then again in Week 5 as the nature of Roland's imagined production changed. In the end, he wrote five different versions of the music for this play-within-the-play, and the music for Miss Beverly had to be reworked as she changed from being an object of lust to a romantic fantasy. Paul has been one of Neil's most longstanding collaborators and he told me that these shifting demands were a familiar part of working with Neil, who likes to keep things open and fluid for as long as possible and to be open to all sorts of suggestions right through the rehearsal period. A friend had coined a Latin phrase, *clam epos*, which means 'epic by stealth' and this seemed to him to constitute an appropriate motto for Neil's process, summing up the way the demands escalate and tasks which seem simple at the outset become increasingly complex and all-consuming. Yet for all these people, designers, technical staff and stage crew, there is pride in being part of the creative team at Belvoir and a deep satisfaction in con-tributing to making work at the theatre they see as being the most artis-tically committed and accomplished in the state, perhaps the country.

I have talked about the inclusiveness that seemed to me to be such a feature of Neil's rehearsal room but it is not easy to describe exactly how it occurs. It emanates from Neil himself and is a central part of his management style. He notices everything, makes personal remarks, asks after family members, notices what people are wearing, and when they have been to the hairdresser. He even commented that I had had a haircut one day, which surprised me given my low profile in the pro-ceedings. I remarked how observant he was and he said in a very matter of fact way 'But that's my job.' It was a telling insight into his practice in that he does indeed apply the same kind of watchful attention to the life of the rehearsal room as to the performances that are being created. His concern for the individuals in the room went far beyond noticing their appearance and he was always prepared to interrupt the work to make personal queries, for instance when Russell had to go to the dentist or when Guy went to a funeral. One day, when Guy and Richard were working on the Daniel scenes, Neil was talking to Richard about something and noticed that Guy had winced. He immediately broke off what he was saying to enquire what was the matter. Guy explained that he suffers from tinnitus as a result of his many years of being a drummer in a rock band and both Neil and Richard then talked in a very concerned way about the possibility of acupuncture to alleviate the problem. He was also generous in acknowledging people's successes: the prize for best actor that had been awarded to Eamon in Western Australia, the fact that Matthew was about to go to London to direct an opera at the Almeida Theatre, the intensely emotional performance Guy had given the night before in *Holding the Man*, the thirteenth anniversary of the death of Tim Conigrave. These kind of comments enhanced the bonds that created a sense of community as well as boosting individual morale.

Neil's practice of inviting the administrative staff to attend the first reading of the play text on the first day of rehearsals and to come to see the final run of the show before it transfers to the theatre is another aspect of the inclusiveness he fosters at Company B. This will be discussed in more detail in the final chapter where I consider the production within the broader context of the theatre community but it is mentioned here as it is indicative of his attempts to ensure that the company staff are kept fully informed about the work that is being created, and that the artists appreciate the wide range of activities carried out to support their work. The effectiveness of the practice was evident in the sense of common purpose I felt every time I went to the offices during the rehearsal period. Everyone, from the publicists to the switchboard operator, would ask anxiously how it was going and there was a buzz of excitement as the idea dawned that the production could well be a big success.

Note

1   *Holding the Man*, as has been indicated already, was not a Company B production but was slotted into the subscription season at the last minute when it emerged that the scheduled production, a new musical by Casey Bennetto, author of the very successful *Keating!*, was not going to be ready in time. It is unlikely that the season would otherwise have included two such thematically similar shows, particularly one directly following the other.

Rehearsal and interaction ritual

> I assume that when individuals attend to any current situation,
> they face the question: 'what is it that is going on here?'.
> (Erving Goffman, *Frame Analysis*)

It is appropriate that the epigraph to the final chapter of this study should be the deceptively simple question that underpins the whole of Goffman's lifelong attempt to understand the complexities of social experience. It stands here as a reminder that the observer who wishes to reach a nuanced understanding of a rehearsal process must continually be asking the same question, and as he or she does so, it becomes increasingly clear that what is going on in the rehearsal room is more than the making of a theatrical production. As Kate Rossmanith showed in her comparative analysis of two rehearsal processes, each production located itself in relation to the broader cultural context of Sydney theatre, and the work of the practitioners was directed as much to elaborating their place within the theatre community as to making a piece of theatre (Rossmanith 2004). I have already indicated that nothing that happens during the rehearsals can be bracketed out as not relevant to the production process that is occurring and, indeed, it is often the exchanges and activities that might be dismissed as peripheral that provide the most fascinating insights into the way the group seems to understand 'what it is that is going on', the hierarchies of power and influence that structure the group, and the way the rehearsal experience is embedded within a broader cultural and social context. For instance, throughout the *Toy Symphony* rehearsal process, there were numerous occasions on which work seemed to stall while Neil and others engaged in animated discussions about good restaurants, where to obtain particular ingredients and the best way to prepare them. Neil is an accomplished cook and connoisseur of good food and wine and his interests were shared by others, notably Richard and Russell. On one occasion, when Kylie thought the interruption had gone on long enough, she asked pointedly whether my book was going to include recipes. Then there was the day Richard brought in a large bowl of tiramisu, made for the group by his Italian wife. The tea break was transformed into a party, everyone gathered in the kitchen, plates and spoons were found, Russell served it out, remembering to include Tess and her team working in Wardrobe. Then he got out his mobile phone and called Silvie to thank her and everyone present chorused their appreciation and thanks. It is a tradition at Company B to provide a cake for afternoon tea if anyone's birthday falls during the rehearsal period (as was the case for both Josh and Guy), yet another manifestation of the family atmosphere Neil is at pains to foster, and on those occasions, too, the sense of group coherence was reinforced.

I would argue that all these kinds of activity served the ultimately serious purpose of creating a sense of community for that particular group of people, coming together from a variety of backgrounds and having only a short period of time in which to establish the social bonds and emotional intimacy that would permit them to work together intensively. The experience of performers and other theatre artists in Australia is one of the rapid formation of groups that work together at a level of physical and emotional intimacy shared by few other professions for relatively short periods and then disperse, perhaps never to work with each other again, perhaps to meet in another combination a year or so later.[1] The on-again/off-again sociality that marks the lives of actors in the contemporary theatre shares certain features with the experience of the tribal groups on whom Emile Durkheim relied so heavily when he was formulating his theoretical analysis in *The Elementary Forms of Religious Life* (1912). For the Arrente people of the Central Desert of Australia, as for the Inuit described by Marcel Mauss (1904–05) to whom Durkheim also refers frequently, seasonal variations in the availability of food created a pattern of life in which larger groupings of people could come together only on rare occasions. It was, however, at these times that the most intensive ritual observances took place, and the year could be seen to be divided between the sacred time of festivals and religious ceremonies and the profane time of the everyday struggle for survival. In Durkheim's analysis, it was the intensity of the coming together that sustained members of the tribe, providing individuals with a sense of their membership of the larger community even though for most of the year they hunted and foraged in small family groups. As he put it, 'Society can revive its sense of itself only by assembling' (Durkheim [1912] trans. Cosman 2001, 259). Durkheim's analysis can also be applied to the situation of actors in the contemporary theatre and I would argue that it is the intermittent opportunity to engage in the intensive creative life of the rehearsal room, more than the nightly routine of performing for an audience for the run of a show, and far more than the fragmentary experiences involved in film or television work, that confers on actors their sense of themselves as actors and as members of a particular and privileged community.

In this final chapter of my study of the Company B rehearsal process for *Toy Symphony*, I am concerned to explore the nature of the group sociality that was created and its function in the overall process, as well as the way the production as a whole can be seen to contribute to the creation of a wider theatre community which itself serves to recognise and validate the work of the artists and the rest of the company staff.

The theory of interaction ritual derived from Durkheim's seminal work and, in particular, Randall Collins's notion of interaction ritual chains (Collins 2004), have been extremely helpful in showing the underlying importance of what might appear to be digressions or discussions with no bearing on the production of the play. They have also helped explain some things I found slightly perplexing at the time. For instance, one evening about halfway through the run, Monica button-holed me in the little backstage kitchen before the performance and, to my dismay, said I had done something that had seriously upset her. In the card I had sent to wish her well on opening night, I had said how much I loved her performance as Mrs Walkham and I mentioned in particular the moment at the end of Scene 8 when she picked up the stapler and the quizzical look she gave it as she walked off. She told me that the upshot of that was that she had been unable to repeat the look and had become self conscious about it. She said that, while the director can make comments about a look or gesture, if anyone else does so, it puts a jinx on the moment and that she had been avoiding me since opening night in case I 'said something else nice about her performance'.

I was of course mortified and later asked Kylie whether this was a well known piece of theatre etiquette that I had transgressed in my ignorance but all she said was that younger actors do not feel the same way. This suggested that I had indeed transgressed some part of theatre lore. Justine, while assuring me that her own performance was sufficiently settled to permit detailed discussion when I spoke to her four weeks into the run, told me that there was an understanding among actors in a show not to comment on each other's acting as that is 'the prerogative of the director and it might seem that the actor was taking a directorial role'. An intriguing thing about Monica's complaint to me was that her gesture and look at the stapler got a big laugh at every performance I witnessed, and her exit often elicited a round of applause as well. So her complaint could not be that the moment was completely ruined as the audience response showed that this was not so. Perhaps it was that, although audiences clearly loved what she did, it was not what she felt she had been doing before I jinxed the moment.

Re-reading my fieldnotes in light of this contretemps, I have found several occasions where Neil or one of the actors commented (usually ironically) on the possibility that his intervention might damage subsequent performances by rendering the actor self conscious. On Day 6, when they were blocking the first scene, Neil said how much he liked the image of alienation and suspicion that Richard had created. He said 'I love the twitching feet, that kind of accelerated foot movement' and then added 'I don't want to make you self conscious'. Later the same day, working on the scene with the lawyer, he said to Richard 'I liked the girlie thing you did with your fingers when you stood up'. Richard denied ever doing anything 'girlie' but when Neil showed him what he had done, he laughed and said 'Now I'll be so self conscious I'll never be able to do it again'. And, indeed, I think he never did repeat the gesture. The rehearsal process involved such detailed commentary on every aspect of the actors' bodily expressiveness that I failed to pick up the implied warning in these little asides. I did, however, make a note of them and they fed into what I came to see as a perplexing inconsistency at the heart of the play. Roland Henning has been afflicted with writer's block because he became self conscious: 'so self-aware that now I can't do anything without questioning it. And when you question your basic instincts that closely, they seize up' yet this is precisely the 'gift' he bestows on Daniel, the acting student. Daniel's speech in the final scene was rewritten a few times over the course of the rehearsals as Michael tried to clarify the character's motivation for agreeing to meet Roland but he never completely resolved this central inconsistency.

In the stop/start reading, Neil asked Guy what he thought Roland had given Daniel and Guy replied 'he made it clear for him that he wanted to be an actor, but to do that means he needs to be honest. He passed on to Daniel the clarity he had got from Nina.' Neil pressed a little harder: 'So there is a self consciousness of motive, a tendency to search for real motive. Maybe that is something Daniel didn't want?' Guy's response was to fall back on the analysis he had already given when they were discussing what the play is really about: 'Daniel is having to unlearn everything he learned at acting school and rediscover what it was that made him want to be an actor in the first place'. On Day 15, they read Michael's reworked version of the speech, which makes clear that Daniel now analyses his own actions minutely, and Richard commented 'so Roland has foisted the paralysing effects of self analysis on to someone else'. Everyone nodded but did not say whether they thought this would damage Daniel or help him to become a better actor. Michael Gow was also aware of the issue and he certainly thought it would be deleterious because he joked later that afternoon that the reason Daniel was not getting work was probably because 'every time he goes for an audition he finds himself asking "why the fuck am I here?"' (Day 15).

It is interesting that different members of the group acknowledged the problem but were somehow able to put it aside and it seemed to me that, notwithstanding all the tweaking of Daniel's big speech, the play never made clear why Daniel now claimed he was grateful to Roland, nor why, if it was a disaster for a writer to be made to doubt his spontaneous, intuitive responses, it would not be equally disastrous for an actor. The blind spot was all the more perplexing given Monica's complaint to me and the perception they apparently all shared about the damaging effect for the actor of being made self conscious. In fact, in making her complaint to me, she actually compared her situation to that of Roland in the play, being made self conscious about his gift and being frozen as a result. I asked her whether this did not apply equally to Daniel and she said that his situation was quite different in that 'he was only being made to question why he wants to be an actor or his motivation for doing things in his daily life'. When I spoke to Guy during the run, he acknowledged that Roland's attack on Daniel would have been destructive ('he had been unable to get out of bed for days') but said that both characters discover the need for honesty and both find a kind of redemption (Roland gets back his 'gift' and Daniel may one day play Treplev). While this is dramaturgically neat, it raises another question as to what precisely Daniel was supposed to have done that needed to be redeemed and whether it could be compared with Roland's dishonesty and cruelty.

The somewhat specious justifications offered by everyone I interviewed, notwithstanding the reservations they may themselves have expressed during the rehearsal period, the sense I had that they were falling back on motherhood statements about the artist's need for honesty, and the fact that none of them seemed prepared even to acknowledge that there might still be a problem suggested something important about the actors' relationship to the work they have created. This was reinforced by the responses I received when I asked about Neil's perception of Roland's sexuality and the erotic dimension to his relationships with Nick, Daniel and Steve Gooding. As has already been shown, Richard was not particularly interested in this aspect of the play, despite a good deal of urging from Neil during the rehearsals. When I interviewed Guy during the run and he told me that he saw Nick as Roland's 'big brother', I reminded him of Neil's frequently expressed opinion that Roland was in love with Nick and that there was 'a dark, shadowy area between them' and then asked whether, in the circumstances, he thought that Richard's and his instincts were more sound than Neil's. He was so nonplussed by the question that I immediately turned it into something less confrontational, fearing I had again transgressed some aspect of theatre etiquette.

The other actors were adamant that there was no attraction between Roland and Daniel either, even though Neil had told them after one performance that on that occasion he really felt that the two would be going home together after their second drink. The most categorical response came from Kylie who said 'Homosexuality is not part of the problem. This is not a play about a homosexual writer with writer's block but about a writer with writer's block.' She somewhat undermined her own assurance by then saying 'I am pleased they didn't make it into a play about homosexuality', thus indicating firstly how open the play was when they began to work on it, and secondly how easily such an interpretation could have developed. For Neil himself, notwithstanding his sense of a yearning for love at the heart of the play, what they ended up producing had a sense of rightness about it, so much so that he really did not recall any sense in which Richard had resisted exploring the character's homosexuality.

All of this alerted me to the way, for the actors in particular, but also to an extent for Neil and others, once the rehearsal period is over and the play has come into existence, the form it has taken is the only one possible. It is as though they cannot permit themselves to doubt what they have done while they are still doing it, and they cannot doubt the morality of the play they have made. They have to think it is good and that it is saying something to which they can adhere. This insight has been endorsed by other theatre practitioners to whom I have spoken, who have confirmed that actors must set aside any doubts they might have or they would not be able to go out on the stage each night and perform. As Kylie said when I interviewed her many months after the production, 'if you open up big questions, the foundations crumble' (Interview November 2010). How much time must ensue

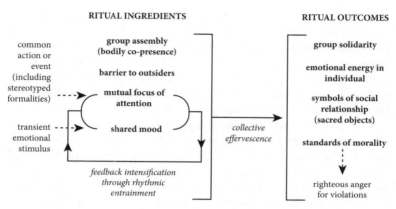

Figure 24. Randall Collins's model of an interaction ritual

before a more nuanced critical judgement emerges is not clear but it is probably several years. During the rehearsals for *Toy Symphony* there were a number of jocular references to a deeply flawed production in which some of them had been involved five years earlier. I think, however, that what is involved goes far deeper than this kind of practical requirement to maintain commitment to the task in hand and this is where Randall Collins's notion of interaction ritual chains becomes particularly relevant.

For Collins, following Durkheim and Goffman, ritual is 'a mechanism of mutually focused emotion and attention producing a momentarily shared reality, which thereby generates solidarity and symbols of group membership' (Collins 2004, 7). His model of the way an interaction ritual functions can be applied virtually without modification to rehearsal. The ritual ingredients, as listed, could almost be a description of the essential elements of rehearsal process: a number of participants gathered together in a particular place from which outsiders are barred, focusing their attention on a common object, the mutual focus of attention intensifying the experience over a period of weeks in the case of rehearsal, and creating what Collins calls 'emotional energy', although in the diagram reproduced above he uses Durkheim's term, 'collective effervescence'. This is totally familiar to theatre practitioners for whom the rehearsal experience is so absorbing, so emotionally and intellectually fulfilling while it is going on that nothing else really comes near it. One director I know told me his wife said that once he began rehearsals for a new production, she knew he would be lost to her and their children for the duration. Even when he was at home, his thoughts and his passion were elsewhere. She used to say it was as though he had a mistress, but she knew she just had to wait for opening night and he would be returned to her. Something of this passionate involvement also affects the mere observer of rehearsal, as I have lived it on many occasions, and the experience is obviously far more powerful for those who are full participants, sharing an intense communal life while bringing their imagination, their craft skills and the deepest levels of their emotional life to the creation of the work.

In Collins's model, the ritual ingredients produce ritual outcomes that include an enhanced sense of self worth and group solidarity both of which are manifested in a tangible way through what he calls 'sacred objects.' The outcome of the rehearsal process is the production and I suggest that in terms of interaction ritual theory, the production constitutes a sacred object for the people who have made it and that it functions as the central symbol of the relationship that existed between them. This explains to an extent the reluctance of the actors to question what they have done, the sense I gained that my questions were somehow inappropriate or that I was being fobbed off with superficial answers. The production they have made has a life of its own, it marks the lives of those who have worked on it (I have already commented on the way that, for members of this group, their own reference points to the past were frequently productions on which they had worked together) and it becomes somehow sacrosanct. The production is of course never totally fixed, it continues to grow throughout the run and performances differ from night to night. Justine told me that one of the great joys of the production for her was that it felt different every time they did it. She said that on some occasions Nina falls in love with Roland, but not every night: 'it happens when we get out there' (12 December 2007). Guy, too, told me that things changed from night to night and that, for instance, the moves in the scene where Daniel is trying to escape from Roland were not set precisely, which meant he had to remain alert and respond to what Richard was doing. He really liked that and felt that if the part were absolutely nailed down, the task of performance would become boring.

It might appear that there is a contradiction between the actors' own sense that the production is a living, organic thing that changes night by night and my perception of it as a sacred object that, once realised, is no longer open to question. I think, however, that the two perceptions are mutually compatible, and that what change are details of emotional intensity, the addition of bits of business (sometimes sanctioned by Neil, like the change of gesture suggested for Dr Maybloom on 'marital problems', abandoned by Russell when it failed to get a laugh, sometimes introduced by the actors themselves, like

Nina's attempts to interrupt Roland during his rant about the writer's creative process), and of course there is the huge variable created by the impact of audience response on the overall experience. What do not change are the larger issues concerning their understanding of the work they have created, their loyalty and commitment to it and to each other. The emotional energy generated between the participants during the run of the play is, however, very different from what occurs in the rehearsal room. When performing at night, the actors may conserve their energies during the day so as to be able to perform at full force when required, but the camaraderie of the dressing room and the emotional high created by good audience response do not come near the experience of the rehearsal process. As I observed it in the case of *Toy Symphony*, once the play opened the energies that had been concentrated in the rehearsal room were dispersed: Neil and Damien went to Houston to do some preliminary work on the opera production they would be doing there the following year, the production staff (as Liam confirmed) were already thinking about the next three productions, the designers were no longer involved and the actors' task was the more mundane one of execution rather than the all-consuming one of creation.

Nowhere is the distinction between the energies involved in rehearsal and performance more clearly delineated than for the actor who is rehearsing by day while performing another show at night. This was the case for Guy during most of the rehearsal process for *Toy Symphony*. It was not until Day 27 that the run of *Holding the Man* was finally over and Guy seemed to be completely reinvigorated by the knowledge he did not have to perform that night. A week earlier, on Day 21, he told me that he was by then 95 per cent focused on *Toy Symphony* and was beginning to find the ongoing work for *Holding the Man* a distraction from what he really wanted to be doing. Then, most revealingly, almost as though that admission had been a betrayal, he said quickly 'don't get me wrong. I still love *Holding the Man* and I'm not pulling back from it in any way.' Guy was, as it were, caught between two worlds, each making demands on his energy, enthusiasm and loyalty and the language he used made him sound like a married man falling in love with another woman. In Antony Sher's account of making his Richard III, his thoughts were consumed by the possibilities of the role long before the actual rehearsals began. He was still performing in *Tartuffe* and David Edgar's *Maydays* in the weeks preceding the rehearsals but what clearly preoccupied him, fired his imagination and even haunted his dreams was the Richard to come. He says in his diary entry on the last night of *Maydays*:

> I feel a sense of relief that it's over. I was proud to be in it and loved the
> rehearsals and early performances. But in these last few, hectically busy
> weeks it felt like climbing a mountain. (Sher 1985, 131)

As other actors have told me, there is no way back to the passionate
involvement of the rehearsal room once the production has opened
and this is perhaps one explanation for the fact that the atmosphere at
the opening and closing night parties was so different. I have already
noted that closing night was relatively subdued compared with the
high octane excitement of opening night, and I think now that this is
because the opening night party is really a rite of passage that marks
the culmination of the rehearsal process, liberating the director and
designers to begin to engage in new creative ventures and signalling the
end of that period of maximum creativity and group solidarity and the
onset of a more normal rhythm of work for the actors and production
crew. In Durkheim's terms this constitutes a move from sacred time to
profane time, and there is no such shift or culmination being marked by
the closing night party. Another reason for the difference in intensity
between the two might be that an excessive display of emotion in respect
of the production that is closing could suggest that the artists in question
do not have any other work in the pipeline. Actors are extremely sensitive to the need to present themselves as much in demand and I noticed
that this fact has even come to impinge slightly on the intense sociality
of the rehearsal room itself, now that mobile phones are an obligatory
part of an actor's equipment. As soon as the rehearsal was interrupted
for a coffee or meal break, actors and others tended to disperse to the
four corners of the room to check their phones for messages and to
make calls. I mentioned this one day to Russell and he concurred that
mobile phones have made an enormous difference to social interactions
in the rehearsal room and that, whereas in the past, people congregated
around the tea urn and continued to discuss issues arising from the
work, they are now in separate corners, talking to their agents. There
was certainly an attempt to impose some control over the use of phones
and if anyone's mobile rang during a work session or they were observed
sending a text message, they had to put a $2 coin in the jar Kylie had
placed on her desk on the first day, the money collected going to charity
at the end of the rehearsal process. These practices are an acknowledgement of the disruption such interventions from the outside cause to the
mood and concentration in the room but it is clear that, given the institutional reality that most actors in Sydney are freelance and getting work
is by no means certain, none of them can afford not to be on the lookout
for more work. The ritual of checking the message bank frequently

during the day suggests, however, that there is also some need for actors to demonstrate to each other that they are in demand.

Collins shows that ritual interaction chains constitute multiple symbols that function as markers of the group and serve to enhance the group's sense of its own identity and legitimacy. I have argued that the central symbol is the production itself but places can also be sacred objects and their importance as symbols for the group in question will be indicated by the fervour with which the group controls access to them and the 'righteous anger' members feel at 'violations' (to use the terms Collins has included in his model). The rehearsal room, the backstage area of the theatre and, in particular, the actors' dressing room are all places that, as I experienced the work process, seemed to me to be over-laid with emotional connotations that exceed the practical demands for safety and privacy. Seeing them as sacred objects in relation to the inter-action chain helps to explain the fact that traditional superstitions asso-ciated with the theatre, while regarded with an affectionate scepticism by many, are nevertheless enforced. Respecting superstitions such as not whistling in the theatre, not saying 'Macbeth', not wearing green, not saying 'good luck' but 'break a leg' (or 'chookas,' which is the Australian equivalent) is part of the way actors signal their membership of a privi-leged group and, indeed, police that membership. As shown with the incident of the school student from Dubbo who whistled during the tech rehearsal, individual members of the group may claim scepticism but when it came down to it, tradition was respected. Monica belonged to an older generation and she, perhaps, felt more 'righteous anger' about infringements than some of the others. She complained vehe-mently to Kylie one day about the presence of an unauthorised person in the backstage area during one of the matinee performances for school students. It is part of Belvoir's practice to invite homeless young people who frequent a local drop-in centre to attend these performances and it appears that this particular boy had been watching part of the show from the vom and had even wandered into the dressing room. Kylie explained to Monica that they had made an exception in the case of this boy who often came to performances and they were trying to make him welcome and give him a place where he could feel safe but Monica's sense of violation was not assuaged.

When I went backstage unannounced after a performance, as I have mentioned earlier in this account, I realised I had committed a serious *faux pas*. Nothing was said and I withdrew immediately but the sense of outrage emanating from all five actors was palpable. They were about to enjoy a glass of champagne together and it was clearly a valued moment of private socialising for this group-within-the-group. Monica used the word 'protocol' when describing the company's unspoken understanding of the director's role and responsibility, and Justine's comment about the 'director's prerogative' indicates a similar awareness of territory and limits. The experience of observing rehearsals and the run of the production showed me that even in the egalitarian, overtly inclusive Company B Belvoir there are nevertheless hierarchies, groups-within-groups and a veritable minefield of unspoken rules and practices. These function not only to exclude outsiders but also contribute to the aura that surrounds certain places, such as the dressing room, and to the creation of a sense of membership of a privileged group that extends beyond Company B and includes the theatre community more broadly. The beliefs, practices and shared terminology, as well as the names of the artists who figured in rehearsal room anecdotes and gossip indicate that the theatre traditions to which this group of artists were laying claim reach back into the historical past of British theatre and that the broader community within which they define themselves includes British and American theatre and cinema. There is a theatre community that extends across the English speaking world to which Australian theatre artists see themselves as belonging and, even though most will never work outside of Australia, their identity is defined to a significant extent in relation to this larger entity.

The rituals in an interaction chain function to create a sense of group membership and solidarity but, as Collins shows, this is by no means incompatible with stratification and conflict. Indeed, he claims that rituals have 'a double stratifying effect: between ritual insiders and outsiders; and, inside the ritual, between ritual leaders and ritual followers' (Collins 2004, 41). This is totally borne out by what I observed in the *Toy Symphony* rehearsal process, where the enclosed space of the rehearsal room was protected from outsiders but where the protocols governing responsibilities within the work process and the hierarchies of respect and veneration created a highly stratified situation notwithstanding the rhetoric of inclusiveness, the laughter and the fun. In fact, the greater the veneration, the greater the sense of self worth conferred on those lower down in the hierarchy by their membership of this privileged group. The network of relationships that existed between various members of the *Toy Symphony* company due to their having worked together on other productions (as shown in figure 4) greatly facilitated the rapid formation of a sense of community amongst the group of people brought together for the intensive period of rehearsal and performance. This network was extended by further bonds created by links to other artists with whom one or more had worked at some time and by their response to theatre, film and television productions they saw. Conversation in meal breaks often revolved around productions they had seen and they were vitally interested in what other actors were doing and who was working where and with whom. It was evident that they, like many other actors, go frequently to the theatre, in particular to opening nights, where their presence functions to celebrate and honour the work of the artists who have made the show in question, as well as affirming the existence of the theatre community to which they belong. This was indeed what seemed to be happening at the opening and closing night performances of *Toy Symphony* where, as I have recounted, the level of excitement was significantly heightened by the well known actors and showbusiness personalities in the audience who, by their presence, were celebrating both the production and themselves.

Other elements in the creation of a sense of self worth among the members of the group include such things as Neil's insistence throughout the rehearsal process on the cultural importance of the work they were doing, the little speeches he made to mark significant stages in their creation of this first production of a new work by a distinguished Australian playwright, and his generous acknowledgement of the achievements and honours gained by other members of the company. When the nominations for the Australian Film Institute awards were announced and it emerged that all the actors in the *Toy Symphony* cast had been nominated for different awards for their film and television work (apart from Guy who had been totally immersed in the Tim Conigrave play all year), there was a significant boost in energy levels and excitement in the room, and a great deal of additional bonding as though the recognition of their peers enhanced the respect they already had for each other's artistry. It became evident to me that the function of such awards and prizes is far from negligible, even among artists who express some scepticism about the criteria and the nature of the jury process. Other incidents involved the expression of support for colleagues in other theatre companies. They were all strong in their condemnation of the Melbourne critic who, after having been admitted as a favour to a preview performance of Michael Gow's production of *Who's Afraid of Virginia Woolf?*, published a negative review before the production had even opened. Everybody in the room wrote personal messages of friendship and encouragement on a group fax for the opening night of *Riflemind* at the Sydney Theatre Company (STC), another new Australian play receiving its first production in that season.[2] In all these ways, the sense of community within the *Toy Symphony* company was enhanced and, at the same time, it positioned itself in relation to the larger theatre community and in particular to the STC, the best funded and most prestigious company in the state.

Judging from the gossip and the joking in the rehearsal room, the STC was the company against which Company B measured itself. Relations with other companies, notably Griffin, were warm, as evidenced by the fact that *Holding the Man* was a Griffin production that had been transferred to Belvoir at the end of its run at The Stables, but it was the STC that figured most frequently in rehearsal room banter. While lighthearted and often self deprecatory, this seemed to function as a kind of group bonding, consolidating the sense of being a valued contributor to a company whose identity was formed in part by what distinguished it from the STC with its more lavish funding and connections to the corporate sector. But there was also genuine warmth and no other company received the imprimatur of a fax from the *Toy Symphony* cast although it is unlikely that there were no other opening nights in Sydney during that six week period. It is an interesting fact that most of the artists who work for Company B Belvoir also work for the STC, sometimes in the same season, and the people I interviewed were well able to articulate what they perceived as the major differences between the companies and what each contributes to the larger entity of Sydney theatre. When I asked people what working for Company B meant to them, I was struck by the frequency with which their definitions of Company B involved contrasting it with the STC and also by the extent to which in their minds, Company B was synonymous with Neil Armfield. Monica said she had found Neil very sensitive to the actor's needs and ready to give approval 'so that the actors feel valued' and for Justine, too, it had been a delight to work with Neil, who 'is able to empower the actor during the process', while for Richard 'Company B is a life raft of a place' to which he has returned for creative sustenance at intervals throughout his career. One of them said that Company B is the arthouse theatre while the STC seems to fulfil a corporate function and another said that while STC productions have bigger budgets, Company B productions 'have heart and are culturally richer'. For members of the production crew, too, Company B represents an ideal model of work in which collaboration is emphasised over hierarchical relations and, as Liam put it, 'everyone's contribution is valued and people feel able to offer'. For him as for other members of the backstage staff, it was not just the work but the way it was produced and, even more interestingly, its social impact that contributed so much to their sense of the place occupied by Company B in the broader theatre community. The idea that the work they produced 'challenges people's attitudes' (Liam) and is 'socially relevant' (Kylie) played an important part in their self image and their sense of being engaged in work of cultural and social significance notwithstanding the low level of remuneration provided by the theatre.

There were many ways in which different members of the company positioned themselves and the work in relation to historical tradition and to the broader theatre community extending beyond the shores of Australia. There was Tess's delight when she discovered that the hat she had found for the Alien Nanny in the wardrobe store had originally been worn by a character in the very first production of Patrick White's *Ham Funeral,* delight that was shared by Neil when the Nanny's costume was first shown. He said the hat should really be in a theatre museum and his response ensured that everyone present took a moment to appreciate the web of connections represented by the faded and fraying ribbons of that little material object. There were also Neil's short disquisitions on the origins of phrases such as 'break a leg' and 'chookas', and the explanation he gave when insisting that the boy who whistled should leave the theatre. And there was the dilapidated scrap of paper that Monica carried in her handbag with the comment by Micheál mac Liammóir that seemed to her to sum up so powerfully the actor's experience:

> But with the actor it is different: we are born at the rise of the curtain and we die with its fall, and every night in the presence of our patrons we write our new creation, and every night it is blotted out forever, and of what use is it to say to audience or critic, 'Ah but you should have seen me last Tuesday.'

I love the fact that she had typed out the quotation and carried it with her for years as it is such a telling example of the sense of connection between actors across space and time, sharing the same anguish of working within the ephemeral.

According to the theory articulated by Randall Collins, there are three orders in which symbols circulate and prolong group membership beyond the period of the ritual itself. Firstly as objects of attention of 'emotionally entrained but otherwise anonymous crowds' and secondly as symbols built up out of personal identities and narratives, and he comments that these 'are two quite different circuits of social relationships' (Collins 2004, 87). Applying this to the rehearsal/performance situation, there is the production itself, the sacred object emerging from the ritual intensity of the rehearsal process, and its nightly iteration to new audiences can be seen to constitute the object of attention in the first order, and then there is the whole gamut of discourse surrounding that particular production as it lives on within the culture and the talk about other performances and the artists that made them that figures so prominently in rehearsal room conversations. These 'third-person narrations', to use Collins's term, constitute the second level within which symbols circulate and it is of crucial importance for the creation of a sense of group membership, hence the amount of time devoted to this kind of talk during the rehearsal process and the amount of emotional energy it generates (figure 15 provides a telling image of the energy that circulates around such narrations). Collins claims that there is a third order and this is the most intimate level of circulation because it occurs within the mind of the individual and is, thus, very hard for the sociologist to get at. He says 'We might as well say that this is a sociology to dream about, and indeed, it encompasses a sociology of dreams' (2004, 99). This reminded me that during the *Toy Symphony* process, three people in the room mentioned that they had had a dream about the work and, for each of them, the impact of the dream was such that they wanted to recount it the next day. On each occasion, the dreamer recounted the dream to Neil and it was Neil who responded even though others were present and able to hear, another example of the way Neil operated as the lightning conductor of the energies in the room.

The first dream was Justine's and it occurred early in the process. On Day 6, as soon as she arrived she told Neil she had dreamt about him. 'You were at my house and we were surrounded by all the toys in the house, and all the actors were there too, and you said we should play with the toys and make them tell a story.' The dream had made her feel very happy and she said that was unusual as her dreams were 'usually disturbing'. The dream seems to contain a reassuring mix of references to her work on *Playschool*, where she is an accomplished and highly successful presenter, and to *Toy Symphony*. The second dreamer was Guy and his dream also involved a house. As he told Neil on Day 21, 'all the cast members from *Holding the Man* and *Toy Symphony* were at a beach house and there was a large sign saying it was Patrick White's first house'. The reference to Patrick White was perhaps triggered by the talk that had occurred in the rehearsal room only a couple of days earlier (Day 19) concerning the connection to the first production of *The Ham Funeral* created by the Nanny's hat, but the dream suggests in a delightful way Guy's perception that what they are doing is an integral part of Australian high culture.

The third dream was mine but I include it here because it differed so markedly from those of the participants in the ritual process and can thus be seen to reveal important features of the way the process was lived and experienced by those involved. In my dream as I told Neil on Day 15, I was in the rehearsal room and Neil suddenly turned to me and asked me to read a part. I had to leave my place on the safety of the sidelines and enter the dangerous space of the 'stage' and, when I picked up the script that was lying there, I found that it was not written in normal prose but was a kind of rebus, the text interspersed with pictures that represented words or phrases. Most of the pictures were photographs of people but, though I vaguely recognised each photograph as being of some celebrity, I did not know any of the names. It was a totally humiliating experience and then, as though my subconscious had not made the point sufficiently clearly, when I went back to my table, a young man was sitting in my place. I said hesitantly 'isn't this my seat?' and he replied with an airy wave 'no, this is where I always sit'.

If Randall Collins is correct about the third order circulation of symbols, then these three dreams contain vivid indications of the sense of community shared by the active participants in the creative process, the house in which they were safe to play and tell stories, the relation of this house to the broader culture, the role of Neil as an authorising and enabling figure, contrasted to my own strong sense of demarcation between insiders and outsiders. The experience of trying to 'read' a text in which photographs of unknown people replace names is comic when recounted (like most nightmares), but was in fact very close to what happened when Neil and the actors exchanged 'third person narrations'. I was always aware that the anecdote contained valuable insights along with the gossip but often did not hear the name or had no idea of the identity of the person to whom they were referring. It is perhaps also interesting that the two insiders who dreamt about the process and felt strongly enough about it to recount the dream to Neil were those whose membership of the group was the most peripheral: neither Justine nor Guy had been in a play directed by Neil, Justine had never performed at Belvoir, Guy was the youngest member of the group. I was of course a total outsider, given a kind of tenuous membership as observer that in fact served to confirm my outsider status. This helped make me aware of the complexities involved in regulating the life of groups that come together for brief but intense periods in which intimacy and emotional trust must be rapidly generated and then equally rapidly dispersed, and where the stability that makes possible such fluctuations is derived from a huge, amorphous, intangible entity conceptualised as 'the theatre community', that manifests itself locally (the 'Sydney scene') and nationally, and more mysteriously, is felt to extend across the English speaking world.

∗∗∗

Reflecting now on the creative process involved in the making of *Toy Symphony* and on other rehearsal processes I have been privileged to observe, I am struck more than ever by the complex nature of rehearsals as they have evolved over the course of the last century and by the role of the director who is the lynchpin of the whole enterprise. In a good rehearsal process, it is the director who stimulates, facilitates and elicits the creativity of a large number of different artists and then somehow draws all these inputs together and shapes them into a coherent work of art. Neil Armfield's particular gift is to do this while enabling each individual artist and artisan to feel they have made a genuine contribution and that without their contribution the work would have been the poorer. Randall Collins's theoretical elaboration of the distinction between 'power rituals' and 'status rituals' and the differing levels of emotional energy generated in these interactions suggests that rehearsal in the contemporary theatre can be seen as a very effective status ritual, 'a situation of emotional entrainment rising to a palpable level of collective consciousness' (Collins 2004, 114) with all the associated benefits of positive self image for the participants and enhanced creative energy released around the group's objective. Some rehearsals function as power rituals, little different from those in operation in highly stratified situations such as the military; this would probably apply to the work of charismatic but autocratic directors like Kantor or Wilson, who strictly control the input of all the contributing artists and workers, subordinating it to their own personal vision, but equally to the large theatre companies in which the director of the production is an employee like all the others and major decisions about programming, budget and personnel are made by head office. By contrast, the *Toy Symphony* rehearsal process, like other successful status rituals, built a high level of collective effervescence, empowering the participants, enhancing their sense of belonging and of the cultural value of their work.

In the introduction to this account, I mentioned my unease with the authorial role attributed to the director over the period of so-called 'director's theatre' and claimed that, in my experience, the authorial process involved in contemporary theatre is far more complex and creative input comes from many sources. The playwright is certainly the author of the script, although as has been recounted in relation to the *Toy Symphony* process, the script itself can be subjected to a significant amount of rewriting by the director and other members of the production team. The foregoing account of the *Toy Symphony* rehearsal process raises questions about the extent to which the director can be said to be the author of the production, even when the director in question is an artist of Neil Armfield's stature and undoubted authority. It also raises questions, and begins to provide answers about what authorship in a genuinely collaborative process involves. This is where, it seems to me, theatre practice has a great deal of value to contribute to contemporary debates about appropriate management systems in institutions and enterprises far removed from the performing arts. Theatre practitioners have, throughout the twentieth century, been evolving protocols (to repeat Monica's term), and whole systems of unspoken rules and practices whereby the director directs but does not thereby infringe the creative autonomy of others. The actors and designers in *Toy Symphony* knew that, by accepting the work, they were tacitly agreeing to take direction from Neil. They not only trusted Neil's judgement but felt that the experience of working with him would bring benefits to them in the pursuit of their craft. While every member of the group, including Michael, knew that it was Neil's vision that was being created, they also knew that this vision was the product of a genuine group process and that the outcome would be affected, sometimes in major ways, by their personal contribution. Working in a process of this sort requires particular skills on the part of the director and generosity of spirit on the part of the rest of the group. There has to be both shared recognition of the utility of the protocols and an allegiance to something greater for which all are prepared to devote their energies and which, in turn, replenishes those energies.

Unleashing the creativity of others does not lead automatically to chaos or anarchy, and complex enterprises can be run without the authoritarian or bureaucratic interference that so saps the energies of the people working in them. I suggest that theatre practice of the sort exemplified by Company B's *Toy Symphony* process constitutes a highly effective model of group creativity, and it provides many insights into ways in which the full imaginative and intellectual potential of a group can be paradoxically both unleashed and harnessed to a common end.

Notes

1   The level of intimacy that is created is doubtless what leads to the frequent use of the notion of family as a means of describing the relationship between theatre practitioners but there is a paradoxical sense of insecurity at the heart of the theatre family, as Camilla Ah Kin has pointed out: 'It is the emotional commitment with the expectation of impermanence that sets a theatre family apart from actual blood family where the depth of connection is assumed to be life-long' (Ah Kin 2010, 9).

2   *Riflemind*, written by Andrew Upton and directed by Philip Seymour Hoffman, had its world première at the Sydney Theatre Company on 10 October 2007. Tess Schofield designed the costumes and Damien Cooper the lighting for the production, and this overlap doubtless added to the sense of connection between the two productions.

WORKS CITED

(NB All translations from the French are by the author)

Ah Kin, Camilla Sobh, *A Chance Gathering of Strays: the Australian Theatre Family*, (Unpublished Masters Thesis, Department of Performance Studies, University of Sydney), 2010.

Armfield, Neil, 'Message from Neil', *Welcome Home Company B*, Belvoir Street Theatre, Sydney, 2007, pp. 5–7.

Armfield, 'Message from Neil', *Company B Season 2009*, Belvoir Street Theatre, Sydney, 2009, pp. 3–5.

Asch, Timothy, 'Collaboration in ethnographic filmmaking: a personal view', in *Anthropologiacal Filmmaking*, ed. Jack R.Rollwagen, New York: Harwood Academic Publishers, 1988, pp. 1-29.

Aslan, Odette, 'Introduction: répéter to rehearse ensayar proben', in *Les Répétitions de Stanislavski à Aujourd'hui*, Georges Banu, Paris: Le Temps du Théâtre, 2005, pp. 17-28.

Atkinson, Paul, 'Performance and rehearsal: the ethnographer at the opera', in *Qualitative Research Practice*, eds Clive Seal, Giampetro Gobo, Jaber Gubbium and David Silverman, London: Sage Publications, 2004, pp. 94-106.

Bablet, Denis (ed.), *Tadeusz Kantor. Les Voies de la Création Théâtrale*, Vol. XI, Paris: Editions du CNRS, 1980.

Banu, Georges (ed.), *Les Répétitions de Stanislavski à Aujourd'hui*, Paris: Le Temps du Théâtre/Actes Sud, 2005.

Bennie, Angela, 'Work, rest, play: Michael Gow's *Toy Symphony* explores the agonising effects of writer's block', *Sydney Morning Herald* (3–4 November 2007), p. 18.

Bly, Mark (ed.), *The Production Notebooks: Theatre in Process*. New York: Theatre Communications Group (Vol. I 1996, Vol. II 2001), 1996 and 2001.

Born, Georgina, *Rationalizing Culture: IRCAM, Boulez and the Institutionalization of the Musical Avant-Garde*, Berkeley/London: University of California Press, 1995.

Bradby, David and David Williams, *Director's Theatre*, New York: St Martin's Press, 1988.

Brecht, Bertolt, *Poems 1917–56* (Edited John Willett, Ralph Mannheim, Erich Fried), London/New York: Methuen [the quotation is taken from *The Curtains* (trans. John Willett), p. 425], 1976.

Brook, Peter, *The Shifting Point: Theatre, Film, Opera 1946–87*, New York: Harper & Row, 1987.

Callow, Simon, *Being an Actor*, London: Methuen, 1984.

Carlson, Marvin, 'Theatre and performance at a time of shifting disciplines', *Theatre Research International*, 26:2 (2001), pp. 137–44.

Cole, Susan Letzler, *Directors in Rehearsal: a Hidden World*, New York/London: Routledge, 1992.

Cole, Susan Letzler, *Playwrights in Rehearsal: the Seduction of Company*, New York/London: Routledge, 2001.

Clifford, James, 'Introduction: partial truths', in *Writing Culture: the Poetics and Politics of Ethnography*, eds James Clifford and George Marcus Berkeley/London: University of California Press, 1986, pp. 1–26.

Clifford, James, *The Predicament of Culture: Twentieth Century Ethnography, Literature and Art*, Cambridge: Harvard University Press, 1988.

Collins, Randall, *Interaction Ritual Chains*, Princeton/Oxford: Princeton University Press, 2004.

Company B, *Annual Report*, Belvoir Street Theatre, Sydney, 2006.

Cox, Brian, *The Lear Diaries: the Story of the Royal National Theatre's Productions of Shakespeare's Richard II and King Lear*, London: Methuen, 1992.

Delgado, Maria and Paul Heritage (eds), *In Contact with the Gods? Directors Talk Theatre*, Manchester: Manchester University Press, 1996.

Delgado, Maria and Dan Rebellato (eds), *Contemporary European Theatre Directors*, Abingdon: Routledge, 2010.

De Lorenzis, Angela, 'Jacques Lassalle: la Ligne d'Ombre de la Répétition', in Banu, *Les Répétitions de Stanislavski à Aujourd'hui*, 2005, pp. 325–33.

Durkheim, Emile, *The Elementary Forms of Religious Life*, Trans. Carol Cosman, Oxford: Oxford University Press, [1912] 2001.

Féral, Josette (ed.) *Theatre Research International*, Special Issue on *Genetics of Performance* 33:3 (2008).

Fischer-Lichte, Erika, 'From text to performance: the rise of theatre studies as an academic discipline in Germany', *Theatre Research International* 24:2 (1999), pp. 168–78.

Foreman, Richard (with Ken Jordan), *Unbalancing Acts: Foundations for a Theater*, New York: Pantheon Books, 1992.

Geertz, Clifford, *The Interpretation of Cultures*, New York: Basic Books, 1973.

Geertz, Clifford, *After the Fact: Two Countries, Four Decades, One Anthropologist*, Cambridge MA: Harvard University Press, 1995.

Goffman, Erving, *Frame Analysis: an Essay on the Organization of Experience*, Boston: Northeastern University Press, 1986.

Gow, Michael, *Furious*, Sydney: Currency Press, 1994.

Gow, Michael, *Toy Symphony*, Sydney: Currency Press, 2008.

Gow, Michael, Interview in *Time Out*, 2010(a), www.timeoutsydney.com.au/theatre/michael-gow.aspx (accessed 21 September 2011).

Gow, Michael, Press release, 2010(b), www.australianstage.com.au/201002243219/news/brisbane/ (accessed 20 April 2010).

Hall, Peter, *Peter Hall's Diaries: the Story of a Dramatic Battle* (ed. John Goodwin), London: Hamish Hamilton, 1983.

Hiley, Jim, *Theatre at Work: the Story of the National Theatre's Production of Brecht's Galileo*, London: Routledge, 1981.

Illing, Robert, 'Haydn's *Toy Symphony*', *Music & Letters* 78:1 (1997) p.143.

Jackson, Shannon, *Professing Performance: Theatre in the Academy from Philology to Performativity*, Cambridge: Cambridge University Press, 2004.

Kinderman, William and Joseph E. Jones (eds), *Genetic Criticism and the Creative Process: Essays from Music, Literature and Theater*, University of Rochester Press, 2009.

Kobialka, Michal (ed. and trans.), *Tadeusz Kantor: A Journey Through Other Spaces (Essays and Manifestos 1944–90)*, California: University of California Press, 1993.

Léger, Nathalie and Almuth Grésillon (eds), *Genesis: Revue Internationale de Critique Génétique* (special issue on theatre), No. 26, 2005.

McAuley, Gay, 'Towards an ethnography of rehearsal', *New Theatre Quarterly* 14:1 (1998), pp. 75–85.

McAuley, Gay, 'The emerging field of rehearsal studies', *About Performance* 6, (2006(a)), pp. 7–13.

McAuley, Gay, (ed), *Rehearsal and Performance Making Processes*, Special Issue of *About Performance*, No. 6, 2006(b).

McAuley, Gay, 'Not magic but work: rehearsal and the production of meaning', *Theatre Research International* 33:3, (2008), pp. 276–88.

McAuley, Gay, 'The Sydney trinity: performance space and the creation of a "Matrix of Sensibility"', *Australasian Drama Studies* 58 (April 2011), pp. 71–87.

Marshall, Norman, *The Producer and the Play*, London: Macdonald, 1957.

Mauss, Marcel and Henri Beuchat, *Seasonal Variations of the Eskimo: A Study in Social Morphology*, London: Routledge, [1904–05] 1979.

Mead, Margaret, 'The art and technology of field work', in *A Handbook of Method in Cultural Anthropology*, eds Raoul Naroll and Ronald Cohen New York/London: Columbia University Press, 1973, pp. 246–65.

Meyer-Plantureux, Chantal, 'Kantor, ultimes répétitions', in Banu, *Les Répétitions de Stanislavski à Aujourd'hui*, 2005, pp. 199–206.

Meyrick, Julian, *See How It Runs: Nimrod and the New Wave*, Sydney: Currency Press, 2008.

Milne, Geoffrey, *Theatre Australia (Un)limited: Australian Theatre Since the 1950s*, Amsterdam: Rodopi, 2004.

Mitter, Shomit and Maria Shevstova (eds), *Fifty Key Theatre Directors*, London: Routledge, 2005.

Mnouchkine, Ariane, 'Le rôle du metteur en scène', *L'Avant-Scène Théâtre*, 526–7 (October 1973), pp. 11–13.

Morgan, Claire, 'Back, in a torrent of words', *Sydney Morning Herald* (9 November 2007), p. 14.

Morgan, Joyce and Garry Maddox, 'Post-dramatic stress plays the villain's role', *Sydney Morning Herald* (2–3 January 2010), p. 13.

Potts, C.M, *What Empty Space? Text and Space in Australian Mainstream Rehearsal Process*, (Unpublished Masters Thesis, Department of Performance Studies, University of Sydney), 1995.

Rabkin, Gerald (ed.), *Richard Foreman*, Baltimore: Johns Hopkins University Press, 1999.

Rossmanith, Kate, *Making Theatre-Making: Rehearsal Practice and Cultural Production*, (Unpublished PhD Thesis, Department of Performance Studies, University of Sydney), 2004.

Roxburgh, Richard, Interview, *Sydney Morning Herald* (9 November 2007(a)), p. 14.

Roxburgh, Richard, Interview Talking Heads, ABC Sydney, 2007(b).

Sanjek, Roger (ed.), *Fieldnotes: the Makings of Anthropology*, Ithaca/London: Cornell University Press, 1990.

Sharman, Jim, 'In the realm of the imagination: an individual view of theatre' (inaugural Rex Cramphorn Memorial Lecture, 1995), *Australasian Drama Studies* 28 (April 1996), pp. 20–9.

Sher, Antony, *Year of the King: an Actor's Diary and Sketchbook*, London: Chatto & Windus, 1985.

Sher, Antony, *Primo Time*, London: Nick Hern Books, 2005.

Sjomon, Vilgot, 'Catching the rare moment', *Tulane Drama Review* II:1 (1996), pp. 102–5.

Stafford-Clark, Max, *Letters to George: the Account of a Rehearsal*, London: Nick Hern Books, 1989.

Stern, Tiffany, *Rehearsal from Shakespeare to Sheridan*, Oxford: Clarendon Press, 2000.

Taylor, Diana, *The Archive and the Repertoire: Performing Cultural Memory in the Americas*, Durham and London: Duke University Press, 2003.

Turner, Victor, *From Ritual to Theatre: the Human Seriousness of Play*, New York: Performing Arts Journal Publications, 1982.

Vince, R.W, 'Theatre history as an academic discipline', in *Interpreting the Theatrical Past*, eds T. Postlewait and B. McConachie, Iowa City: University of Iowa Press, 1989, pp. 1–18.

Vitez, Antoine, [*Théâtre/Public*, 64–5:July 1985] 'Un regard médiumnique', reprinted in Banu, *Les Répétitions de Stanislavski à Aujourd'hui*, 2005, pp.147–55.

Wesker, Arnold, *The Birth of Shylock and the Death of Zero Mostel*, London: Quartet, 1997.

Whitton, David, *Stage Directors in Modern France*, Manchester: Manchester University Press, 1987.

INDEX

Note: Page references in *italics* refer to illustrations